FEAR AND ART IN THE CONTEMPORARY WORLD

CATERINA ALBANO

REAKTION BOOKS

Published by
Reaktion Books Ltd
33 Great Sutton Street
London EC1V 0DX, UK
www.reaktionbooks.co.uk

First published 2012

Printed and bound in China by Eurasia

British Library Cataloguing in Publication Data
Albano, Caterina.
Fear and art in the contemporary world.
1. Fear in art. 2. Art, Modern – 21st century – Themes, motives.
3. Art and society. 4. Psychology and art.
I. Title
704.9'4915246-dc23

ISBN 978 1 78023 019 1

FEAR AND ART IN THE CONTEMPORARY WORLD

CONTENTS

INTRODUCTION

We see a talking head: the American scholar Noam Chomsky. Off-screen, a woman's voice asks about politics, environmental issues and economics. The overall subject of the interview that constitutes the video work *Chomskian Abstract* (2007) by the British artist Cornelia Parker is an analysis of today's ecology of fear, which, as the artist puts it, '[draws] on a sense of apocalypse – death and resurrection'.[1] Chomsky traces the origins of the contemporary culture of fear in the United States back to the dawn of North American history and highlights it as a recurring motif in popular imagination, including fiction and film. It is a story in which the impinging threat of destruction by a menacing 'other' is averted by technological advancement and the triumphant intervention of a heroic figure. This narrative runs through the account of the annihilation of Native Americans and gives way to the Japanese threat during the Second World War, followed by the panic over Cuba during the Cold War period, and more recently to Saddam Hussein's alleged menace. Quoting Chomsky, fear is a 'constant theme, sort of a steady sort of current – you know, which can always be stimulated when needed by cynical leaders with usual public relations techniques'.[2] The political and mass media manufacturing of a culture of fear is a means for conformity and the maintenance of the status quo. *Chomskian Abstract* is both the portrait of an intellectual and a reflection upon the contemporary culture of anxiety or 'fear society' as a relevant theme that sees scholars and artists alike interrogate the pervading emotion of our time.

Since the 1990s sociologists have claimed the conceptual consolidation of what has variously been defined as an 'age of anxiety', 'risk society' and 'culture of fear', whereby, as the sociologist Frank Furedi notes, 'the growing usage of the term "at risk" expresses cultural attitudes towards everyday life. It is symptomatic of a tendency to regard a growing range of phenomena as threatening and dangerous.'[3] Such a tendency suggests that fear 'serves as framework through which we interpret a variety of experiences'.[4] In a study of contemporary fear in the United States, the historian Peter Stearns identifies three main strands that differentiate it from the past and involves an evaluation of personal anxieties and external risks: heightened concern for children, the media's strategic uses of fear, and collective reactions to danger, especially in terms of foreign threats.[5] These strands, not dissimilar to those in Europe, have developed against unprecedented conditions of security and general safety, raising questions about the management and manipulation of risks, dangers and prejudices. A fleeting look at newspaper headlines maps an ever-present landscape of impinging epidemics, health risk factors, growing percentages of anxiety-related disorders, environmental disasters, racial preoccupations, economic uncertainties, increases in criminality and violence and widespread terrorism alerts.

If today's bogeymen are paedophiles and Muslim terrorists, an ensuing feeling of anxiety, a 'liquid fear', to use Zygmunt Bauman's metaphor for our pervasive sense of uncertainty and insecurity, insidiously shapes how we live.[6] The individual counterpart of the cultural phenomenon of fear is a gamut of emotional and cognitive experiences. Sensations, feelings and thoughts all converge to create fear scenarios, as we wrestle with daily incidents and encounters, and our own inner landscape of anxieties. While we locate phobias in specific, identifiable 'objects', anxieties are undetermined and encompass a spectrum of feelings and thoughts that reveal our perception of ourselves and others, of the environments that surround us and of the ways in which we evaluate reality. Fear engulfs our most intimate inner world and the ways we shape it, calling upon both our inner and our outer defences.

In this panorama where subjective experience and socio-cultural constructs coalesce to produce today's feelings of fear and anxiety, we may ask what is the role of the arts in general, and of the visual arts in particular, given the cultural predominance of images in popular media such as film, video and advertising. Themes, including paranoia, trauma, terrorism and the concept of 'fear society' itself, the overall topic of a pavilion at the 59th Venice Biennale in 2009, have been the subject of numerous exhibitions and art projects. Historical concepts such as 'the Gothic', 'the Sublime' and 'the uncanny' have been invoked anew, as both themes and theoretical references, creating a varied, multiform and multifaceted landscape of artworks that interrogate the current culture of fear. Throughout this study, we shall consider the contemporary culture of fear through the lenses of contemporary art, not as a survey but rather as a reflection upon the role of images in the shaping and contestation of this culture. Contemporary art lends itself to a broader consideration of the salience of the visual in the contemporary imaginary through its absorption and formal re-elaboration of various forms of cultural production in the broadest sense. Through and within contemporary art we can see reflected tendencies that happen elsewhere in culture. It is my intention to establish a dialogue between art practices and the culture they stem from and encapsulate, between artists and ourselves as viewers, spectators, critics and, most of all, as the participants in today's anxieties. We will consider the implications of such a culture and question how art may critically contend with it. How, for instance, did an emotion become the zeitgeist of our time? And in which ways do the incorporation and manipulation of strategies of representation mobilized across culture help us to interrogate the visual rhetoric that underpins the current 'culture of fear'?

A 'Culture of Fear': An Emotion and the Zeitgeist of an Epoch

Fear is regarded as an emotional state linked to strategies of survival. Although there is little agreement among psychologists, brain scientists, philosophers and historians on how emotions may be defined, there is a general recognition that an organism responds to a real or presumed danger with a state of alertness that triggers the defence mechanisms of the body across the neural pathways of the brain, metabolically, physiologically and, ultimately, psychologically. The uncertainty of peril, as much as the immediate recognition of a threat, is important in the triggering of brain responses that lead to the cognitive assessment of the situation and the adoption of defensive reactions. These reactions include the 'fight or flight' produced by fright, but also the physical and mental sensations of paralysis and dejection that accompany the experience of fear.[7] This psycho-organic picture acts as a model for the complex processes that underlie the multilayered feelings of tension, alarm, nervousness, distress and trouble that disturb, sicken, unnerve, torment, agitate, confuse, upset, anguish and pain us. Those feelings that we may recognize as fear are those that make us tremble, shrink, hesitate, withdraw, worry or doubt. Whether the risk is real or imagined, external or within, in our minds, conscious or non-conscious, the very perception of threat arouses our defences. These defences may be physiological and psychic, but also social and cultural. Following this model, the contemporary 'culture of fear' or 'age of anxiety' or 'risk society' appears as a culture that has become consumed by its own perception and response to the potentials and uncertainties that it has forged for itself. It is like an organism that has entered a default state of alertness, of constant unrest and disquiet, triggering anxiety, obsession and paranoia. This is not completely unintentional, not completely hazardous or accidental. It might be a fitting feeling, though a consuming one, towards pressing change and undefined threats. Nonetheless, it denotes the sensation and sentiment of our time.

Throughout history, individuals have always experienced dread and panic, been concerned about or felt threatened by certain groups or certain situations, by natural and human-made forces. We have always existentially 'trembled', as Bauman puts it, in front of the uncontrollable force of fate and the menace of death and disease.[8] Across the centuries we have told stories of fear and horror to mitigate, to come to terms with or to disavow our angst. Fear has been used as a political means of aggression, of exploitation and of coercion, as a force of control but also as a propeller for change and renovation. Whether seen at the origins of social aggregation or of political division and power, fear has circulated across culture, seeping into its layers and affecting the ways in which people perceive themselves and their circumstances. Certain historical events have had lasting shocking effects. The French Revolution, for example, deeply troubled Europe well into the nineteenth century. The two World Wars, alongside more recent conflicts and atrocities, still lurk with traumatic feelings in the imagination of the twenty-first century. Never before has the potential of devastation and destruction been so overwhelming. Old terrors appear in new forms, renewing pre-existing fears, making us tremble anew.

Commentators argue that fear as it appears in contemporary Western societies is, however, of a different kind or rather the result of shifts that have no parallel in the past because they involve the unprecedented development of globalized power structures brought about by market capitalism and the development of a high technology culture that has altered socio-economic dynamics.[9] Indeed, the extent and rapidity of change engendered by scientific and technological advancements throughout the twentieth century has impinged on old certainties and shaken established assumptions in ways that have been exciting, groundbreaking and tantalizing but that could also seem daunting and unsettling. Whether on the macroscopic scale of the state and society, or at the level of the individual, the potentials of expansion and less constrained forms of organization have resulted in feelings of profound anxiety. 'The free-floating dynamic of fear', according to Furedi, 'is promoted by a culture that communicates hesitancy and anxiety towards uncertainty and continually anticipates the worst possible outcome'.[10] For Bauman, the emphasis on the perception of life and reality has moved 'from the area of security (that is, of self confidence, and self assurance or their absence) to that of safety (that is, of being sheltered from, or exposed to, threats to one's own person and its extinction)'.[11] Increasingly, terms such as 'risk factors', 'risk-groups' or 'vulnerable groups', and 'risk-conditions' have ambiguously entered the vocabulary, positioning risk as something to be avoided rather than a challenge to be welcomed.

The spectres haunting late modernity are many and varied. Food, people, living environments or technologies can all bear the signs of real or potential threats that cause us to take defensive actions or responses, including prevention, control, prohibition and eviction. Fears of pollution and contagion have acquired new cultural currency stemming from climate change, GM crop production, risk-related substances in the foods we eat (pesticides, high quantities of fat, sugar, salt) or in the toxic air that we breathe. At the same time, ever-scarier epidemics of 'new' viruses, such as the recent H5N1 avian flu and H1N1 swine flu, are pending menaces. Yet 'epidemic panic' also surrounds conditions such as obesity, whose 'infectiousness' spreads across the psychological, social and economic layers of societies.[12] Ideologically, fear of metaphorical contagion also pervades the perception of national boundaries, despite, or indeed as a consequence of, the great mobility of people and goods across continents and nation states. This anxiety is signalled not least by immigration policies and the marginalization of immigrants and refugees. It is also accompanied by a pervasive suspicion of strangers, in contexts that feed into systems of surveillance, including omnipresent CCTV cameras, capsular protection of living environments, the negotiation and monitoring of public spaces and other forms of social control, such as online sex offenders' lists and the tagging through mobile networks of protesters. We are continually finding new ways in which to keep a fearful eye on one another. Indeed, what we are experiencing is a *privatization* of public fears and a projection of private ones into the public spheres by rendering them the blueprint of daily interactions.[13]

Personal uncertainties concerning professional and economic security, old age, relationships and most aspects of our private lives equally undermine confidence in our prospects for the future and in solid belief systems, rendering failure ever more daunting and destructive, psychologically and practically. Both individually and collectively fear defines a 'cultural script' that endorses the rules and meanings of our daily life.[14] Our behaviour spirals in forms of defensiveness, feelings of inadequacies, displacement and disquiet further prompting fear and anxieties. According to Bauman, 'Fear has now settled inside, saturating our daily routines; it hardly needs further stimuli from outside, since the actions it prompts day in, day out supply all the motivation and all the energy it needs to reproduce itself.'[15] Political rhetoric, media discourse and institutionalized attitudes promote the proliferation of this phobic climate. They underline a 'rhetoric of fear' through words and images, verbal and visual narratives that impose upon the diversified, fragmented, idiosyncratic and contradictory legacy of post-modernity an overarching interpretation of reality. Though always partial, being rooted in readings that prompt defence responses, this interpretation sanctions the script of which we are perhaps unwillingly, though unavoidably, enactors, spectators, critics or casualties. Cultural scripts engulf us. They also offer mirrors through the cultural products that they create: contemporary art is one of them.

In this discussion I suggest that the kernel of the contemporary visual and verbal rhetoric of fear can be located in the late nineteenth century with the consolidation of modernity, though earlier signs were visible. In this period the concept of emotion as a physiological and psychological event free from moral and spiritual considerations emerged across the relatively new disciplines of psychology, physiology and evolutionary studies. Accordingly, fear was understood as a basic emotion that denoted a primal, almost feral, condition. Inadequate to the modern civilized man, it was identified with children, 'savages' and women. Fear was thus culturally repressed within the disciplines that substantiate the current understanding of this emotion in neuroscience and experimental and cognitive psychology. Photography and scientific film were part of the visual tools that informed, supported and documented the modern notion of fear, and which are still part of today's scientific currency. They constitute standard tools for the recognition of fearful faces and the supposed detection of facial signs denoting untrustworthy people, and are part of the visual practices of somatic codification in criminology and other biometric forms of classification of the criminal body. Film and photography have also played a key role in the study of trauma and stress-related conditions, presenting the visualization of 'fear states' as both critical and salient to the current understanding of fear.

Modernity also brought about the conceptualization of anxiety as a state of prolonged susceptibility to fear, worry, uneasiness, preoccupation and dread that are not related to any specific external danger but connected to an internal angst that concerns the self and its being in the world. At the core of modern neurosis, anxiety defines a disquiet that encompasses the excessive charge of modern urban living. It suggests the brittleness and fragmentation that threatened to rupture subjectivity in the forms of railway shock, shell shock and trauma, and which still reverberates in today's anatomized and disjointed experience of the self whose stories are ridden with shame and anxiety. Gothic tropes surface anew to give form to the ghosts of modern and late modern sensibility, rendering new technologies the sites of old and new horrors. The uncanny similarly emerges as a fitting aesthetic category but also a real experience in which old, familiar fears appear in new, unfamiliar guises, whereby displacement becomes a form and condition that would epitomize post-modernity. If the Sublime has returned within critical theory as a useful way of conceptualizing to address contemporary experiences of terror, the uncanny is no less invoked to help us to unravel the tenuous boundaries between the real and the virtual, and to consider the interface of science and technology with nature within contemporary sensibility. The visual referents for these frightening feelings include photography and the moving image, but also the hybrid use of the ready-made and found object, of the machine, and of architectural structures as components of a modern aesthetics that manipulates things, images and spaces to affect meanings and explore visual currencies. In the slippage between continuity and difference, the complex construct of feelings that makes the contemporary 'culture of fear' takes shape and presents itself as a script that, among others, is visually saturated. Hence, it is pertinent to the nature and the role of imagery in this script, and to the necessity of asking whether the 'culture of fear' can be mapped onto an 'aesthetics of fear'.

Is there an 'Aesthetics of Fear'?

The French art historian and theorist Paul Virilio has accused contemporary art of inhumanity, arguing that it is 'basically terrorist and terrorized' in its appropriation and glamorization of images of violence and revulsion. Virilio's critique stems from an ethical position that seeks a re-evaluation of humanism vis-à-vis the horror of violence and the deathly silence that surrounds it, despite the 'vociferous sonority' of contemporary art.[16] As John Armitage maintains in the introduction to Virilio's *Art and Fear* (2003), 'Virilio considers that contemporary artists have abandoned their function of continually reassessing the creative practices and sensibilities, imagination and cultural meaning of the advanced societies.'[17] This abandonment results in 'pitiless art' denoted by 'terrorist aesthetic procedures and the premeditated termination of the enunciation of silence'.[18] In the phrase 'terrorist aesthetic procedures' Virilio (as quoted by Armitage) refers to a proliferation of images and practices of aggression, violence and voyeurism devoid of empathy. The 'premeditated termination of the enunciation of silence' contrasts with Adorno's famous declaration of the impossibility of poetry after Auschwitz, hence the impossibility of art to comprehend and bear witness to the Holocaust's legacy of horror. This imposition of silence is antagonized for Virilio by an attraction towards the thrill of terror that characterizes much of contemporary art and which manifests in an acute solipsism and the embracing of techno-science. Contemporary art becomes the vehicle of a new terror that for the critic is both dangerously subversive and, in general, ethically futile, which in turn may be formalized into a contemporary aesthetics of fear.

While Virilio denounces contemporary art as presenting a non-critical as well as amoral endorsement of popular culture and techno-science, contemporary art is also seen to be inadequate in responding to the impact of violence brought about by the War on Terror. According to the political theorist Susan Buck-Morss, language and images have been appropriated by the rhetoric of fear in ways that render them subservient instruments of this rhetoric. 'Language – the tool of thought, and image – the tool of cognitive perception, are being appropriated today by discourses of power in a very particular way, one that negates their usefulness for *critical* practices of theory and of art.'[19] Buck-Morss is wary of the encapsulation of art within the control of the 'art world', dominated by the forces of the market and by the validation of art practices through the recognition accorded by privileged channels such as art galleries, museums and art fairs. Hence, while Buck-Morss argues for an art world independent from 'disciplinary' regimes, a space of aesthetic experience, of 'affective, sensory cognition – that involves making critical judgements about not only cultural forms, but social forms of our being-in-the-world', she also sees art as disappearing in a fragmentation of forms and practices.[20] As Buck-Morss argues,

> But if in the present political climate all of the cultural space of the global public sphere becomes subject to appropriation by power, if it is impossible to exist there on terms other than those set down by institutions of cultural control, then this potential has a very slim chance of being realized.[21]

Implicitly, another kind of aesthetics of fear is suggested, one of impotence and disappearance. This aesthetics is different from the one argued by Virilio, who sees contemporary art as complacent to violence. In this instance the extremism and manipulative supremacy of the rhetoric of fear renders contemporary art as superfluous and self-mirroring.

Drawing on an argument presented in relation to cinema, in particular to horror film, we may propose another way of looking at a supposed 'aesthetics of fear'. The film historian Adam Lowenstein has re-evaluated the role of horror film, suggesting its cultural significance vis-à-vis trauma and the legacy of horrors and violence in history. Lowenstein argues that the excitement of horror film is based on the use of practices and conventions that exceed narrative and involve 'bodily sensations' as well as 'cognitive responses, such as memory and identification' from the spectator: horror films 'frighten us in ways that are both visceral and cognitive, personal and historical'.[22] For Lowenstein, the cinematic image is capable of shocking us, in Walter Benjamin's original sense of both provoking a sensory reaction through an overstimulation, and of acting as a catalyst for our attention and curiosity. Horror sequences also invoke Benjamin's idea of the allegory 'as a radical disruption of conventional historical continuity'.[23] Lowenstein invokes 'the allegorical moment', the shocking collision of film, spectator and history, in the moment when the image viscerally affects the spectator through non-narrative registers, and argues that such an instance enables a deferred re-presentation of history.[24] This deferral immediately incites both emotional and intellectual reactions to the image. Indeed, the allegorical moment represents the destabilizing encounter with horror as a 'moment of danger', in which 'trauma entails an opening out to complex and often contradictory representations, where unexpected recombinations and disfigurements of history can occur'.[25] Hence, for Lowenstein the depiction of fright and dread in films such as George A. Romero's *Day of the Dead* (1985) and *The Land of the Dead* (2005) visually mediates historical experiences of trauma that impinge on American consciousness, respectively the Vietnam and Iraq wars. These films enable an 'aesthetic experience' whereby the spectator can feel as well as cognitively know fear, and process other, non-fictive horrors through the imaginative scenario of the film.[26] This dynamic actualizes 'points of contact' in the fictive horror of the moving image, 'between past and present, between film and history'.[27] The affective response to these 'points of contact' is diverse and multiform, since the image encompasses 'a wide range of possible affects including (but not limited to) horror, dread, disgust, and anxiety', and also 'empathy, anger, amusement, and admiration'.[28] The image thus presents the spectator with a 'shocking confrontation and/or playful encounter' with art 'illusion'.[29]

The term 'aesthetics' etymologically reminds us of the arousal of sensory responses (whether in terms of pleasure, displeasure, pain or other sensations), of a form of knowledge that pertains to the senses, to the emotive self as much as to intellectual judgement.[30] Fear equally solicits somatic and psychological reactions, at the boundaries of exhilaration, disturbance and pain, of thrill as well as of profound abjection, as it traverses organic and mental layers both literally and figuratively. Neuroscience tells us that fear is an organism's defence response, which in humans instigates cognitive processes of memory, assessment and decision-making.[31] Affective states and cognition, feeling and thought, as the Swiss psychologist Jean Piaget asserts, cannot however be separated: 'affectivity and intelligence are indissociable and constitute the two complementary aspects of all human behaviour'.[32] In claiming for contemporary art an 'aesthetics of fear' we argue for an art that affects the viewer in multiple and even contradictory ways, for an art that provokes responses and that, as Lowenstein suggests of horror film, thrills and shocks – stirring the body and the mind alike. It is this kind of aesthetics of fear that we have to talk about as central to contemporary art and to artworks that are neither complacent to violence nor impotent in the face of terror.[33]

The comparison of horror film and contemporary art is pertinent on many levels. Not only is the contamination of artistic genres and modes of cultural production (high and popular culture) integral to contemporary art practices in forms as diverse as video art, installation, digital and web art, the role of the viewer is also increasingly comparable to that of the spectator as their position can be physically as well as emotionally and intellectually predicated by the artwork. The alertness to visual cultural practices, their shaping of ways of seeing and hence of interpreting through the exploitation and manipulation of the affective potential of images is equally relevant to artists and artworks that interrogate the systems and modalities of culture. In proposing a dialogue between contemporary art, the contemporary 'culture of fear' and the viewer, we aim to uncover the interface of these components, so as not to celebrate, defend or refute an 'aesthetics of fear', but rather to interrogate the very possibilities and potentials of such an aesthetics.

Bodies, Objects, Narratives, Spaces

I navigate my way through the contemporary culture of fear through the lens of contemporary art using four broad categories that correspond to the four chapters in this book: bodies, objects, narratives and spaces. Interlaced, overlapping and mutually related, the chapters act as a compass or framework through which to visit fear as anxiety and phobia, paranoia and apprehension towards the other, as trauma, as the uncanny, and the Sublime, as dislocation, displacement and abjection.

The chapter entitled 'Bodies' considers phenomena such as 'fat phobia', 'beauty terror' and anxiety-related disorders to address the body as a contested site of anxiety in contemporary culture. It also examines the phobic construction of the other – as the criminal or the terrorist – in terms of prejudiced readings that are interwoven with racial and other forms of discrimination. The chapter questions the centrality of physiognomy in the construction of fear, examining the role of photography as a scientific and cultural means of giving fear a face. The label 'at risk group' is equally interrogated, as it instigates the facile juxtaposition of victim and predator in the circulation of feelings that fear entails. 'Bodies' suggests that fear defines physical and ideological boundaries of the body and of the self, and the chapter looks at the ways in which these boundaries are made in terms of phobic attitudes or practices, such as fear of pollution and contagion.

The second chapter, 'Objects', considers the centrality of the object as a site of contemporary sensibility and art practice, calling upon the concept of the uncanny to explore individual as well as historical fear and its representation through memory. Already formulated as an aesthetic category in Sigmund Freud's first enunciation, the uncanny has emerged as a potent referent for assessing today's 'aesthetics of fear'. This is expressed in the unsettling qualities of the unhomely brought about by dislocation and traumatic memories, and by the motif of the ruin as a vehicle for addressing historical terror and terrorism and the re-emergence of old fears in the topical currency of ecological disaster and climate change.

'Narratives' examines the role of the image – in painting, photography, film and video – as inherent to the construction of knowledge of the self and society alike, and focuses on the antithetical experiences of horror as thrill and trauma. The chapter investigates the centrality of the visual as a narrative mode that shapes mental and cultural constructions of reality, the ways in which we imagine and recount fear. The shock effect of the image as inherent to modernity is further revisited in relation to virtual reality as a new area of sensory overcharge and affective visuality. The chapter also questions the representability of trauma within the narrative frameworks of guilt and shame, and considers it vis-à-vis the disruption of the affective potency of the moving image, through the creation of Lowenstein's 'points of contact', in which past and present, memory and emotion, artwork and history both overlap and emerge.

The last chapter, 'Spaces', focuses on the implosion and homogenization of the contemporary notion of space and questions the extent to which disorientation is a condition of late modernity. Traditional notions of spatial fear, such as vertigo, agoraphobia and claustrophobia, are revisited in relation to current uncertainties of living, to surveillance practices, to feelings and experiences of dislocation and of displacement. The Sublime as a critical category is invoked to account for terror and horror, in relation to both nature and history. The notion of ruin returns here in terms of how space has been contaminated by human horror and ecological cataclysms, by political terror and existential angst. The chapter asks: what are the contemporary characteristics of desolation and ruin, what typifies the empty space of awe and terror of our time? It also looks at the dominant implementation of surveillance as an instance of a scared and scarring society, in which suspicion and uncertainty undermine trust, and considers the remapping of urban and domestic spaces that results from disorientation as a condition of living.

Central to the discussion of an 'aesthetics of fear' is the encounter of the viewer and the artwork, the allegorical moment, in Lowenstein's words, when the image, the spectator and the present (as well as history) meet, when the 'aesthetic experience' unravels affectively and cognitively, such that it is viscerally felt and intellectually appreciated. Aesthetic experience is grounded in the artwork's ability to jolt, thrill, disturb and even amuse, but it also pertains to the questioning, interrogation, reflection and contemplation that the beholding of the work enables and causes. Indeed, as we move through bodies, objects, narratives and spaces, we shall conjure the presence of the viewer and the significance of her responses.

Although the artists and works considered here are numerous, they far from exhaust the rich, international panorama from which they have been chosen. To include them all would have been impossible. Those selected for focus were chosen either for their salience, or for an artist's consistent engagement with the subject. Names that recur do so to suggest the intersecting of certain themes and, inevitably, there are omissions. Nonetheless, the diversity of medium, approaches and critical insight has been a constant guide. Throughout, the discussion of the artworks is integrated and woven in the structure of the chapters and the exposition of the argument, not as illustrations, but rather as the catalyst for a critical discussion of the current climate of pervading anxieties. The context is interdisciplinary and embraces a broad landscape of sources, so that the history of medicine (particularly the history of emotions), the history of art and culture are considered alongside psychology, neuroscience, sociology and philosophy.

The cultural historical framework of the book aims to capture 'points of contact' between art and culture and society, present and past, the work and the visitor. The attempt is not to draw a comprehensive picture, but rather to trace moments in which ideas and affects coagulate, as suggested, through 'shocking confrontation and/or playful encounter' with contemporary art: FEAR/REAR reads

Bruce Nauman's famous neon artwork. Is flight the only response to a culture of fear?

ONE

BODIES

During *Rhythm O* (1974), a six-hour performance, the artist Marina Abramović passively lay down as the audience freely acted on her body with an array of objects including paints, nails, a feather, chains, a pistol, flowers, a needle, a flute and wire. Initially cautious and restrained, the audience's actions on Abramović's body became increasingly aggressive: the power relation moved from the performer to the spectator, and Abramović lay at the mercy of the audience.[1] Discomfort, humiliation, pain, aggression and fear were part of the affective currency of the work, which rendered the artist's body a medium and an object, exposing its vulnerability. Unlike performances of self-inflicted harm, the artist was neither in control of the audience's intention nor her own resilience. In this uncertainty, in the gap between the enactor (fearsome) and the receiver (fearful), the self and the other, between intention and reception, lies fear as the alarmed apprehension of what is or what could be.

Fear, as the historian Joanna Bourke observes, is primarily an emotion 'about the body – its fleshiness and precariousness'.[2] In its most basic form of sudden fright, fear ensues from the activation of the amygdala – a primitive part of the brain that modulates vigilance and arousal levels towards external stimuli, mobilizing the defence mechanism in the body before the potential danger is fully cognitively assessed.[3] However, fear is not merely an evolutionary response to a presumed threat. It is also a mental and cultural construct in which manifests the interface of body and mind, self and other, consciousness and non-conscious. Fear is felt within, through and across physical, mental and cultural layers, implicating the body both as the internal reservoir of anxieties and as the external referent of apprehension towards others. Fear also happens and is shaped within and across culture through the specific systems of knowledge that define it. In this chapter, we shall explore bodies of fear, entering their 'fleshiness and precariousness'. This journey traces the historical arrival of the 'emotion of fear' within evolutionary and cognitive models, and the ways in which these discourses have affected our current understanding of fear and anxiety, as expressed in terms of anxiety disorders, fat-phobia and beauty terror. We shall further investigate the making of the 'criminal body' as a site of anxieties, and the articulation of the affective boundaries of fear on which the tension between the self and the other is shaped. To conclude this section, we will also consider the fear of pollution, as the perceived threat to the boundaries of the bodily envelope.

The Making of Fear

The psychologist Jerome Kagan refers to fear as 'an alpha emotion', both 'archaic and modern'.[4] If the concept of anxiety, as a form of fear whose object is undetermined and elusive, is intrinsically modern, fear, as we know it, is also a modern notion of the new sciences of physiology, evolution and psychology, which in the second half of the nineteenth century conceptualized the blend of affective states that we recognize as the 'emotion' of fear.[5] Accordingly, fear is understood as archaic, the legacy of an ancient history of human development, a basic, primal, instinctual and feral response to danger that is aimed at survival. These attributes make it somehow outmoded in the modern context, where different kinds of 'defence mechanisms' – to borrow Freud's phrase – seem to be required. Thus, this emotion becomes disturbing and obnoxious to a modern sensibility. Old and new fears coalesce in the nervous bustling of metropolises, in the exciting but also disconcerting encounter with the machine in the many cycles of technological revolution, in the diagnosis of psychosis that began to highlight behaviours and feelings whose morbidity was tenuously separated from normality.[6] As well as archaic, therefore, fear emerged as a 'modern emotion', rooted in the shaping of subjectivity, latently present in both culture and the self. Given this tension between old and new, a few historical considerations are necessary to outline this 'alpha emotion', to borrow Kagan's phrase, and the 'fleshiness and precariousness' of the body that characterizes it. Three key images, or shall I say three faces, illustrate this brief excursus into the making of modern fear: the photograph of an elderly man, a drawing of a woman named Margherita, and Edvard Munch's painting *The Scream* (1893–1910).

Historically, painting, sculpture and acting appear emphatically to quote each other, to underscore a shared social idiom of bodily postures and expressions that medicine and philosophy substantiated and referred to when discussing the expression of emotions. Hence, the face was compared to a canvas on which the 'image of feeling' was depicted through an alignment of sensation and expression.[7] Well into the second half of the nineteenth century, the iconographic representation of fear was typified by five characteristic features: the contracted immobility of the whole body, in which movement is suspended and all functions seem to arrest, the expressive opening of the mouth in a terrified suppressed scream, the dilation of the pupils and widening of the eyes in a fixed darting gaze marked by the frown of the eyebrows, a general paleness with occasional shots of blood in the white of the eye, and the erection of the hair.[8] Due to the convulsive contraction of the whole body imbued with pain, the expression of fear climaxed in an agonizing feral scream, displaying a disturbing brutality.[9] Traditionally associated with sin, the face of fear incited dread in the observer and was invested with an inherent cultural nervousness onto which apprehension for moral perdition, or other anxieties, including various embodiments of problematic otherness, could be projected.

The consequences of the codification of the 'face of fear' are far-reaching, and continue to influence current studies on emotions that substantiate our innate ability to read the micro-facial movements

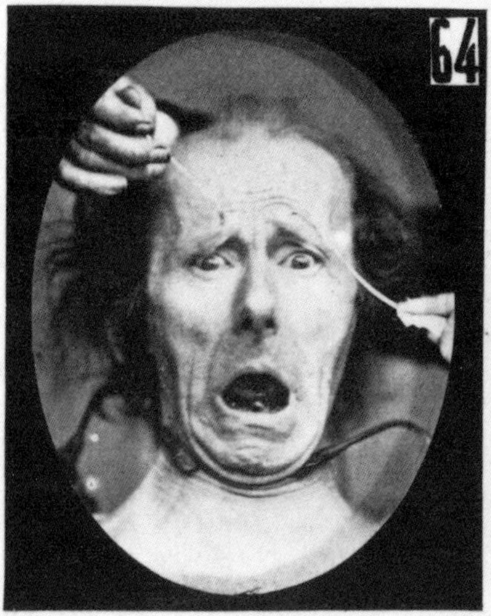

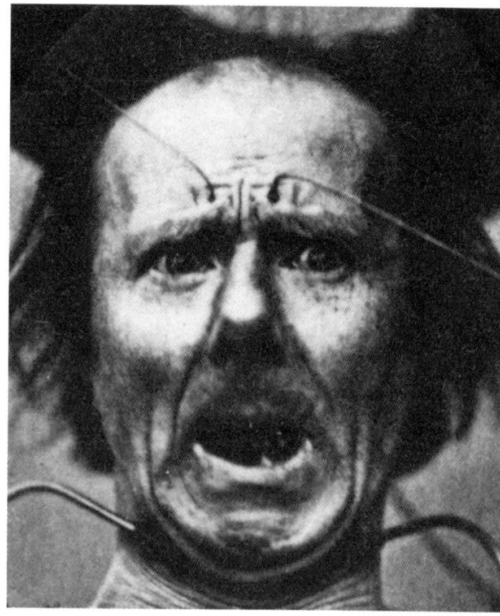

1 & 2 Guillaume-Benjamin-Amand Duchenne de Boulogne, Plate 64, 'Terror', and Plate 65, 'Fear and Horror', from *The Mechanism of Facial Expression* (1862).

believed to interact with affective responses. This research is indebted to Charles Darwin's evolutionary theory of the expression of emotions and his use of the new medium of photography in *The Expression of Emotions in Humans and Animals* (1872), the first scientific treatise to deploy photographs – alongside engravings. Darwin expressly opted for photography to illustrate human emotions as part of an overall narrative strategy in which the theoretical premises of the evolutionary basis of expression are visually supported.[10] Despite the deliberate move to distance his studies of emotion from the visual tradition that had upheld it, Darwin's treatise nevertheless endorses the longstanding characteristics ascribed to fear. For this study he chose photographs taken by the French physiologist Guillaume-Benjamin-Amand Duchenne de Boulogne (1806–1875) for his treatise *The Mechanism of Facial Expression* (1862). In these images, the face of an elderly man contracts under the effects of electro-stimulation. As Darwin claims, these photographs, though 'eye-catching and even shocking . . . are pliable. They allow the viewer to project onto them what he or she wants to see, thus engage the viewer on his or her terms.'[11]

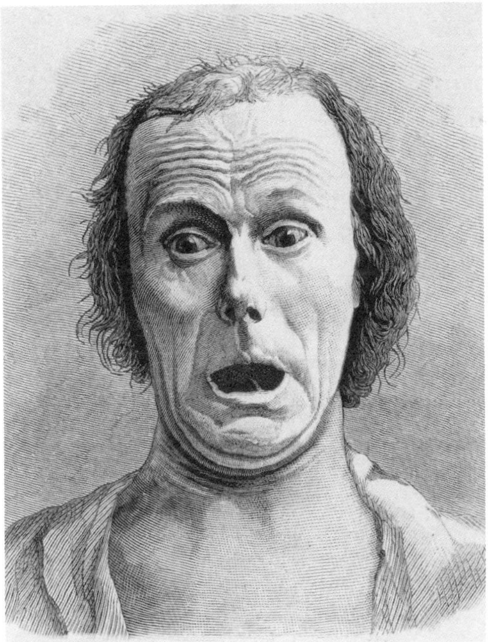

The choice of Duchenne's photographs and its justification are relevant because the pictures are highly contrived images, which are useful to authenticate a theoretical idea and which, in the case of fear, are dense with implications.

Duchenne's pictures belong to a series showing the sequential gradation of the expression of fear under the effect of localized electro-stimulation. This process triggers an increasing contraction of the *platysma myoides*, which the French physiologist regards as the 'muscle of fear', such that the subject's facial expression alters from one of frightened astonishment to terror.[12] As Duchenne explains, the traits of fear are

3 Guillaume-Benjamin-Amand Duchenne de Boulogne, *Terror*, wood engraving after a photograph, *The Mechanism of Facial Expression*, 1862.

> drawn by all the features of his face being pulled down obliquely and by the elevation of the skin on the anterior part of his neck. This gaze, terrified and *transfixed*, shows only the origin of the danger that menaces the man . . . aware of the torture to which he has been condemned.[13]

As he unpeels the expressive movements of fear to the camera, Duchenne's visual dissection gradually disfigures the face in an ever more horrendous mask. As he writes, 'in Plates 64 and 65, the horrible pain of torture has been added to the expression of this terrible emotion. This expression must be that of the damned' (illus. 1 and 2).[14] Duchenne's photographs are both *mise en scène* and documentation, at the same time the product of an aesthetic and scientific project that bears references, as he claims, to the expression of emotion painted by the old masters.[15]

The images prove to be pliable to Darwin's intention. They grant a supposed 'universal' reading of the expression of fear, highlighting features that can be detected in animals as well as in humans. They reinforce assumptions about the expression of fear that are culturally rooted in the iconographic tradition indirectly quoted by Duchenne as a terrifying and disquieting spectacle. These images also establish an expression for fear that still recurs within current scientific practice, since standard photographs employed to illustrate this emotion display the same emphasized traits. Yet Darwin had the originals altered and specially engraved, removing the electrodes and generally smoothing the facial distortion, possibly to flatten the shocking effect. As a result, Duchenne's original photographs appear to be tamed. The troubling qualities of fear, as dehumanizing and uncontrollable, are subdued (illus. 3). This alteration matches Darwin's text, which both points to the primal, feral state of fear and implicitly holds it back. Following Herbert Spencer, Darwin explicitly reads the expression of fear as a manifestation of the primitive man: 'Many savages do not repress the signs of fear so much as Europeans. They often tremble greatly . . . With savages, the sphincter muscles are often relaxed, just as may be observed in much frightened dogs, and as I have seen with monkeys when terrified of being caught.'[16] The reverting towards an ancestral and animal-like condition (the loosening of physical control) and the faltering of rational faculties (the loosening of mental control with the prevailing of the irrational) betray a troublesome regression to earlier stages of human development, to uncivilized or morally inadequate expressions of individuality, and towards the dark chambers of insanity. Fear was, in other words, associated with otherness.

Darwin's alteration of his photographic sources are instances of keeping at bay cultural ghosts and visually endorsing the danger of troublesome feelings that lurk within us.[17] The Darwinian physiologist and anthropologist Paolo Mantegazza (1831–1910) maintains that, for humans, fear is a habitual mode in women, children and feeble men who lack moral and physical strength. Unsuitable to masculinity and modern society, fear had to be repressed with feelings of self-dignity and honour.[18] The listing of women, children and 'feeble men' – a category that implicates Jews, the mentally ill and homosexuals, as well as other discriminated people – delineated standards of physical, social and moral vulnerability. Those in this category were often marked with the title 'degenerate', such that social threats were written into the notion of a defective, under-developed, morally corrupted and contagious body.[19] Fear could thus be classified as a primary emotion, primeval and ancestral, a state to be repressed, but as one which also defined cultural boundaries of otherness whenever the other became 'imbued' with fear.

Paradoxically, fear has re-emerged from this cultural repression as the dominant affective response of late modernity. Today, the labels 'at risk' or 'vulnerable' designate the susceptibility of certain groups to becoming or being troublesome, and also the menace that such people represent. The labelling identifies the most vulnerable and powerless members of society, as well as the most potentially dangerous, such as sex workers, transsexuals, drug abusers, the homeless, the mentally ill, children and young people, to name a few.[20] Whether seen as 'vulnerable' or as 'potentially dangerous', as the sociologist Deborah Lupton argues, 'special attention is directed at these social groups, positioning them in a network of surveillance, monitoring and intervention'.[21] As society tackles the implications of this designation, the psychological understanding of fear continues to encompass facial movements and the capacity to 'read' faces, maintaining the 'face of fear' as an ambiguous referent alongside other bodily signs.

In the 1890s, the French criminologist Alphonse Bertillon (1853–1914) was the first to develop an anthropometric system for the codification of criminals. It was based on a method of measuring and photographically documenting external bodily features including height, weight, the colour of the iris, the size of the skull and of the nose, fingerprints, the shapes of the mouth and ears. Photography endorsed this tagging of bodily traits by acting as a normative tool and was standardized according to specific visual strategies (in the instance of faces: frontal and profile; direct light, neutral background).[22] Hence, photography became 'the product of a disciplinary method' that formalized an empiric vision of the body and 'the related notion that images, like graphs, could work without text and become a controlled lexical space'.[23] Body morphology presupposed in fact an objective means of identification, a demonstration of identity in which detection, observation and investigation concur.[24] Further linked to atavism, which used evolution to explain the 'criminal body', the method supposes a double logic of 'diagnosis and prevention' that draws attention to both the criminal and the social environment, and which identifies the somatic features of the criminal in ways that still resonate today: 'We may be joined with the past by a certain kind of anxious faith in the body – in the potential to signal social dangers, and in its habit of testifying or confessing.'[25] Penile plethysmography to monitor the blood flow in the penis of sex offenders, and facial thermography, PET scans and DNA evidence to identify chromosomal patterns or genetic markers that indicate a predisposition to alcoholism, are among contemporary means to make the body a readable indicator of difference and danger.[26]

Parallel to the evolutionary study of fear is the investigation of its physiology and the measurement of the organic changes that occur in a state of fright, such as those in heartbeat, respiration, blood flow and adrenalin release. Within these studies, the preludes to the contemporary developments of neuroscience and experimental psychology, fear became contingent on the formulation of new ideas of consciousness, increasingly divested of spirituality, and inscribed within organic throbbing and fluctuation. This fear constantly dwelt at the boundaries of the non-conscious and of the conscious in the flow of stimula, sensations, and physical and mental responses, of the emergence and dissipation of ever changing inner representations that give form to feelings, thoughts and memories.[27] One of the pioneers in the study of fear was the Italian physiologist Angelo Mosso (1846–1910). As he states in his 1886 treatise on the subject, 'It is in the tissues, in the properties of the living substance which constitute the vital machine, that we must seek the reasons of numerous phenomena which Darwin deduced from external causes, natural selection or environment.'[28] Mosso swiftly traverses bodily tissues to capture the increase of blood flow and the expansion of the blood vessels in the brain under stress. He looks for the physiological dynamics that make fear a perceptible physical and mental experience. Setting a precedent to current fMRI and PET brain imaging, Mosso was the first scientist to glimpse the living brain and graphically record fear:

> It suffices to increase or diminish in a slight degree the rapidity of blood penetrating to the brain, in order to cause an immediate change of our 'ego'. The equilibrium of the molecules in the organs where consciousness has its seat is greatly disturbed by causes which scarcely affect the functions of other parts of the body . . . If I were asked which of the functions of the organism were most sensitive to the slightest organic change, I should, without hesitation, answer – *consciousness*.[29]

Among Mosso's unpublished papers is an engraving that he had made of Margherita, one of the three patients discussed in his treatise on fear and whose throbbing brain he was able to observe (illus. 4). The picture shows a modestly dressed elderly woman with a fracture on her scalp. Her hands rest on a medical instrument on top of which stands a skull with a hole in the forehead.[30] Margherita was affected by syphilis, which had corroded the frontal bone of the skull, revealing the brain through a fissure. During an experiment intended to measure the pulsation of the brain, carried out in the office of Mosso's colleague, the anatomist Carlo Giacomini, the graph registered a sudden increase in blood pulsation and in brain size, despite the apparent tranquillity of the patient. When Mosso enquired what Margherita was thinking, the woman replied that she had been looking absent-mindedly at the bookshelves in the office and saw a skull among the books. The sight had frightened her: a distressing reminder of her condition.[31]

The montage of the engraving condenses the episode in a visual memento mori: Margherita gazes down at her splintered skull. The moment of perturbation is also one of self-consciousness, of the ego's throb of change at the emergence and dissipation of fright. According to the neuroscientist Joseph LeDoux, whose research has extensively focused on fear, the 'feeling' of fear occurs when cognitive and emotional information – the non-conscious bodily and brain responses to an

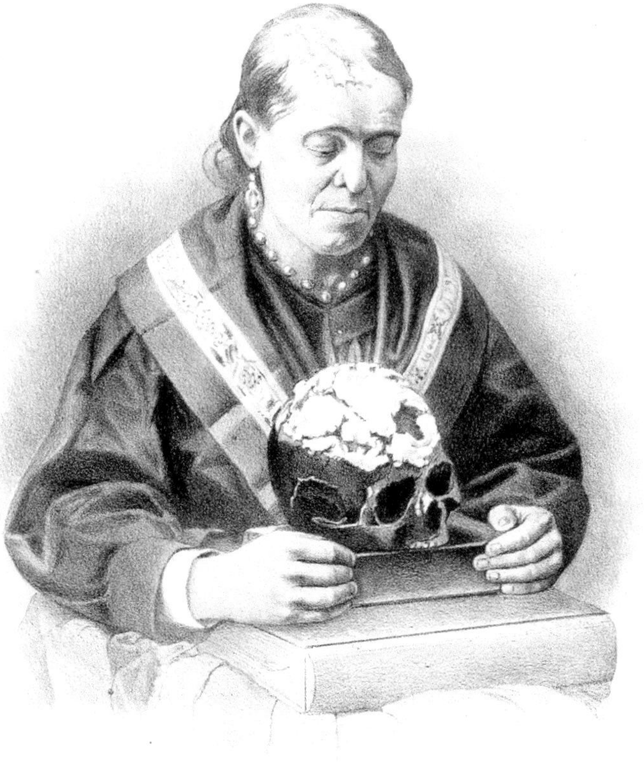

4 Anonymous, *Portrait of Margherita*, one of the patients discussed by Angelo Mosso in *Fear* (1886).

external stimulus – are brought together in a sustained mental representation. This inner picture or imaging is meant to focus the attention of different parts of the brain in order to activate conscious responses. It imbues the experience with the specific quality of what we call fear – as this emotion impinges and interferes with the continuous unfolding of memories on which subjectivity is based.[32] According to this model,

Margherita's experience is explained by stating that the visual stimulus of the glimpsed skull is worked through the fear-system, triggering the bodily reactions captured by Mosso. These reactions are matched by non-conscious brain responses, such as the activation of the vigilance-processing circuitry with the release of hormones to focus attention. The stimulus is worked through memory processes shifting towards consciousness. A mental representation is formed and tinged with the colour of fear. This internal picture is cognitively articulated in a thought that has specific meanings for the subject: Margherita fears her own mortality. Her contemplation of death is both recognizable and particular. In the brain, the 'feeling' of fear forms in the same way in all humans, and yet it is unique to her experience of being Margherita and to the specific interpretation that she confers to it. The moment of consciousness is also one of subjectivity. This picture could have, however, revealed another kind of fear, and another concealed yet menacing presence within the self.

Angst adumbrates the theatre of repetitions and conflicts that characterize the self through the persecuting disquiet of unconscious fears. As the painter Edvard Munch (1863–1944) writes in his diary:

> I was walking along a path with two friends – the sun was setting – I felt a breath of melancholy – Suddenly the sky turned blood-red – I stopped and leant against the railing deadly tired – looking out across flaming clouds that hung like blood and sword over the deep blue fjord and town – My friends walked on – I stood there trembling with anxiety and I felt a great, infinite scream through nature.[33]

A devastating scream metaphorically lacerates one of the best-known paintings of modern times. In Munch's *The Scream* (1893), the sinuous lines composing the riverbank landscape melt in the red condensed marks of an agitated sky (illus. 5). A skull-like head emerges: the eyes wide open are like desolate cavities; the mouth, a gap, exposes the alienating fissure of modern subjectivity. The face of fear distorts itself into new deformations and fluidities that allude to the fragmented self of modernity but also to the 'liquid' subjectivity of our time. A recurrent motif in Munch's work, anxiety infuses with unfathomable apprehension the anonymous crowd of *Despair* (1893–4) as well as the introverted gaze of the artist's self-portraits. This anxiety bears the stigma of vertigo, what the Danish philosopher Søren Kierkegaard (1813–1855) describes as existential dizziness: a fear of falling into an abyss of choices, into a void of meaninglessness, into existential angst.[34] Indeed, these images foreground the feeling of anxiety as a distinctively modern kind of fear.

5 Edvard Munch, *The Scream*, 1893, oil, tempera and pastel on cardboard.

In theorizing the concept of the psychoanalytical unconscious at the beginning of the twentieth century, Sigmund Freud (1856–1939) addressed the unconscious components of fear and their conscious manifestations. In *Beyond the Pleasure Principle* (1920), Freud distinguishes fear, dread and fright, and writes, 'Fear represents a certain kind of inner state amounting to expectation of, and preparation for, danger of some kind, even though the nature of the danger may well be unknown.'[35] Unlike fright, which is characterized by the surprise of a sudden presence of danger, and dread, which is always directed towards a specific object, the nature of fear is 'to be *non-specific* and to have no object'.[36] Biological, evolutionary and psychological understandings converge in the analytical assessment of fright and dread. By being 'non-specific', fear instead accounts for both expectation and the emergent notion of anxiety. It is bound to an undetermined and possibly unknown danger tearing the subject between the latent uncertainty of the future and the painful repetition of the past.

Within the triad configuration of ego, id and superego, the ego is the 'locus of fear', and the threats it faces are internal as well as external.[37] For Freud phobias, obsessions and paranoia are indicators of processes in which repressed fears are displaced and manifested, as he theorizes through the aetiology of neurosis. Ultimately, fear 'is *re*produced as a state of affect on the basis of a pre-existing memory-image', a state that is 'innate in the human psyche as the result of a primal traumatic experience' that is 'reawakened as memory-symbols'.[38] The birth process is the original fearful event that unconsciously tears the tissues of the inner life and that confers upon the experience of fear its characteristic features. The etymological meaning of the term 'trauma' is 'wound', and an inner

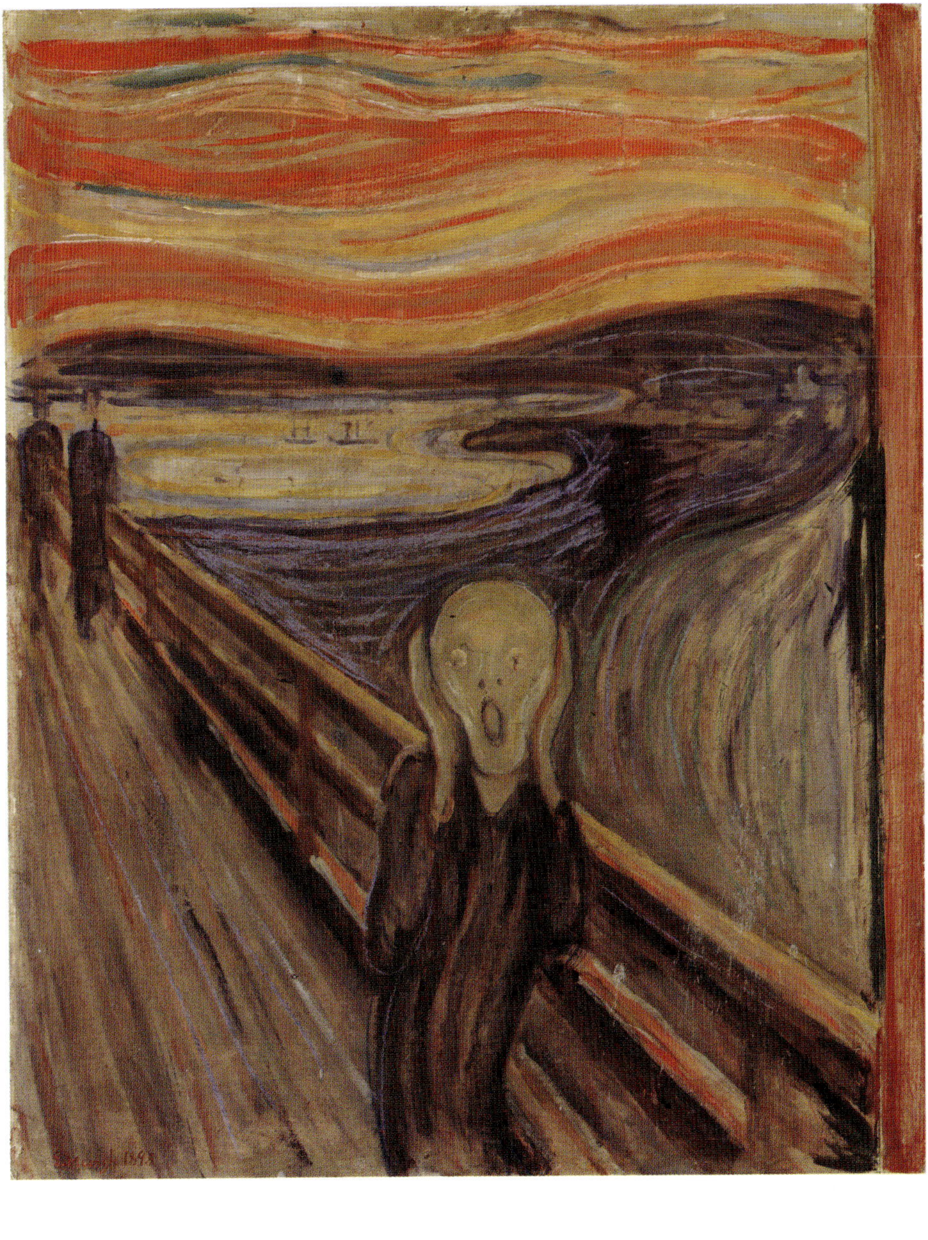

wound defines the subject through the first paradigmatic danger faced by the ego. On a psychic level, fear cannot be escaped. As Freud puts it, fear shares 'the destiny of other affects', haunting the modern subject.[39] Anxiety – fear that lacks a specific object, or 'the refusal to know what we are frightened of', is reframed within psychoanalytical theory in terms of repetition, which confers onto it an internal, psychic, repressed object.[40]

According to the psychoanalyst Adam Phillips, 'Psychoanalysis, in all its versions, is a story about what there is to fear; like the symptoms it can sometimes explain, it is grounded in terror.'[41] Indeed, in our psyche, as Phillips further argues, 'fear is constructed through the ways we protect ourselves from it . . . Psychoanalysis can show us, from developmental theory and reconstruction, how we construct our fears (like precious artefacts), but it cannot always show us, though it usually wants to, what it is that we are usually frightened of.'[42] As in the case of evolution, fear is positioned as a constitutive and displaced state of subjectivity. The tension between conferring a specific object to fear and its pervading, yet elusive, enveloping are tied to matters of consciousness and ways of knowing (hence of internal self-narrative). This 'ironic form of self-protection', this pervasive anxiety, enfolds bodies; it alienates objects and environments, producing stories and prompting the defensive barricading against suspicious others. Beyond it linger feelings of angst, disorientation, estrangement and uncertainty. It is in this context that we position our discussion of fear and of the bodies, objects, narratives and spaces that characterize it.

As these preliminary considerations suggest, contemporary fear is epistemologically as well as physically and psychologically intrinsic to body-ness. Yet, the body is also a source of concern and distress, making it a repertoire of old and new fears. In the last decades, the visual arts, for which the body has historically been a privileged subject, has delved into physicality with renewed emphasis across practices as diverse as performance, video art, installation and bio-art, as well as painting and sculpture. The result is a rich panorama of artworks that unravel the fleshiness and precariousness of fear. The galvanic distortion of Duchenne's face of fear, the palpitating frightful awareness of

Margherita and the unnerving anguish of Munch's paintings return in the diverse and multifaceted guises of conceptual art through photography, installation and video to interrogate the systems of knowledge that govern current fears. Our discussion moves now from anxiety directed towards the self and one's own body, to anxiety towards the other and the circulation of fear across bodies, and the threat felt towards bodily boundaries in relation to contagion.

Bodies of Anxiety

Paranoia and other anxiety disorders, including obsessions, phobias, panic disorder, post-traumatic stress disorder and obsessive-compulsive disorder affect one out of ten people in the UK in ways that interfere with 'normal life'.[43] This entails anxieties directed towards the self, living environments, past experiences, whereby things, situations and other people are perceived as dangerous. The aetiology of these disorders encompasses the feeling of anxiety that affects, both ideologically and psychologically, modern individuality and sensibility. Its figments and figures are many and multiform. What stigmatizes contemporary angst is a concern with corporeality, the private and the social body. Indeed, we live in a time of 'body scare', whether in terms of disease, self-perception or contagion. 'Epidemic' panic surrounds a broad range of psychological, physiological and psychosomatic conditions. As a contested site of fear, the body acts as a double mirror in which the internal state of anxiety reflects and endorses cultural preoccupations, and vice versa.

Freud compares the internal splitting of mental illness to a crystal that breaks along invisible internal cleavages integral to its structure.[44] This image of splitting aptly conveys the fractures that have expanded beyond mental illness to encompass the widespread anxieties of late modernity. These anxieties pervade the work of artists that contend with the experience of being, including figures as diverse as Philip Guston, Bill Viola or more recently André Butzer. It also informs artists who in recent years have focused on the body as a medium and the subject of their work. They are many and their practice wide-ranging: works by Korean artist Byung Ho Lee, British artist John Isaacs and American artist Tony Oursler are representative examples in which to explore the cultural clefts that make today's anxious bodies.

The ways in which we feel and experience our bodies is, according to the psychoanalyst Susie Orbach, both the sign and the product of being ill at ease in our skin. This uneasiness manifests in an obsession with the physical self and the attempt to manufacture our appearance as artefact through diet, cosmetic surgery, strenuous exercising and other forms of bodily enhancement: 'there is a new franticness surrounding the body induced by social forces which are absorbed and transmitted in the family, where we first acquire our bodily sense'.[45] We are thus prey to a pervading 'beauty terror'. This perception of the body betrays an experience of corporeality as 'a menace'. It signals a painful searching for a lost sense of the 'body' that, as Orbach claims, resides in our physicality as well as in the mind.[46]

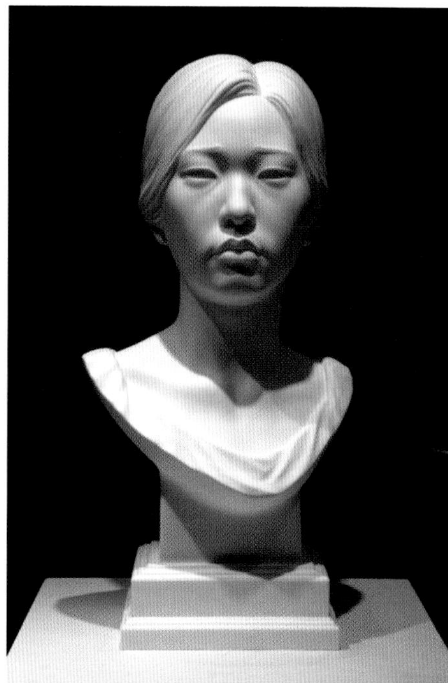

In *Vanitas Bust* (2010), Byung Ho Lee captures this collision by exploiting both traditional visual canons of Western beauty and the new technologies that support the quest for the perfect appearance, and which foreshadow new frontiers of body enhancement. Based on classical features, which are increasingly fetishized in countries such as Korea and Japan, Byung Ho Lee's silicone bust eerily wrinkles into old age and then rejuvenates through the pumping and suction of air. Although the face is East Asian, its features are quite undistinctive, following the requirements of global uniformity driven by the consumerism proper of 'beauty terror' (illus. 6). *Vanitas Bust* enacts for the viewer the promises of advertisements for cosmetics. It is saturated with the desires for a fabricated appearance, the mask of eternal youth, but also with the anxieties inherent in the need to appear 'young and beautiful'. The reversibility of the process is thus the more disquieting as the bust ages, and transforms itself into another uncanny version of itself. The title reminds us of transience, impending mortality and futility, but also of narcissism, the 'ego's ideal', and the anxious attainment of an impossible object of desire. It suggests that beyond the possibilities and potentials of enhancement and physical alteration lies the question of 'who am I?', which is today rephrased, according to the philosopher Renata Salecl, 'in the demand "I need to reinvent myself"'.[47] The pressure to be acceptable to others is parallel to that of creating a likeable other for one's self, as a struggle of reinvention, but also of compulsive obsession and dissatisfaction. Under the overwhelming encouragement

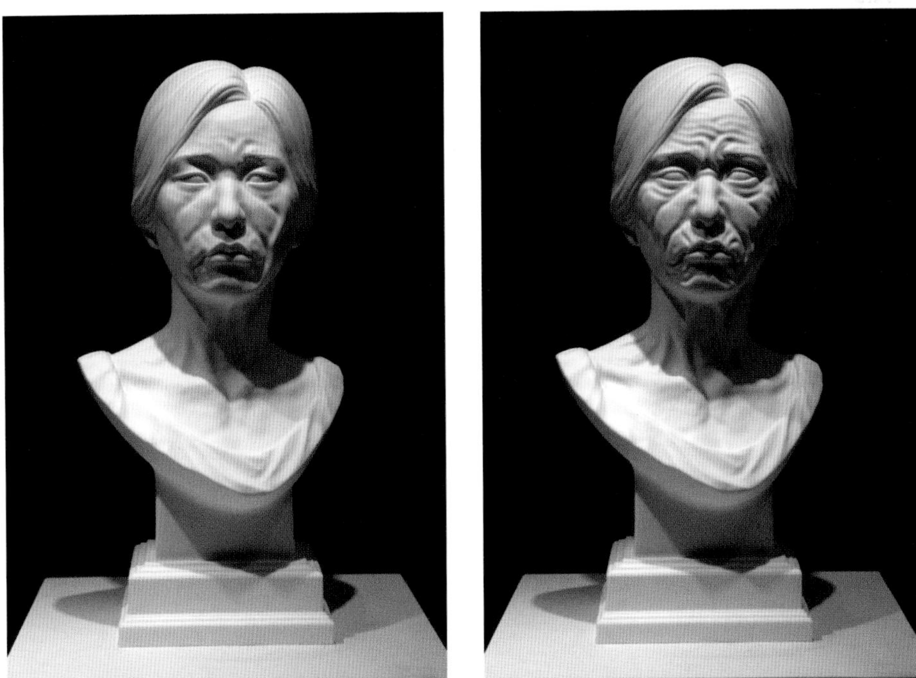

6 Byung Ho Lee, *Vanitas Bust*, 2010, mixed media.

to remodel oneself through clothes, cosmetics and plastic surgery, physical appearance becomes a quest for oneself that is often riddled with anxiety.

7 John Isaacs, *I can't help the way I feel*, 2003, wax, resin, polystyrene and steel.

The emphasis on external appearance as a means of fashioning one's identity, and the related vogue for dieting, date from the 1870s, when the interests of medical practitioners converged with those of the developing food industry, and claimed the obese as candidates for treatment, endorsing the association of unhealthy fleshiness with ineptitude, laziness, lack of will and moral lethargy. As the historian Sander Gilman states, 'Fat is dangerous. Dieting is modern.'[48] Today, the menace of the imposing presence of the obese body is hailed as social panic while visual icons promote thinness. The overly thin and overly large body act as cultural symbols of a widespread 'fat phobia'. They signify – not unlike the nervous body of hysteria – defiance as a form of in-corporation, exposing the alluring and revolting boundaries of consumer culture. By powerfully embodying physical, ideological and normative boundaries, they both contend with and transgress the paradigms of good and bad diet, of exercise and health, of physical and psychological control or a lassitude towards physicality. They intimate an ambivalent obsession and uneasiness towards corporeality, towards a body that is canonized and abused in equal measure. The artist John Isaacs has considered the stigmatization of the obese body, and the anxieties that psychologically characterize this condition, in large wax figures whose 'fleshiness' reminds us of the intrinsic embodiment of this feeling. In *I can't help the way I feel* (2003), the sculpture conjures this tragic alienation in the erupting and engulfing growth of the flesh in which the head is seemingly trapped, and under whose weight diminutive legs disappear (illus. 7). The eerie resemblance of wax to the rolls of skin bears out the individual plight and cultural stigma of obesity. The artwork confronts us with the overt visibility of a body that is felt to be too noticeable, too indulgent and too unruly, while begging for recognition. For Isaacs, physicality becomes the metaphorical landscape of the individual's affective struggle, and of her emotional incapacitation onto which feelings of failure are projected. The defiance attributed to being overweight is internalized, perpetrating the moral

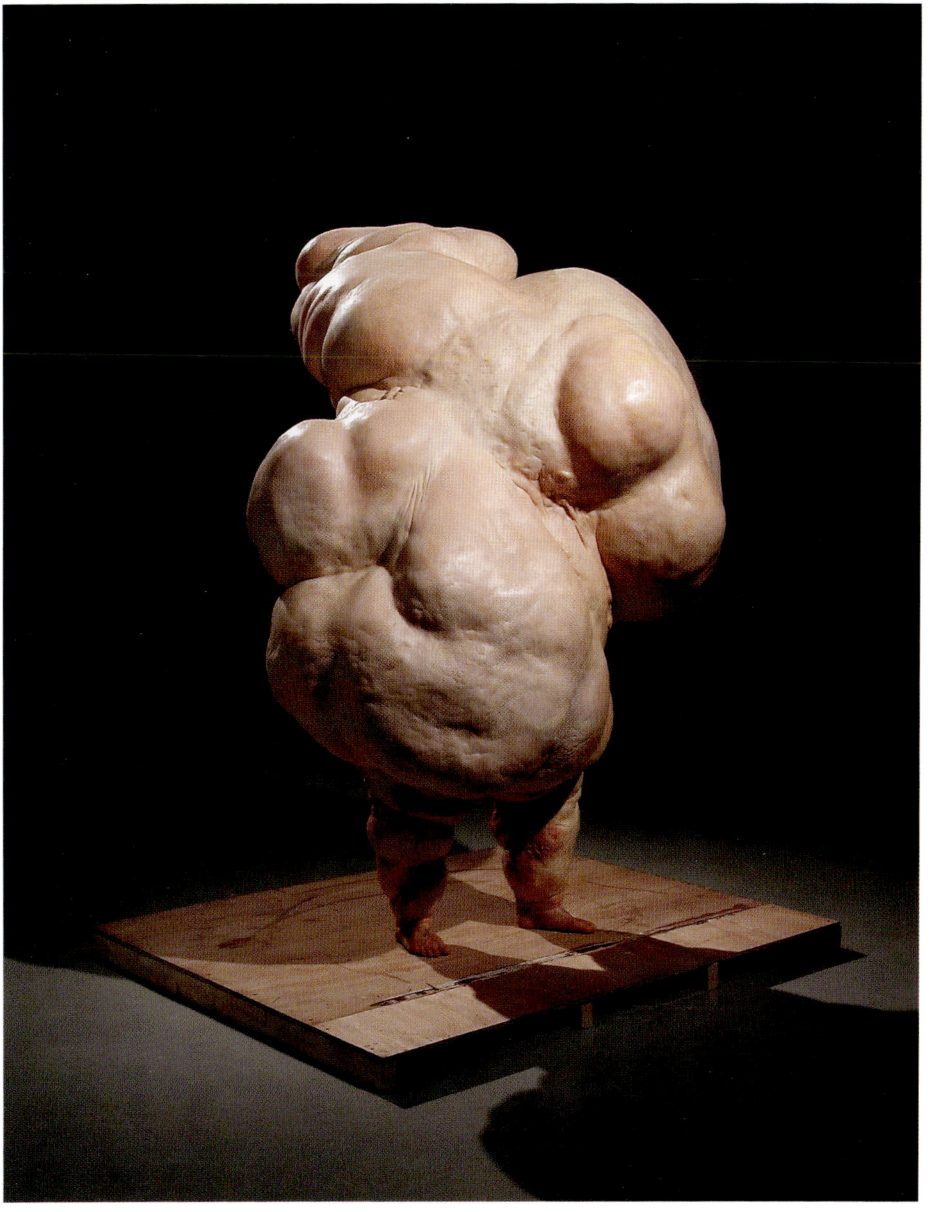

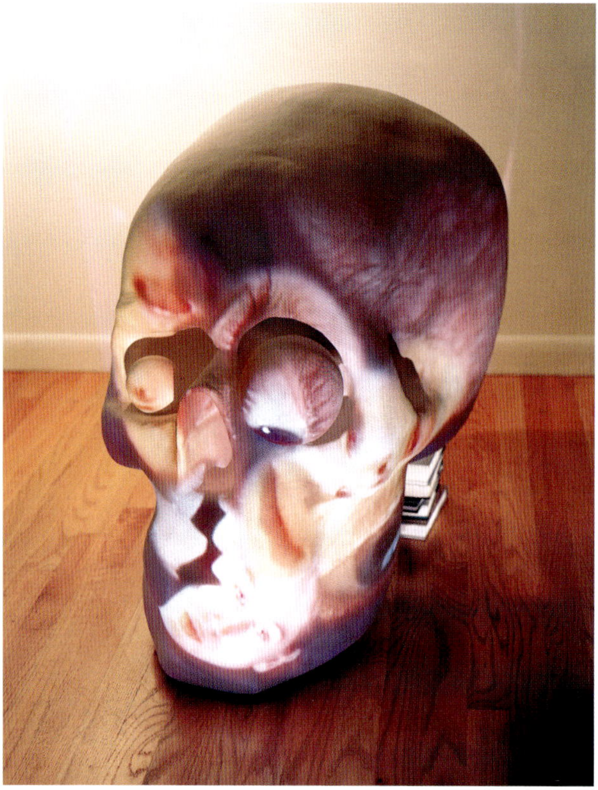

8 Tony Oursler, *Mutant Skull*, 1998, part of the *Still Lives and Skulls* installation, projection on foam and resin sculpture, audio component.

panic of overflowing fleshiness.[49] Shame weighs down this massive figure of wax, suggesting the vulnerability of a body that fears itself.

Both Byung Ho Lee and Isaacs point to the precariousness of physicality, of its external, potentially malleable surfaces, and to the displacement of a quest for subjectivity that teeters between phobia and obsession. This is the mayhem of hallucinatory impressions, of fragmented voices, of split bodies and disconnected figments created by Tony Oursler. Throughout his career, Oursler has explored the neurotic, twitching, spasmodically repetitive and sensorially heightened inner landscape of anxiety-related conditions. Giant ovoid and bodiless faces, enlarged floating eyeballs and mouths, or doll-like puppets with large

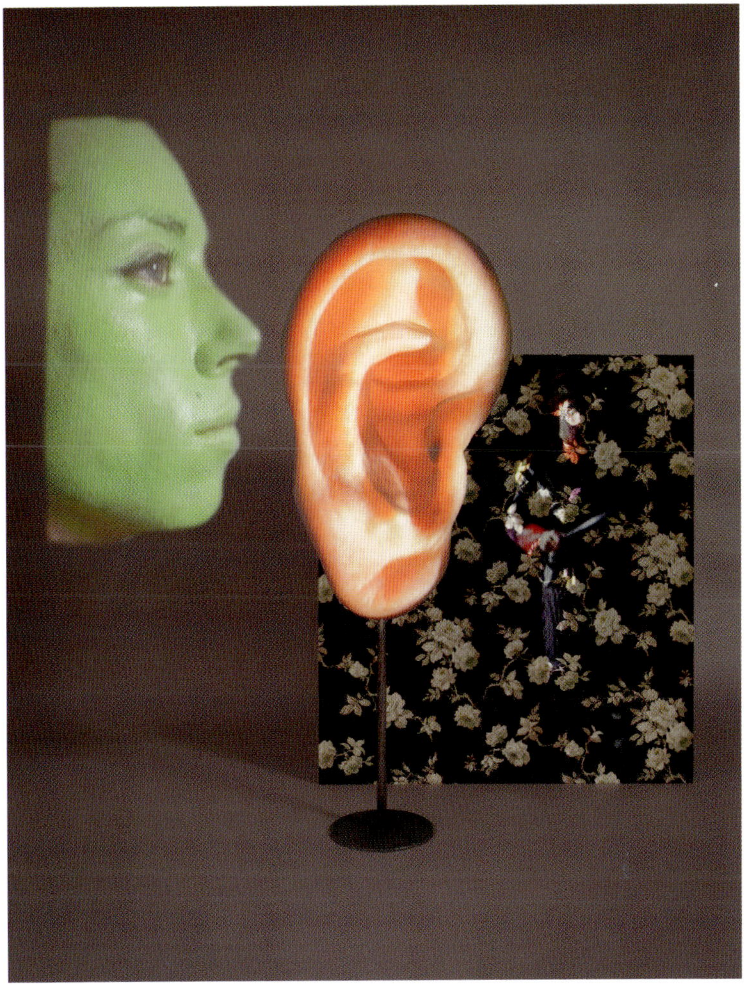

9 Tony Oursler, *ASL*, 2008, video projection, audio, resin, metal, wallpaper installation.

heads and inert bodies, are the grotesque screens of projected images, of distorted sounds and voices, through which the artist conjures eerie psychosocial bubbles of fractured violence and trauma (illus. 8 and 9). These visual and oral 'ephemera', to borrow Siri Hustvedt's description of her auditory hallucinations, suggest a time 'when consciousness recedes and my mind seems to jump on two wholly separate tracks: the heard and the seen'.[50] Oursler's forms are intentionally dysmorphed – distorted and dysfunctional. Phobias, addictions and paranoia are typical themes of his works, which consistently maintain a hallucinatory and nightmarish quality. Tall, diaphanous cigarettes accompanied by the sound of smoke being inhaled, and an enlarged mobile phone that babbles disconnected messages, are instances of the psychological dependency, obsessive desire and anxiety-related addictions that take control of our life. Compulsively, Oursler situates his work within the realm of neurosis, in the fracturing cleavages of the self where fear appears. He shows us the blurring points in which the subject disappears to a place of retreat but also of groundless obsessive anxieties or paranoia. Oursler's puppets, blown-up heads and anthropomorphized objects rephrase for our time Munch's vertiginous disorientation and the startled awareness of Margherita. They reflect the inner split that anxiety has traced within subjectivity and display the many defences that this frightened self forges.

Faces of Fear

Marcus Harvey's painting *Myra* (1995) is a portrait of the notorious child-murderer Myra Hindley, based on newspaper photographs and composed with children's handprints (illus. 10). When it was displayed at the *Sensation* exhibition at London's Royal Academy in 1997, the work caused outrage. On the first day of the exhibition it was damaged by repeated attacks, part of a campaign for its withdrawal on the grounds of its immorality. The *Daily Telegraph* labelled Harvey 'infamous'. One of the attackers claimed 'more people should be given the pleasure to throw things at it'.[51] Years later, a fleeting image of the work, which appeared in a video by the British Tourist Office to promote the 2012 London Olympics and presented at the official closure of the 2008 Beijing games, still caused indignation. But can an image really be so provocative? Evidently, the crimes to which it refers are felt as especially offensive, and blinding to the nature of the image itself. A comparable example is the consternation that followed the publication of Marguerite Duras' fictional evocation of Christine V, the presumed murderer of her four-year-old son, published in *Liberation* in July 1985. Both texts –

10 Marcus Harvey, *Myra*, 1995, acrylic on canvas.

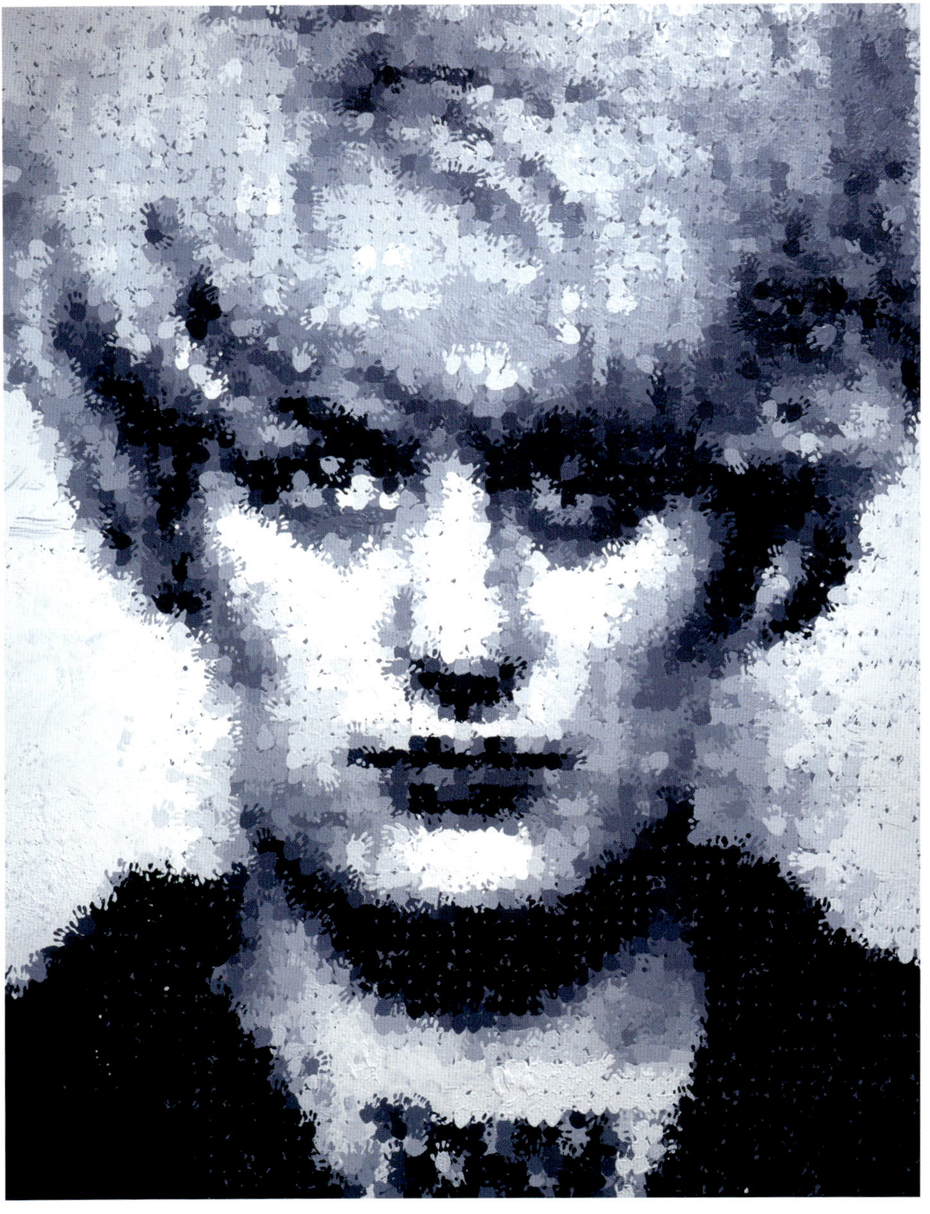

the literal and the visual – are based on news and draw a picture that treads ambiguously between verisimilitude and representation, between reality and fiction, between assumed ways of seeing, of constructing appearance, and an attempt to look beyond, challenging the 'picture'. For Duras, Christine V is 'sublime, forcément, sublime'.[52] The latter's act forcefully encompasses horror, unavoidably making us look and ask how and why, while remaining unfathomable.

Harvey's painting also forces us to look, to face, both literally and metaphorically, the supposed monster, and to notice the tiny marks that compose her image. At the Royal Academy the canvas was displayed on the floor propped against a wall. It invited the viewer to move closer, inspect the enlarged surface of the face in detail and to recompose it mentally. The painting is an image of images. It is transitional, derivative, referential and composite, overtly suggestive of its formal qualities – frontal, enlarged, pigmented, two-colour, head only and so on. The transition from reproduced photography to the canvas implies a transfer of medium and of the cultural values attached to such a movement. It also suggests a reflection upon seeing as an affective process that draws attention to the psychological veracity with which the act of seeing a face is endowed. Who do we see? What does the expression of the depicted face display? What can we deduce from the portrait if we are ignorant of who Myra Hindley is? Almost by default, *Myra* was invested with the symbolic power of images to evoke. As Duras writes about Christine V, the painting metaphorically became 'sublime, forcément, sublime'.[53] Removed from the specific context of the case, *Myra* is merely a portrait of a face open to multiple interpretations. But can we ascribe a face to fear?

If historically fear had a face in the expression that was codified across science and art, the ascription of a face to fear in the features that inspire suspicion, uneasiness, anxiety, and even dread and terror, concerns the recognition of the fearsome. To what extent such an act of recognition is to be imputed to an evolutionary inherited ability and to what extent the process is culturally encoded and developmentally learned is a matter of debate, bringing back issues concerning images and their pliability within scientific interpretation. Since Darwin, as already

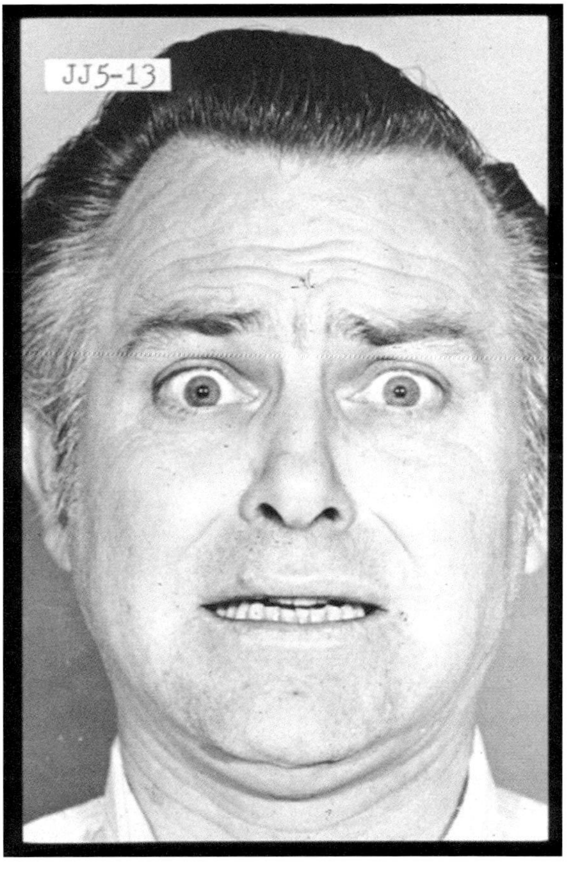

11 Paul Ekman and Wallace V. Friesen, 'Fear', photograph from FACS.

suggested, photographs have supported a reading of fear that has positioned it within an evolutionary scheme. Psychologists Paul Ekman and Wallace V. Friesen have further developed the Darwinian hypothesis of a hardwired model of primary emotions including fear, based on the recognition of involuntary micro-facial movements. The Facial Action Coding System (FACS) uses sets of photographs selected and categorized according to laboratory controlled identification of emotional states in faces (illus. 11). Extensively used in psychological experiments, these photographs feature, among other places, in trials designed to test the recognition of untrustworthy faces, shifting the emphasis of the 'face of fear' from the fearful to the fearsome.[54] Despite the criticism that they have garnered, detractors also deploy these pictures to suggest that, as in the case of Duchenne's images, they are pliable to interpretation, raising the question of the nature of this pliability.

Formally, the photographic image is sanctioned by the 'pose', an inherent feature that, as Roland Barthes argues, fixes an intention. The pose stands as 'an intention of reading', the instant when 'the real thing happened to be motionless in front of the "eye" in the arrest that constitutes it'.[55] The reciprocity between the 'real' face and the actuality of the image is captured in the moment of seeing as it seizes its object in the picture. The image freezes a moment in time, a face, a fleeting expression, and denotes a relation between the observer and the observed that is far from exhaustive or univocal. If we relate Barthes's notion of the pose to the specificity of scientific pictures of facial expressions of fear, the face is 'posed' in an arrest that is dictated by the requirements of the investigator according to existing intentions of the reading. These intentions vary according to protocols and theoretical frameworks, and can also be inferred according to established standards and consensus. Not only is any facial expression inherently unstable and nuanced, its recognition also lends itself to complex contextual factors. The pose – the instant when the real face stood motionless in front of the eye – repeats itself in front of the viewer: the visual strategies that determine it also sanction its reading, or do they?

Ironically there has hardly ever been consensus about the photographs meant to indicate fear – those used by Darwin and those in Ekman's and Friesen's series – yet they have grounded the centrality of the face as a discreet space of enquiry and formalized the recognition of the fearsome. For instance, they are used to support research aimed at developing tools for the detection of terrorists. Photographs of supposedly 'neutral' faces similarly appear in other kinds of experiments. In separate studies in which white Americans were presented with photographs of African American people, it was proved that the participants showed signs of alarm in the brain with the activation of the amygdala. These results matched those of a parallel bias test that implicitly measured racial prejudices in the participants, suggesting a presumed state of alertness at the sight of certain types of faces. This kind of research opens thorny areas of investigation not immune from ethical, psychological and social questions.[56] It also brings into question the possible interference resulting from the visual standardization of faces (i.e. light, frame, exposure) in the denotation of certain visages as 'fearsome'. The pose makes us look at the affective tension between the image and the labelling, between the intention and the reading.

Artists have investigated the significance of the pose by variously using and intervening in the visual features through which images of faces and bodies are standardized across scientific disciplines and practices of surveillance; in order to shift or challenge the intentionality of reading embedded in certain kinds of pictures. From Andy Warhol's famous, blown-up photographic series *Thirteen Most Wanted Men* (1964), which used police photographs of criminals, to Keith Piper's more recent video works based on immigrants' identity format photographs matched by CCTV footage of their movements, artists have subverted the 'controlled lexical space' of the photographic image.[57] They have invited the viewer to reassign meaning beyond its common designation, whereby the characterization of dangerous groups refers both to expert opinion and to individual judgements involving appearance, social class, ethnicity, sexual preferences and personal interactions fostered by culturally ingrained assumptions.[58] Similarly, the African American artist Lorna Simpson appropriates the standards of anthropological and criminal photography, such as the parallel use of frontal and profile pictures, in a series of works that questions racial and gender identity. Simpson deliberately masks part of the face, thus directing the spectator's attention to the mechanism of framing (illus. 12). The formal construct, rather than the subject, of the image becomes the focus of reading as we are asked to consider modes of looking and the culturally conditioned recognition of traits embedded within them. As the art historian Lisa Saltzman remarks apropos of the work of another African American artist, Glenn Ligon: 'Blackness is that marker of difference that makes certain subjects visually recognizable and socially legible, it is also blackness that renders certain subjects ultimately invisible,

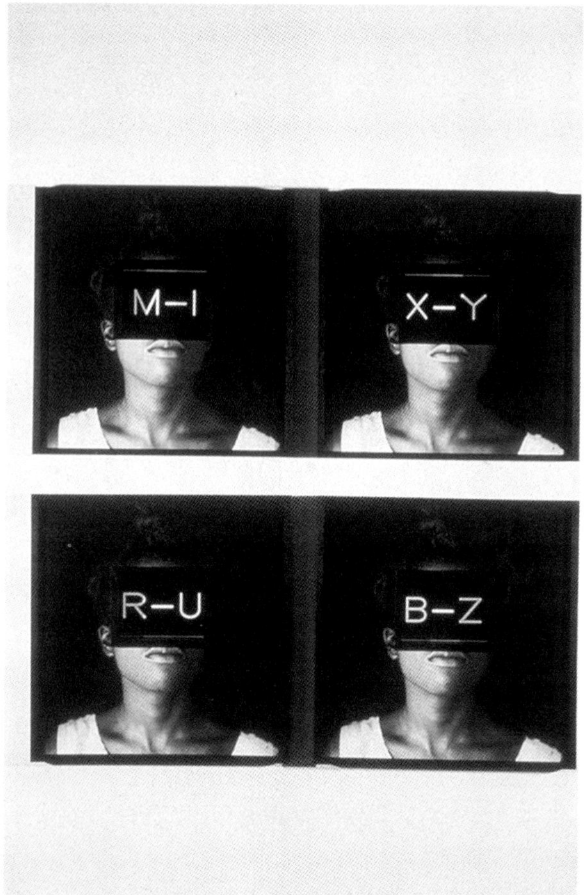

12 Lorna Simpson, *Proof Reading*, 1989, 4 black and white silver gelatin prints, 4 engraved plastic plaques.

spectral – a presence that haunts American social history and the white cultural imaginary.'[59] Simpson invokes the momentousness of photographic exposure as being one of definition, and intervenes in sanctioning the readability of the pose so as explicitly to destabilize it. Her work implicitly comments on the visual framework that informs other kinds of standardized, and hence supposedly 'neutral' photographs, such as those used in psychological experiments concerning the recognition of or reaction to faces. At the fore is the relation between the image and the viewer and the readings that such relation entails, the one framed within and those projected onto the picture. Intentionally, the artist renders these readings opaque. In so doing the affective response to the pictures ambivalently treads upon the cultural assumptions that corroborate our fears. Simpson exposes crystallized practices of seeing and the associations that stigmatize such practices, asking us to become aware, not of what, but *how* we see, of the biases and anxieties that we project into faces.

Similar problems transpire in relation to supposedly less 'standardized' and more heterogeneous kinds of photographs, such as those published in newspapers, proving that the pose, this formal definition of seeing, is equally at stake. The tenuousness of the attribution of meaning to faces and of the framework that culturally confines these readings is evinced in *The New York Times Project* (2003), a work including drawings and performances by the Finnish performance artist Pia Lindman, which explores the media manipulation of emotion following the September 11th attacks. The work is based on photographs published in the *New York Times* between September 2002 and 2003, portraying anonymous people in states of anguish, distress and despair, in places as diverse as the USA, Afghanistan, Iraq, Sudan, Palestine, Israel and Bali.[60] The artist questions and deconstructs assumed interpretations of bodily signs, as she reenacts and videos the expressions captured by the camera, and retransposes the video recording in a series of outline drawings that she then uses as guidelines for her performances (illus. 13). By divesting the pictures of a narrative context, she upsets univocal interpretations. Lindman's grimaces

13 Pia Lindman, from the series *Black Square*, pencil on vellum, 2003.

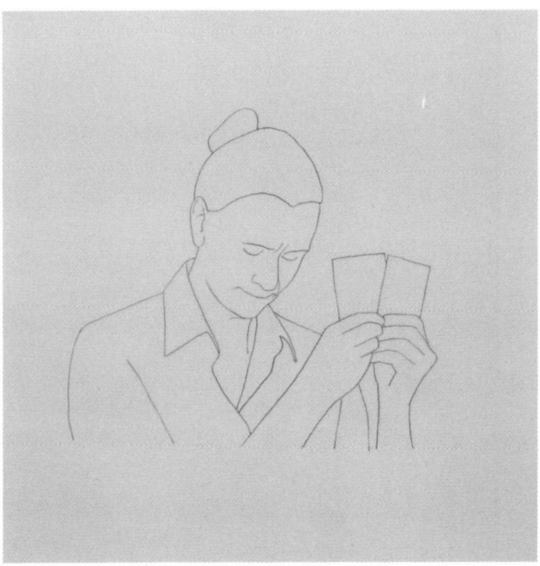

and gestures are laconic, resisting straightforward paradigms of signification.[61] The artist teases out the ingrained tenuousness of considering expression to be a sort of language, a code that mediates between the subjective and the objective, the inner and the outer, the physiological and the cultural, thereby unleashing some of the complexities implicit in the attribution of meaning to expressive movements.

It is not only the outward event of facial movements that is relevant to the contextual situation in which they feature. Their significance may also vary for the individual experiencing them, according to her belief system, inner wishes and conflicts, or other internal and external conditionings. Similar parameters equally interfere with and determine the observer and the act of seeing. Indeed, for some psychologists, facial movements are not unintentional, hardwired manifestations of a specific internal state that we call 'fear', but rather meaningful behaviours aimed at communicating a particular condition in relation to a designated context, for which there are multiform ways of emoting 'fear' according to the intention and context of those interacting.[62] Lindman makes us aware of the shifts and transitions that may occur through the processes of deconstruction and re-presentation that her work undergoes, signalling a formal diversity of patterns ranging from static to moving images, from photograph to drawing, from recorded enactment to re-enactment. From this process, divergent features and meanings emerge that confront the constitution and distinction of categories of visualization and interpretation as sites of exposures, interpolation and layering of meanings.

Embodied Fear

The shaven-headed man in Willie Doherty's video *Non-Specific Threat* (2004) faces the viewer with all the currency of the cultural ambiguity and ambivalence surrounding homosexuality, terrorism, crime and, more generally, how the other becomes an embodiment of our inner fears. It does so, not by overtly posing the issue, but rather by implicitly deploying a subtext of prejudices, anxieties and resentment. The video

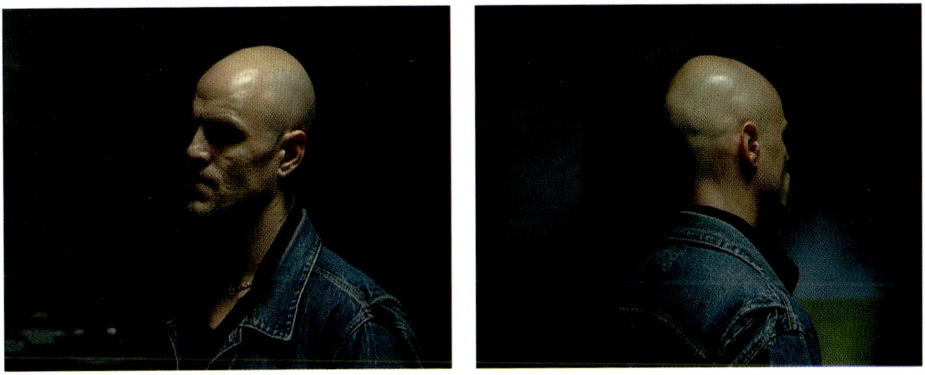

14 Willie Doherty, *Non-Specific Threat VIII (indifferent cruelty)*, 2004, c-print mounted on plexiglass (edition of 3).

shows the young man alone in a derelict space, possibly an industrial warehouse. The camera spans his face and head, revealing bumps and marks that are for the viewer to interpret, all while scrutinizing him for signs of danger (illus. 14). A voice-over claims, 'I am the depiction of everything you despise . . . I am the embodiment of all your fears.'[63] But whom do we despise most? Who is the embodiment of our fears, both conscious and subliminal? Perhaps the answer is an individual who embodies for us the signs of fear, a signifier onto whom we project overt or unspoken anxieties. He can be anybody: a terrorist, a gay man, a criminal, an 'I' who 'disappears in a crowd', and who is hence the more dangerous, being anonymous and unknown. As Doherty comments:

> I was very happy that *Non-Specific Threat* was read from a queer perspective. In a way it is so obvious. Such a reading was something that I was conscious of at the time of making the work. *Non-Specific Threat* is concerned with how we project our fears and anxieties onto an unknowable other.[64]

When we interrogate 'the face of fear', we are confronted with the cultural making of the other as dangerous and the acknowledgement that certain groups feel menacing, thus endorsing existing prejudices and anxieties. The visual ambiguity that characterizes Doherty's video is the more provocative as the viewer projects upon the man a specific 'threatening' identity, a supposed recognition of danger. At the fore is the positioning of menace in the gap between the face and the gaze, the frisson of an intention of reading that facial expression entails. In the encounter between the image and the viewer a slippage or interference occurs. Fear is embodied, but what are the insinuations of this embodiment? What do we see in a potential Islamic terrorist, or youngsters at risk? How culturally fraught is the recognition of the threatening other?

The headline of *The Times* on 31 March 2009 read 'The Face of Terror'. The accompanying photograph showed one of the militants who laid siege to a police academy in Lahore during his arrest. The *Oxford English Dictionary* records the entry of the term 'Islamophobia' in 2001 as an instance of a contemporary racial phobia. Historically, however, Muslim culture has embodied an otherness to Christianity from its onset, representing contested attitudes that were pivotal in the making of the 'West'. In the attribution of the 'face of terror' to a supposed Islamic enemy, a sort of cultural repetition is enacted that exposes the irritability of the boundaries on which cultural identity is generated. This translates to other phobic attitudes and anxiety towards race, gender and the like, unravelling the cultural constructs that inform images and the implications of emotional responses to a 'dangerous' face, whether derived from concerns surrounding terrorism, criminality, racism or homophobia. In the artwork *Dying Gauls* (2005–6), which uses plaster casts of the faces of Hellenistic sculptures, the German artist Sophie Ernst superimposes on them the faces of men from Lahore whose recorded voice-overs discuss ideas about life, death and afterlife. The projected faces match the still features of the plasters, layering movement and instability on the facial contours (illus. 15). The artwork refers back to classical originals that were commissioned to celebrate the victory of the Greeks over the Galatians in Asia Minor. The sculptures endorse the heroic nobility of the defeated warriors, as well as epitomizing what was other to Ancient Greek culture: the non-Greek, the barbarous. The layering of cultural references is evident in the overall series of which *Dying Gauls* is part, which further uses plaster casts of ancient busts of Persians, Amazons and giants that coincide with well-established stereotypes of antiquity adopted in the late nineteenth century to represent gender and racial otherness. Historically, the Persians stood for the feminized East, both alluring and immorally dangerous; the masculinized warrior woman was adopted to epitomize the emancipated modern woman; and the uncivilized giant represented not only the bogeyman of folklore, but also a category encompassing both the 'historic' other (the prehistoric man whose features, for modern evolutionary science, are traceable in the tribal man) and the other within society (people of colour, criminals, the disenfranchized). Ernst's technique of aligning and freezing superimposed features thus suggests a continuum of embodiment. It displays a mythology of enemies in which the present Islamic threat is culturally situated and immortalized as a personification of danger in Western perception.

The vulnerability of designation of a 'dangerous other' acquires new prominence when it regards those that are considered most 'at risk'. Contemporary preoccupation with children's and young adults' safety manifests in the home, in the playground, at school or on the Internet, and permeates every aspect of social and cultural life. Youngsters' physical and emotional integrity may be put at risk in the various spaces that they inhabit, and therefore demands surveillance. At the other side of the 'at risk' equation, youth criminality is an impending social problem. Young offenders are increasingly perceived as a serious social threat, judged by London's Metropolitan Police as second only to terrorism. According to an article published in the *Observer* on 19 January 2009, young urban gangs have been linked to Muslim activism, adding to the already present danger of drugs, violence and sex offences the potential recruitment into terrorist units. Though contested as part of a pose 'to gain street credibility and trade on false perceptions about links to terrorists', distinct sources of risk and fear converge in one recognizable group, highlighting the cultural dynamics that intervene when danger is embodied.

In *Bare Dust* (2000), film-maker and artist Shona Illingworth explores the double implications surrounding the social perception of 'groups at risk' by working with teenagers from a council estate that forms part of a regeneration programme in Hackney Wick in East London, one of the epicentres of youth violence in the city. Illingworth focuses her

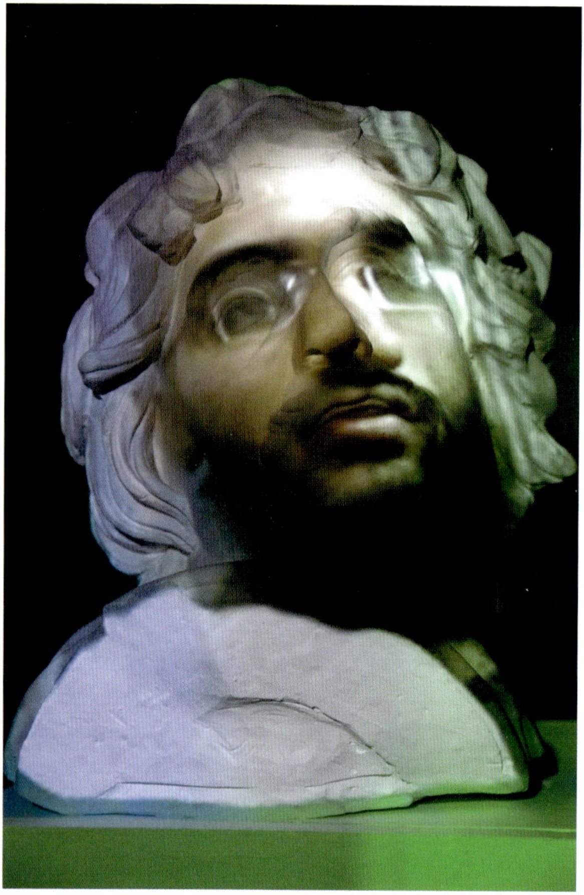

15 Sophie Ernst, *Dying Gauls*, 2005–6, projection on plaster cast.

lens on the tense dynamics of fear and aggression as she follows some of the teenagers, relentlessly showing their kicking and running feet as they practise their skills (illus. 16). The feet barely touch the ground that bears the footprints of one of the estate's demolished buildings, repeatedly displayed as it collapses. The ground is sinisterly inscribed in the subliminal evocation of the ruin. It is also a perimeter that denotes through disappearance the alienating experience of immigration embedded in the politics of dislocation that so prominently affects contemporary subjectivity. This desolate ground marks the limits of the youngsters' mobility, demarcating their power of action: beyond they are vulnerable and the prey of other gangs. The threat that they embody gives way to their fears, voiced in the concern for the safety of their mothers and sisters. As their game has no plot and is never-ending, without prospect of a solution, the fragmented account of their experience reveals anxieties and powerlessness. Apart from the physical dexterity needed to run with the ball – possessed by many young boys and men – what these young people doubtfully articulate is the dream of becoming a footballer. Yet the running feet also suggest and produce the emotive charge of antagonistic feelings, evoking both vulnerability and menace. To be 'at risk' is, therefore, to inhabit the ambiguous boundaries that delineate danger and protection, aggression and vulnerability.

In a study of 'gang cultures' in Britain that draws comparisons with research carried out in the USA, the sociologist John Pitts looks at the complexities of these cultures across changing scenarios of organized street crime and of the dynamics that lead young people to join gangs. Issues of ethnicity are intermeshed with the economics and politics of marginalization, future prospects and social representation. Within this context, young people's affiliation to gangs is part of an affective process marked either by a desire of inclusion and success, a fatalistic answer to circumstance, or a response to fear that further spreads dread and social angst.[65] This complexity resonates with discussions of

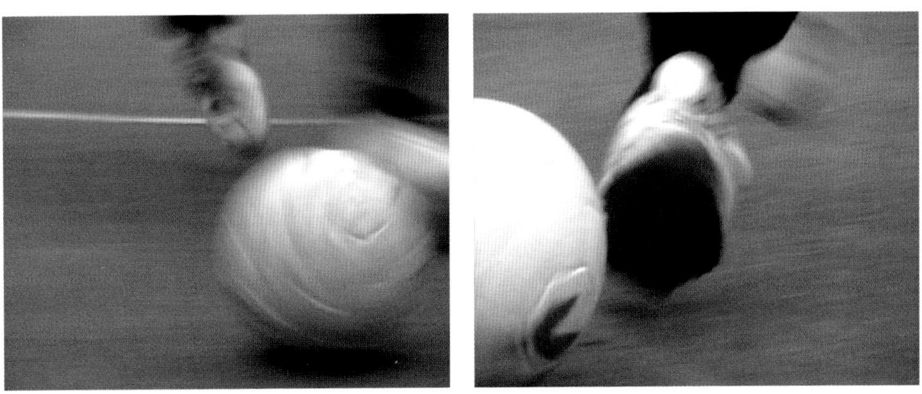

16 Shona Illingworth, *Bare Dust*, 2000, digital video stills.

African American constructions of masculinity. Thelma Golden, the art historian and former director of the Studio Museum in Harlem, comments that 'black masculinity represents an amalgam of fears and projections in the American psyche which rarely conveys or contains the trope of truth about the black male's existence', and which results in over-representation, simplification and demonization.[66] It is a picture punctuated by stereotypes, as the work of Lorna Simpson demonstrates apropos of black femininity. By disrupting the narrative flow and simple means of identification, *Bare Dust* raises similar questions about young gang culture in Britain. It allows for ambiguities, blending biases and anxieties to convey the tattered ground of dislocation, and exposes fears and fantasies that are too 'bare' not to be frightening. Illingworth's subjects are denuded and worthless, but also excessive and empowered, as one of the young men says, 'there's nothing here, just bare dust'.[67]

In her study on the politics of emotions, sociologist Sara Ahmed introduces the chapter on fear with the fable of the black boy and white boy that the French Algerian sociologist Frantz Fanon narrates in his seminal work, *Black Skin, White Masks* (1952). When the black boy meets the white boy, he shivers with fear, which the white boy mistakes for anger and reacts by displaying his own fear. As Ahmed comments, neither body generates the emotion; rather, they display the opening up of 'past histories of associations' in which the circulation of emotions and their related reading is embedded.[68] These histories and the associations that they engender do not only affect the borders between the self and the others but also the ways in which we objectify fear. Our anxieties are indeed shaped 'by histories that "stick", making some objects more than other fearsome'.[69] The location of these objects and the modes through which they are recognized reflect cultural practices of categorization. The result is stories and praxis that 'stick'.

In his work, the German artist Gerhard Lang has consistently questioned the tools of bodily classification and standardization that inform criminology and other disciplines. Lang is attentive to the consequences of a normative reading of the body, those exposed by photography, and those already present in its precursor, the death mask. In *Provincia Adumbrata: Encounters in the Realm of Shadows* (2007),

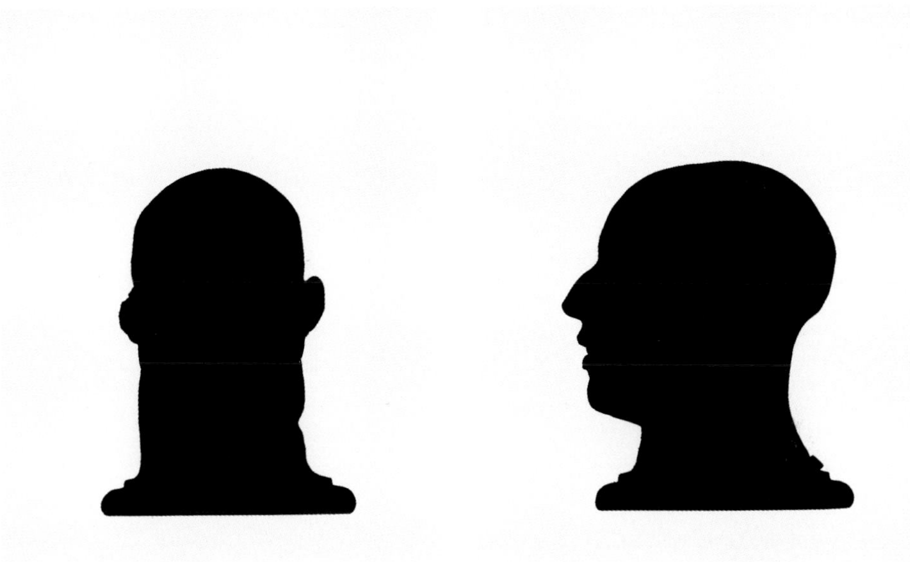

17 Gerhard Lang, DM7 front and profile, from *Provincia Adumbrata: Encounters in the Realm of Shadows*, 2007, knife cut.

Lang creates a haunting landscape of shadows based on the silhouettes of 34 plaster casts. The casts are taken from a collection of nineteenth-century phrenological heads of judicially hanged individuals, whose culpability was not always clear and in some cases is still a matter of debate. Originally displayed at Newgate prison and now at the Crime Museum (Scotland Yard) in London, the casts were originally made for the detection of signs that could reveal the 'criminal' and define readable traits of deviance. Lang traces and cuts out the silhouettes of the busts, paying close attention to the idiosyncratic forms and marks of the individual heads (illus. 17). The medium is a formal and conceptual layering of historical references and the dubious claim of phrenology as a system of knowledge. It also reminds us that the twenty-first century is not immune from the search of physical signs of otherness. The final work envelops the viewer in insubstantial presences, on which shadow casts shadow, and profiles overlap. These unstable encounters regard absences as well as presences, unsettling contours of meaning as the past projects into the present and vice versa, such that the embodied enters into contact with its warped disembodiment. Shadows belonging to the ghostly are at the same time inherently bound to the properties of the corporeal and the material.

Provincia Adumbrata goes beyond the specificity of the phrenological project to interrogate the affective circulation that defines somatic and cultural boundaries and the reading of difference through which fear and anxiety shape the body of others. The images evoke and invoke spectral presences. The mythical embodiment of fear clashes with the ghost of knowledge, posing anew the predicament of the 'systems' that regulate bio-surveillance in relation to today's means of brain and DNA tagging. These technologies iterate practices regulating the identification of a 'suspect population'. According to some commentators, these systems provide an addition to 'qualitative variable knowledge of suspect populations already constructed through highly localised, informal and often unreliable information – thus providing more information on groups already targeted'.[70] Especially problematic is the implementation of extensive national and international databases of DNA profiles that support and regulate the current 'culture of crime control' implemented by the police.[71] Ethical questions concern the storage and accessibility of information provided by these databases, which also include the DNA of non-offenders. These questions, as the authors of a report on genetic information and crime investigation published in 2004 note, 'become more urgent with increased storage and speculative searching of the DNA of individuals who have never been charged with, let alone convicted of, a recordable offence'.[72] They involve complex issues of individual information privacy, since DNA gives access to knowledge not only about the individual but also their relatives. Currently these databases use non-coding areas of DNA, but advances in technology may, however, lead to the risk of other forms of information becoming available, including 'genetic risk factors, phenotypical information, and "genetic ancestry"'.[73] The act of defining the dangerous body thus expands into the recognition of external traits to our genetic make-up, mobilizing ever more sophisticated technologies of surveillance as fear figuratively circulates in the deepest tissues of our societies.

In a performance at Tate Modern in 2008, the Cuban artist Tania Bruguera had the audience in the Turbine Hall herded by guards on horseback. The guards implemented the same techniques used for the control of riots, moving the crowd with fierce authority. The performance mobilized feelings of fear, passive compliance, and perhaps even resistance, as well as overtly enacting upon dynamics of power relations and control. Fear, anxiety, nervousness and dread are part of the affective currency exploited and explored in Bruguera's performances and installations. Her various interactive works involve the visitor posing for photographs with semi-tamed animals beneath a portrait of the founder of the Soviet secret police, or being put under the blinding light used for the interrogation of prisoners while hearing the sound of rifles being loaded. Bruguera interviewed visitors to an installation held in the Frankfurt Bürgerhaus Gallus, where the 1963 Auschwitz trials took place, and over-imposed their replies with original testimonies. Overtly unsettling the 'safe' role of the spectator, this artist creates disturbing and ambiguous situations that trigger uncertainty, discomfort and angst.[74] The weakened position in which the visitor finds herself addresses the institutionalization of power through threat, insinuating modes of prevarication and the troublesome feelings that this engenders through a momentary shift of perspectives.

The Polish artist Artur Żmijewski is renowned for his experimental film work based on staged situations with non-actors, which critically contest established relations of power and the inherent affective interaction in human exchanges. These stagings reveal culturally ingrained dynamics of action and reaction, comparable to Ahmed's model of emotional circulation. In *Repetition* (2005), a work with which the artist represented Poland at the 51st Venice Biennale, Żmijewski interrogates the revelation of abuse in prison camps such as Abu Ghraib and Guantanamo Bay. The work restages the American psychologist Philip Zimbardo's renowned experiment to assess the effects of prison life, both on the inmates and prison staff, in which Zimbardo created a replica of a prison below the Psychology Department at Stanford University.[75] The shifted sense of reality in the participants to the Stanford experiment was noticeable. As Zimbardo observes, 'After observing our simulated prison for six days, we could understand how prisons dehumanize people, turning them into objects and instilling in them feelings of hopelessness'.[76] As for the guards, ordinary people could also be transformed 'from the good Dr Jekyll to the evil Mr Hyde'.[77] In discussing crime prevention, criminologist Paul Ekblom draws attention to emotions, including fear, excitement, guilt and shame, as part of the ways in which offenders feel and experience themselves.[78] While these emotions can sustain prevention if they are recognized and used constructively, those who designate the dangerous also rely on a gamut of emotions and readings of signs in their own judgement. Fear is thus incorporated, displaced and intensified, not only by those who fear but also by those who are perceived as the 'object' of fear.

For *Repetition*, Żmijewski invited unemployed Polish workers to participate in the work and divided them in two groups: the guards and the prisoners. The pressure of the situation, as in the Stanford example, produced determined behaviour and emotional interaction. Participants were also coaxed by the artist, who remained a hidden but powerful presence throughout, epitomized by the impinging presence of cameras all over. The resulting film exposes this affective collision between the participants and the artist and the role of surveillance practices. *Repetition* sets itself overtly as a re-enactment for the camera. Filmed from multiple perspectives, in its final rendering it betrays the visual conditioning that informs surveillance. The art critic Anthony Downey observes that, 'As an aesthetic form, [surveillance] implicates the viewer from the onset in its panopticised rhetoric and the implications of guilt that it places (rightly or wrongly) on those who are being viewed'.[79] Surveillance thus establishes boundaries of presumed culpability, acting as a technology of knowledge between the observed and the observer, between a guilty and a judging party.

This dynamic results in a rhetoric and aesthetics that 'imbricates the observer within a system of knowledge that includes the production of criminological, juridical and sociological models for the study of normative and, crucially, aberrant forms of behaviour'.[80] The intentionality of the act of seeing inherent to the making of images is still critical. As in the case of Lang and Bruguera, the artwork is a 'repetition' of visual practices that interfere and interact in the affective circulation of fear. And fear, as Sara Ahmed observes, involves boundaries not by defending those that already exist between the subject and others, but rather by establishing new ones – by continuously redefining practices of categorization and the biases that they endorse.

Contagious Bodies

In 1998 the artist Anthony-Noel Kelly was tried for smuggling human remains for use in body casts. Kelly is one of many contemporary artists whose work employs blood, skin, hair, placenta and other organic matter. The deployment of material that it is often regarded as disgusting, revolting or repulsive transgresses boundaries of comprehension as well as moral and other codes of social praxis, since it presents the body in its uttermost fleshiness and precariousness, as an ambiguous artefact both abhorred and awesome. The popularity of Gunther von Hagens's display of plastinated corpses in poses similar to those of historical écorchés reveals a fascination with the macabre through simulacra that blur the distinction between reality and representation, between the biological and the artificial. This uncertainty reproduces the uneasy contestation of the corpse already evident in historical wax models and preserved human specimens. Fashioned in lifelike poses and adorned with lace and beads, eighteenth-century anatomical models aestheticized and sanitized death by rendering the corpse and the decaying flesh a beguiling spectacle and astonishing sight. In this aestheticization historians have read an attempt to dissolve the fear of disintegration and decaying of death, and a disavowal of cultural taboos and unconscious anxieties represented by the corpse and the pollution of bodily matters.[81] Fear of pollution and contagion entails the body and most specifically the definition of its boundaries: if death retains spectral qualities that neither science nor technology have exorcized, then corpses, blood, bodily fluids and excrement continue to occupy a borderline position within contemporary culture and are linked to notions of disgust, repulsion, filth, pollution and risk in ways that are socially, politically and even morally problematic.

The Mexican artist Teresa Margolles deploys these liminal products (water used for cleaning a morgue, blood and human remains) as the material and subject of her art, to explore the politics of marginalization through a form of physicality, a manifestation of the body that is borderline and hence culturally dangerous. *Lengua* (*Tongue*) (2002) shows the embalmed and pierced tongue of a drug addict, sold by the family of the deceased to pay for the funeral (illus. 18). It critically points to violence, dispossession, exploitation and inequality, and enacts a displacement from the margins to the centre, complicating further inherent fears that surround the corpse.[82] Margolles unapologetically exposes

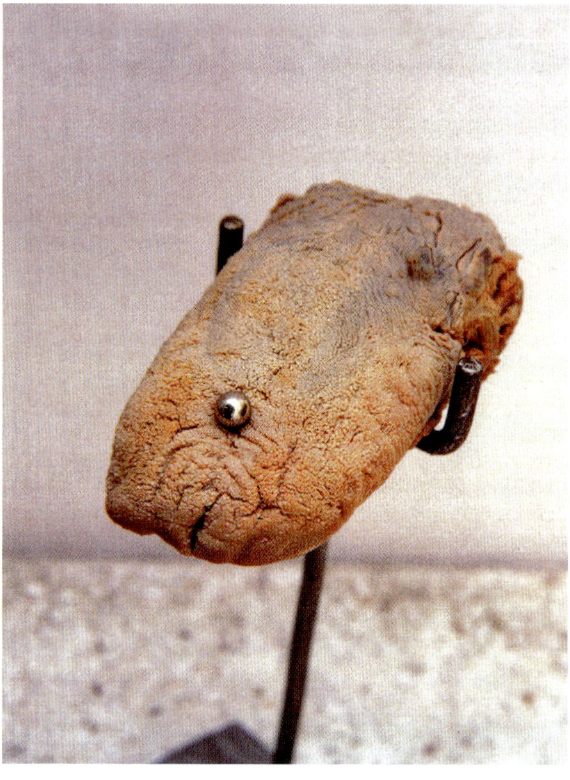

18 Teresa Margolles, *Lengua* (*Tongue*), 2002, perforated tongue with piercing from a teenager murdered in a street fight.

what is repressed and silenced in contemporary culture, what belongs to the margins of societies and is located at the periphery of the so-called developed world. The work contends with the horror of dismemberment and fragmentation, with a cultural as well as psychic violation of borders, as instances of displacement and pollution. It reminds us of Walter Benjamin's claim that the image of the corpse is able to capture all that is both 'sorrowful and unsuccessful' in history and 'the biographical historicity of the individual', thus standing meaningfully between the subject and history.[83] This conceptual and physical liminality renders *Lengua* a potent image through which to question notions of cleanliness, order, safety and aesthetics as established standards of sanitation, propriety and safety, and to interrogate the cultural tenets implicated in the fear of pollution, when the contaminating body is always liminal.

In her seminal study of the anthropological concept of pollution as a cultural construct through which notions of danger are established, Mary Douglas contends that the nineteenth-century discovery of bacterial transmission and infection has deeply influenced contemporary ideas of filth, which are now articulated around 'the knowledgeable pathogenic organism'.[84] However, as she argues, despite this new definition, dirt still retains the cultural attribute of being 'matter out of place'.[85] As she puts it: 'if we can abstract pathogenicity and hygiene from our notion of dirt, we are left with the old definition of dirt as matter out of place'. For Douglas dirt can, in fact, be understood as a 'by-product of a systematic ordering and classification of matter, in so far as ordering involves rejecting inappropriate elements'.[86] The 'residual category' of filth – connoting also a danger – potently interferes both physically and symbolically with the margins of acceptability, cleanliness, order, safety and beauty, producing ambiguity and confusion. Accordingly, nineteenth-century science offered a new and revolutionary explanation to the origin of contagion through germ theory. External microscopic pathogens, the theory uncovered, could affect humans and animals by entering the body, in many cases putting the pathogenic vector, as it were, in circulation through contact.

Germ theory was central to the development of contemporary ideas of hygiene and indeed to changing our notion of cleanliness. It offered systematic means of sanitary prevention and treatment, but it also epitomized the scientific and technological endeavour to control matter and systematize ideas of danger and risk that are still recognizable today. Imperialism coincided with the implementation of new practices of domestic sanitation as well as with new ideas of safety and protection. Hence, soap 'emerged commercially during an era of impending crisis and social calamity, serving to preserve, through fetish ritual, the uncertain boundaries of class, gender, and race identity', since it established social and moral as well as hygienic barriers against external pollution – whether of dirt or other 'polluting' bodies.[87] Cholera, which resulted from contaminated water, was one of the most devastating epidemics to ravage Europe throughout the nineteenth century. The historian Richard Evans recognizes the political consequences of the bacterial origins of the disease in his study of cholera. Although referring to the German context, a similar picture applies elsewhere. Evans writes that, in the 1880s, 'the idea of a deadly bacillus transmitted by carriers and infected individuals throughout society had an obvious relevance to bourgeois and official fears of the peril of socialism.'[88] Germ theory provided an analogy that endorsed the identification and fight against social and moral defiling caused by degenerative 'matter' both internally and externally. This reflected broad anxieties towards the existing imperial notions of marginality, since cholera originated in Asia, and also towards the puzzling, corrosive effects of a changing social fabric.

The symbolic content of germ theory is no less relevant today than it was in the past. From the mid-1990s fear of epidemics have become central to international politics in ways comparable to environmental danger, terrorism and other forms of transnational threats to national security, since it acts as a catalyst of socio-economic and political change.[89] The uncertainties concerning the aetiology, lethality and vector of transmission of the pathogens are common at the insurgence of epidemics, affecting responses both on an individual and collective level. The unfolding of recent epidemic scares, including HIV/AIDS, SARS, H5N1 avian flu and H1N1 swine flu, are indicative of conflicting responses in which individuals' beliefs, scientific knowledge, information and official interventions have been at odds.[90] While flu epidemics are cyclical, the etymology of the name from the Italian *influenza* (also meaning influence and manipulation) suggests the power to affect and condition, to determine reactions and responses. Transmission migrates literally as well as figuratively from the periphery to the centre and back again. The origins of the epidemics are often situated at the encroaching fringes of Europe and the United States: SARS started in China, H1N1 in Mexico, and the controversial narratives of the HIV virus betray a similar story in the supposed transmission from Africa, via Haiti to the United States.

Viruses and bacteria attack membranes, and circulate through physical, national and social borders. Transmission occurs through the 'abject' channels of bodily fluids, including blood, breast milk, saliva, mucus and tears. The NHS campaign to combat the spreading of swine flu in the UK reads: 'If you could see the germs, you'd see how quickly they spread', and 'Catch it. Cough or sneeze into a tissue. Bin it. As soon as you can. Kill it. Kill the germs with soap and water or use a sanitiser gel.'[91] The response to germs resonates with aggressive protection. Faced with the dangerous substances of abjection and with the uncertain grounds of visibility and recognition, the reaction is one of defence, making questions of prevention and containment across physical and ideological borders as important today as in earlier times.

A case in point is offered by an artwork that was contaminated during an exhibition:

> The Victimless Leather was quite sick in the last few days . . . although the cells seem to grow very well, we had a small fungi infection which we treated . . . but I am afraid that in so doing we introduced some bacterial contamination which is much harder to treat. So it seems that we will now need to add ethanol and fix the specimen. A new jacket will be installed at the beginning of January. This is the nature of this beast – every time I show this work there are new challenges and stories – I like the fact that in a show titled Medicine and Art there was an actual attempt of providing medicine to a living art work . . .[92]

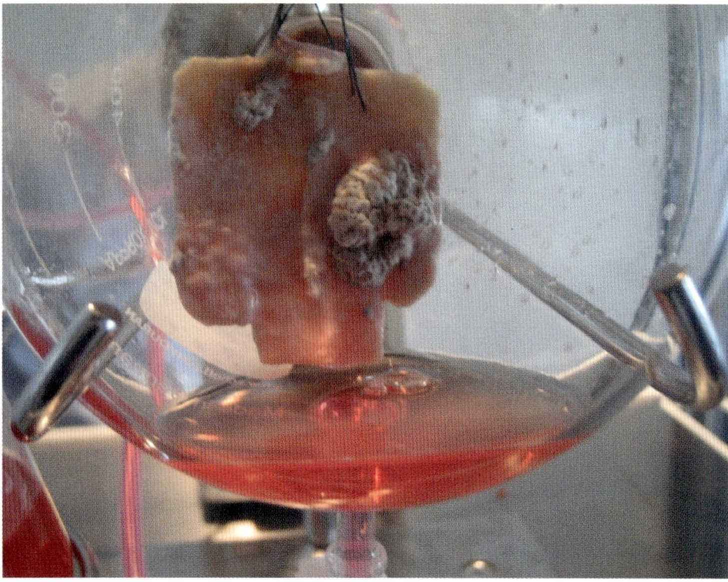

19 *Victimless Leather* – A Prototype of Stitch-less Jacket grown in a Technoscientific 'Body', the Tissue Culture & Art Project (Oron Catts & Ionat Zurr), 2004–2010, biodegradable polymer skin and bone cells from human and mouse.

The Victimless Leather Project is a live installation of a grown co-culture of human and mouse cells, a collaboration between Oron Catts and Ionat Zurr for the Tissue Culture & Art Project (TC&A), hosted by SymbioticA at the University of Western Australia (illus. 19). Its 'living condition' has exposed the work to infection and bacteriological contamination in a short period of time. Pathogens endanger the sterile microenvironment of the artwork in ways that may not be apparent to the visitor. And yet *The Victimless Leather* is 'affected' and 'has to be treated'. This vulnerability to pollution treads across physical and ideological layers of visibility and of signification of this hybrid organism. The work itself is the result of a palpable and yet microscopic process of growth. At stake is the susceptibility of the clean, uncontaminated, pure and pristine qualities of matter, whether in the form of object or body (*The Victimless Leather* is both artefact and body), to the insidiousness of pollution and contamination represented by molecular organisms such as germs, fungi, bacteria and viruses. Mutable, and mutating in conjunction with the environment, pathogens evoke evolutionary and historical morphing and act as a persistent threat that, like repressed toxic material, can infect and affect.

Scientific visualizations of viruses, often enhanced through artificial colour and virtual models of the chemical composition of the molecules, represent the margins of organic matter. Using such imaging as a referent, Luke Jerram has produced a series of three-dimensional glass-blown sculptures that include the HIV virus, E.coli virus, and avian and swine flu viruses (illus. 20). Different levels of detail, shape and dimension create a varied 'menagerie' of labyrinthine and spiky transparent forms, both beautiful and surreal, giving form to the phantoms of contagion. While Catts and Zurr's living cells evoke the fear of contamination as an 'affective' condition of the work, Jerram's sculptures turn 'dangerous' invisible threats into elaborate translucent surfaces. Both artists prompt a consideration of the notions of membranes, boundaries and borders. Catts and Zurr's cells are hybrid,

20 Luke Jerram, *E.Coli*, 2009, glass.

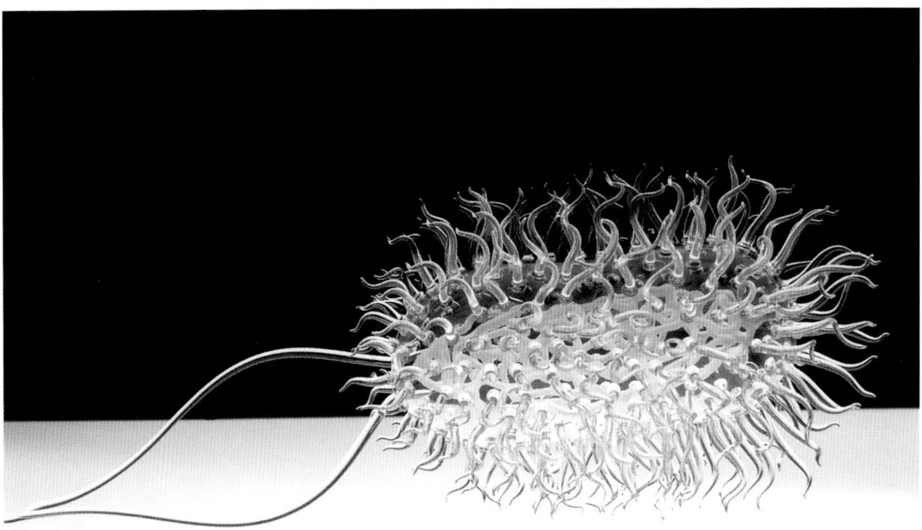

the product of genetic manipulation of organic matter at cellular and tissue level. As such they already stand for the anamorphous, malleable forms of biology and culture. They contain the seeds of the exciting and confusing ambiguities embedded in biotechnologies that irritate and infectiously affect boundaries. Both Catts and Zurr's and Jerram's artworks evoke the invisible and yet alarmingly contingent menace that resides and endangers the borders of perception, order and control with the power of contaminating, infecting, spreading and disseminating.

TWO

OBJECTS

In 2010 artists Amelie von Harrach and Damian Le Sueur developed a site-specific installation at the Science Museum in London, whereby the artists adopted the visual trope of the mirror and turned it into an unsettling object: the mirror does not reflect back and the visitor sees her face disappearing in a blank surface. CCTV cameras frame the mirror, alluding to the artificial gaze of surveillance that pervades public places. *Un-known* (2010) is a reflection on perception at the interface of old and new technologies, and on the eerie encounter with *things*. The work exploits the unnerving relation with the material world to interrogate the collapse of familiar certainties.[1]

The continuous interaction with inanimate objects is an intrinsic part of our daily experience. Yet these dealings can be imbued with uneasiness, concern, apprehension and feelings of estrangement, impotence and loss. Objects expose a relationship to the environment that is tainted with fear. To understand these feelings, we need to consider our physical and metaphorical relations with things. We need to look backwards at the affective responses that the advent of science and technology caused from the Enlightenment onwards, and at the ways in which these responses defined modernity. We need to look at the individual's relation with things and the emotional investment of memory and loss. And we need to interrogate the contemporary role of objects and our positioning towards them. If the individual possessions of the victims of Auschwitz and the ruins of the Twin Towers attack are the physical reminder of trauma, objects are endowed with a dread that exceeds materiality and that shapes the contemporary imaginary.

Indeed, from the late 1980s the uncanny has been invoked across theory to articulate the disquieting experience of post-modernity. In an era of impasse, but also of strenuous rationality, the uncanny offers itself as a useful way to account for an elusive but perceptible and persistent sense of alienation and dislocation. The anxious fluidity of the present is both anchored and contradicted in the material world, in technically sophisticated and yet potentially dangerous objects. As Nicholas Royle has remarked, the uncanny exposes an impasse of the defining categories of reality and reveals a crisis of borders and frames.[2]

In talking about objects the focus is on the relationship between the subject and the environment and on the ways in which this translates in unhomely material configurations, whether in the face of experiences of dislocation, disempowerment and violence, of social isolation, inequality and marginality, or in relation to the impinging threats of terrorism and natural calamities. In other words, the focus is on the contemporary aesthetics of the uncanny.

The Uncanny Object

The formative nucleus and cultural referent for the feelings of estrangement that so potently characterize modernity can be located in the late seventeenth and the eighteenth centuries, when scientific knowledge began to gain epistemological prominence and thereby undermine the longstanding correspondences between the natural and supernatural that for centuries had governed the understanding of nature and the position of humans within it. With the consolidation of scientific knowledge, nature is taxonomically classified and its phenomena explained according to physical laws, or those of the chemical principles that underpin the transformation of substances and the manufacturing of materials. The referent for the natural world is no more a greater cosmological order, rather the order of nature itself, as it can be unravelled by reason. Electricity, magnetism and chemical transformations are understood as the hidden forces that move and shape matter.

The cultural relocation during the Enlightenment of what had traditionally pertained to the categories of the sacred, of the supernatural and of the superstitious at the boundaries of knowledge was, however, not without consequences: the 'aggressive rationalist imperative of the epoch . . . also produced, like a kind of toxic side effect, a new human experience of strangeness, anxiety, bafflement, and intellectual impasse.'[3] The systematic 'quest for law' of modern science resulted in a picture of reality that 'teetered on the brink of nothingness. Rather than rational reassurance, the invisible realm revealed through scientific discovery generated a sense of deep uncertainty, an entrance into a new, unfamiliar world that seemed ghostly and insubstantial.'[4] Such feelings of uncertainty, these 'shadows of fear', to use Immanuel Kant's phrase, affected and became constitutive of modern consciousness. They gave rise to the ambivalent attitudes towards the manifold progressions of modernity including industrialization, technological advancement, urbanization, capitalism and the consolidation of scientific knowledge in its many facets.[5]

The machine – whether in the form of the mechanical loom, the steam engine, the automobile, mechanical weapons or the telegraph – presupposed new forms of interaction that were as exciting as they were intimidating. J.M.W. Turner's painting of a locomotive in *Rain, Steam and Speed – The Great Western Railway* (1844) captures the spectral potency of the machine. The changing glow of light is intensified by the powerful effect of density produced by the steam. The dark looming silhouette of the steam engine menacingly speeds forward in the cloudy and heavy atmosphere, ready to engulf the viewer with ponderous force. Turner's close observation of light, informed by the theories of Isaac Newton and Johann Wolfgang von Goethe, betrays the awe of the scientific gaze. Yet his painting also endorses the haunting sentiments of an epoch. He captures the shadows of fear that the new bore within it.

Similarly, for nineteenth-century audiences photography provided a mirror image of reality whose visual replication was felt as both wondrous and baffling.[6] The microscope in the early eighteenth century and the X-ray machine in the first decades of twentieth century similarly produced new kinds of images and disclosed new aspects of the physical world, pushing the boundaries of the visible beyond normal perception in ways that were both tantalizing and perplexing as they penetrated the layers of the material world and revealed the ghostly outlines of interiority. The telegraph, the telephone and later the radio and television also bore the sign of the 'spectral' due to the particularity of electronically mediated sound and images that made them seem insubstantial and unrelated to physical processes.[7] They enabled previously unthinkable forms of disembodiment that could be perceived at the limits of the real and the imagined. The experience could become hallucinatory, and the 'thing' could be conducive to the creation of fears.

Implicitly, Sigmund Freud's 1919 essay on the subject foreshadows the spectral connotations of materiality that haunted modernity, and confers on it aesthetic potential. For Freud the disturbance of the uncanny is bound to a momentary dissipation of the boundaries of the real and to a destabilizing experience of one's environment.[8] Though psychoanalysis seems little concerned with the material world, its development coincides with the twentieth century's industrialization and the advent of the mass-made product as the symbol of consumer culture and modern alienation. The 'thing' increasingly becomes loaded with negative ideological connotations and contaminated by the affective mark of estrangement that renders it a potent cultural and artistic referent. Perhaps not accidentally, in the 1930s the object emerges as both medium and new artistic form within the Surrealist movement, bringing the 'thing' to the fore of art practice with the found object and the ready-made.

Inherently ambiguous and potentially destabilizing, the Surreal object oscillated between 'psychological primer, subjective expression, commodity fetish and designed product', the aesthetics of which resided in the act of transformation that it had undergone, either of use or of the artist's intervention, typically the mixing of materials (such as hair and fur) and forms into heterogeneous combinations.[9] This resulted in 'associative links, material contrasts or anthropomorphic representations' that visually resonated with Freud's elaboration of the unconscious and turned everyday objects into sinister artefacts.[10] Technology also potently lurked with menacing spectrality, as artists revelled in the latent aggressiveness of engines, contraptions and devices. Man Ray's *Cadeau Audace* (1921) and Jacob Epstein's *Torso in Metal from the 'Rock Drill'* (1913–14) are indicative of artefacts that carried the unnerving suspicion of disruption and distortion (illus. 21). They bore the signs of estrangement – doubles or surrogates of an already unfathomable reality.

Contemporary art has not abandoned the exploration of the thing as a means to interrogate the present and the contours of reality. On the contrary it has made the object an even more potent expression of the pervading feelings of anxiety that haunt society. The reinterpretation of materiality is still firmly located in the affective manipulation of texture, scale and form, as well as in the fascination with the erupting energy of automation, the transformation of physical states and the insinuating presence of digital technologies.

Examples are various. For instance, in the ongoing series *Powerless Structures* (1997–), the artists Michael Elmgreen and Ingar Dragset alter furnishings by 'rupturing their generic finish, dimensions and usage, to articulate the anxieties and frustrations inherent to political and social structures'.[11] Doors are cracked, chained together; clocks are jarred or broken in half. The frisson exposes the constraints, tensions and subversions of spatial and temporal demarcation through flaw, fracture and impracticability. Tony Oursler's ghostly, large-scale projections, evocative of eighteenth-century phantasmagoria, and his exploration of cyberspaces in works exhibited at the interface of the art gallery and Internet, conjure the aesthetic potential of the 'uncanny valley' in artificial three-dimensional sculptures. The Australian artist Stelarc, renowned for his performances that investigate the boundaries between physicality and robotics, exploits the potential and uneasiness of our encounter with avatars and replicants, stretching the unnerving slippage generated by cybernetics.[12]

The Japanese artist Kenji Yanobe, likewise, references both Japan's high-tech industry and *manga* pop culture to address impinging fears of

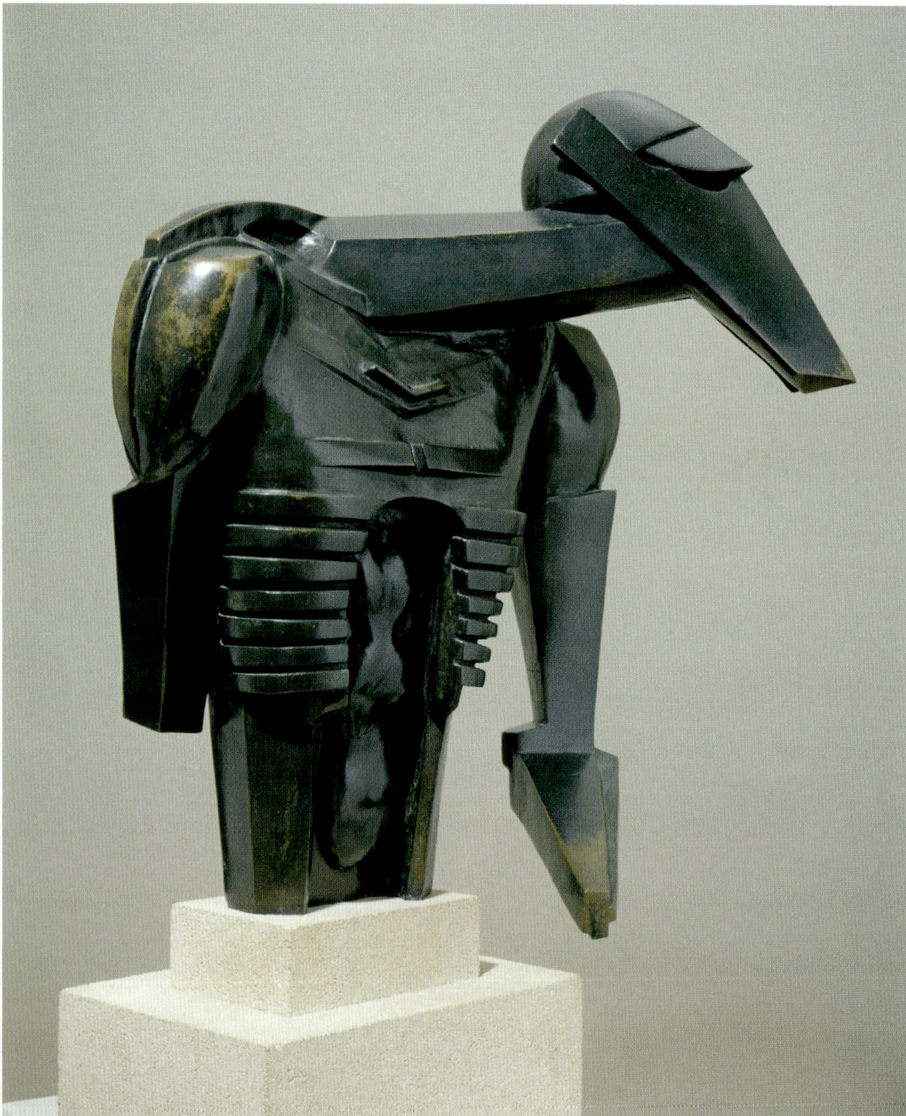

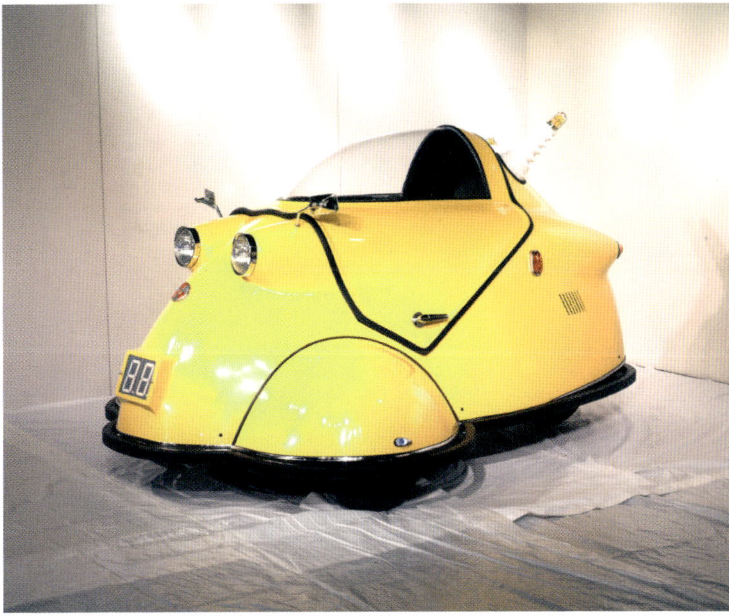

22 Kenji Yanobe, *Atom Car (Yellow)*, 1998, Geiger counter, FRP, motor, other media.

nuclear threat and the danger of mass contamination through terrorist bio-warfare. Yanobe builds uncanny machines in the shape of atomically resistant robotic suits, masks and even cars (illus. 22). The artist invokes end-of-the-world scenarios that reflect a double-edged perception of technology and its possibilities. Yanobe's work suggests an otherness that has been critically aligned with the stereotypical Western perception of Japanese culture, but it also betrays the preoccupation of what in Japan is known as the 'atomic Generation', who grew up at the convergence of post-war recovery and technological advancements. His three-dimensional cyborgs are fictions and artefacts; they are 'objects' that conflate real and imaginary fears.[13]

More broadly, in the current panorama of contemporary art, three main kinds of objects can be identified as catalysts of the uncanny: those that articulate a personal experience of the uncanny, whether centred around individual fears, memories, feelings of dislocation or marginality; those that address lingering traumatic memories and the

21 Jacob Epstein, *Torso in Metal from the 'Rock Drill'*, 1913–16, bronze.

problems surrounding testimony, documentation and remembrance; and those that explore the inherent potency and menace of the object itself, either by looking at the impact of transformation and erosion on the material, or by exploiting the manipulation of context and display. Conceptually and aesthetically interwoven, these three groups have reconceptualized the ready-made and found object, mobilizing the concept of the uncanny as a potent cultural and aesthetic feature for our time.

The Uncanny Object

The Brazilian artist Lucia Nogueira (1950–1998) has described her own work as emerging from the disruptions of the ordinary:

> I sometimes think that my work is all about gaps. For instance, you have routine in your life that carries on and suddenly something happens, and that breaks the line. I think that my work is very much connected with what happens when that line is broken, and the 'what happens then'. What happens in that gap.[14]

Nogueira physically incorporates ruptures in the internal structure of her works, often creating a moment of impasse and disturbance as she brings the inert to life with the sudden activation of mechanic objects. The strategy recalls Freud's remarks about the uncanny feelings caused by automata. This moment of frisson is contingent on the quality of feeling that it creates, to its emotional alienation. As the psychoanalyst Michael Parsons observes, 'The uncanny does and does not belong to everyday life. It is an ambush, making what should be familiar feel suddenly spooky and dislocated. Such eerie moments are not quite part of ordinary experience, and yet the feeling is recognizable. This is normal abnormality.'[15]

In the essay on the uncanny, Freud recalls two autobiographical events to reawaken the feeling and transpose himself into the peculiar sensation of the uncanny. He remembers his younger self lost in a provincial town in Italy, aimlessly walking the same streets, where prostitutes appeared at the windows: 'A feeling overcame me which I can only describe as uncanny.'[16] Like mannequins, the prostitutes at the windows were equivocally disturbing, and Freud felt entrapped in a labyrinth of streets that looked alike. Later on in the text, Freud recalls the disturbing impression of fleetingly gazing at his own reflection in a mirror while travelling on a train and not recognizing himself. In both occurrences, the temporary experience of disorientation and uncertainty suggests a rupture or disconnection in the flow of sensory apprehension and cognitive recognition. As an aesthetic device, the uncanny is similarly tied to a visceral sensation that overcomes the subject and produces a temporal gap between past and present, reality and imagination, memory and fantasy. In E.T.A. Hoffmann's tale of 'The Sandman', the text that Freud analyses in his essay, the recollection of childhood's fears is pivotal to the story's unfolding and to 'a peculiarly violent and obscure emotion' that foreshadows the uncanny effect of the narrative.[17] Literature was for Freud a fertile terrain for the uncanny. Throughout the twentieth century, the cultural preoccupation with 'things' has positioned the material world as a significant referent of unsettling feelings, and rendered artefacts central to an 'aesthetics of the uncanny'. The uncanny has, in fact, moved beyond the 'test of reality' argued by Freud: as Parsons states, 'It is not in the end possible to separate, as Freud wished to, the uncanny as an aesthetic quality in works of art from the uncanny as a subjective experience in real life'.[18] Both seem eerily to co-exist and interweave in our lives.

Repressed fears and the menace of their resurfacing are potent motifs in the work of the French artist Louise Bourgeois (1911–2010), who, building on from a Surrealist legacy, has mapped the psychic scenarios of the mind by morphing everyday objects into the frightening projections of her inner landscape. Throughout her career, the artist has both literally and metaphorically woven, stitched and embalmed her dark inner fantasies and conflicts out of cloth, wood and metal. Ordinary things have been turned into the unordinary and disturbing furnishings of dreams and of childhood's memories.

Fear and the frightening disfiguration of domesticity are the subject of the series *Cells* (1990–93), composed of lifesize steel frame cages often featuring discarded doors and windows, in which old pieces of furniture, including mirrors, beds and wardrobes, stitched dolls, casts of body parts and hanging clothes stage nightmarish scenarios. As the artist states, 'Each *Cell* deals with fear. Fear is pain. Often perceived as pain, because it is always disguising itself.'[19] Bourgeois' cells are both claustrophobic spaces and uncanny objects. Densely filled with domestic things, they act as the inanimate and yet potently vivid duplications of inner fathoms, substantiating the projections of subliminal fears that move beyond the personal experience of the artist to interrogate the actuality of this emotion and its relation to pain felt or inflected.

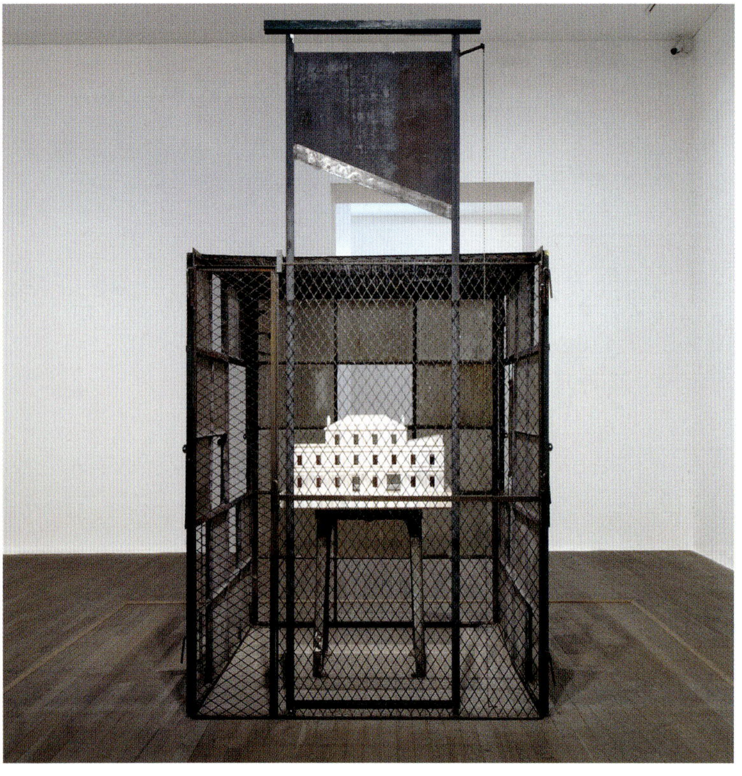

23 Louise Bourgeois, *Cell (Choisy)*, 1990–93, marble, metal and glass.

Cell (Choisy) of 1990–93 features, for instance, a miniature version of the artist's childhood house threatened by the blade of a guillotine (illus. 23). Whether in the form of repressed anger or a hysteric seizure, embodied in a decapitated male figure, pain and fear distort, amputate and trap at the blurring of reality and imagination, where objects sinisterly provoke the viewer, subverting assumptions and diverting her from familiar experience. As Bourgeois comments on *Cell (You Better Grow Up)*: 'First there is fear, the fear of existence. Then comes a stiffening up, a refusal to confront the fear. Then comes the denial. The terror of facing ourselves keeps us from understanding and subjects us to the repetition of acting out. It is a tragic fate.'[20]

Bourgeois calls upon the psychic realm of fears as a shared and yet intimate experience. She uses mirrors that superimpose one with the

24 Detail of Louise Bourgeois, *Cell (You Better Grow Up)*, 1993, steel, glass, marble, ceramic and wood.

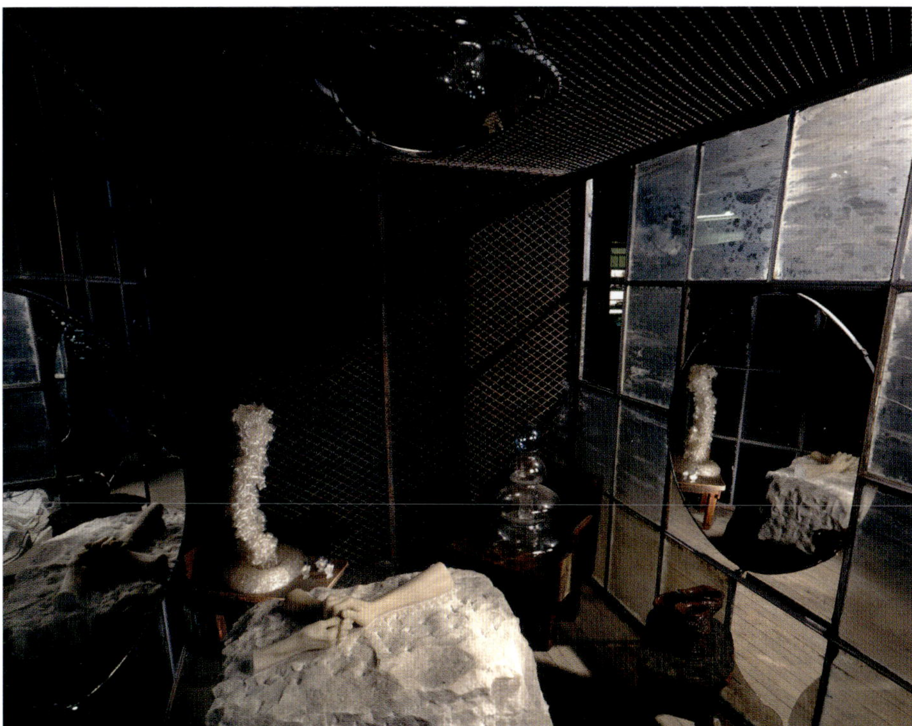

other to reflect difficult realities that one has to face and fills the space of physical and psychological entrapment of the cell with distorted imageries (illus. 24). The artist transforms domesticity into a frightening space where ordinary objects linger threateningly, by allusively rehearsing 'a tragic fate' made up of haunting memories. Following Freud, Bourgeois may be considered to be re-enacting the past, to be acting it out as a 'vivid way of remembering'.[21] Conversely, her work may be read as a figuration of angst that reflects upon fear's psychic experience of entrapment, paralysis and castration. In Bourgeois' art this is culturally located within a shared iconography of objects (well known from film and museum displays if not the family attic), which acquires new actuality in the demythologization of the domestic sphere. In the series *Cells*, Bourgeois uses old things. Yet her dollhouses, evening gowns or perfume bottles are not nostalgic, rather they stand as clues that evoke spooky sensations of the world and embody the subject's eerie relations with the past on the stage of the mind. This encounter with the unconscious is both scary and provocatively enriching: 'The potential value of uncanny experiences lies precisely in the way that they escape the boundaries of our habitual world-view. It may be eerily disturbing to found oneself operating outside one's awareness. But it may also reveal new inward horizons.'[22] The uncanny thus challenges us, and its aesthetic 'regression' is rich with unsettling promises.

The evocation of childhood memories, of repressed thoughts and the physical sensation of childhood 'aesthetic experiences', is no less firmly located in the material world and our scary, distorted perceptions of it for the American artist Mike Kelley (1954–2012) and the French artist Annette Messager. Both artists draw on this uncanny aesthetic experience to give shape to the haunting ghosts of adulthood. As Kelley writes: 'Such past feelings (which recur even now in my recollection of them) seem to have been provoked by disturbing, *unrecallable* memories. They were provoked by a confrontation between 'me' and an 'it' that was highly charged, so much so that 'me' and 'it' became confused.'[23] For Kelley, the bewildering 'muted horror' of the uncanny gives 'goosebumps' and is 'spine tingling'. It is a gut sensation that endures, in the artist's words, 'the feeling of callable fears, expected as an atmosphere that was "creepy" or "weird"'. [24] Déjà vu and déjà vécu – the threshold separating the self and the thing blurs, the 'I' and 'it' become indistinct, awakening uncomfortable sensations of the unhomely. Kelley reminds us that the uncanny belongs to the historical as well as to the psychological formation of subjectivity. Highly personal, 'the uncanny is an experience of being after *oneself*, in various senses of the phrase. It is the experience of something duplicitous, diplotic, being double.'[25]

Indeed this uncertainty is stylistically integral to the 'mixings, deformations, and transformations of the genre' that characterize Freud's essay on the uncanny.[26] The interpolation of etymologies, direct quotes and other textual references layers the internal structure of the essay suggesting a convergence of form and content. It is as if Freud was not only explaining the uncanny negation of the familiar, but also evoking its unnerving and disorientating feeling within the text, and between the subject and the text, between the text that Freud is writing (his essay on the uncanny) and the one he is reading (Hoffmann's 'The Sandman').[27] The visual correlate of Freud's textual mixing and deformation are optical effects, hybrid assemblages, distortions of scale, animation and duplication.

The work of Kelley and Messager follows trajectories that are not dissimilar to those traceable within Freud's essay. Both artists wilfully mix texts, images and objects, creating artworks that tread the boundaries between the real and the imaginary. They use large soft toys, stuffed animals and sinuous waves of fabric to explore memories interpolating biographical references with pop culture, fairy tales and political references. For Kelley, the recollection of the goosebump feeling of childhood is permeated by the preoccupation with the dialectics of power and the loose bolts of the scaffoldings of social and cultural mores. Messager scrapes off the eyes from the photographs of children in supposed family albums, stitches fabrics and embalms dead sparrows, providing them with mechanized automation (illus. 25). She shifts meanings and forms producing chimeras, automata and figures suspended between humour and disturbance. The result is a cabinet of curiosities for our time, filled with odd relics and strange objects, embodiments of fears that are both archetypal and deftly contemporary.[28] Daunting is the

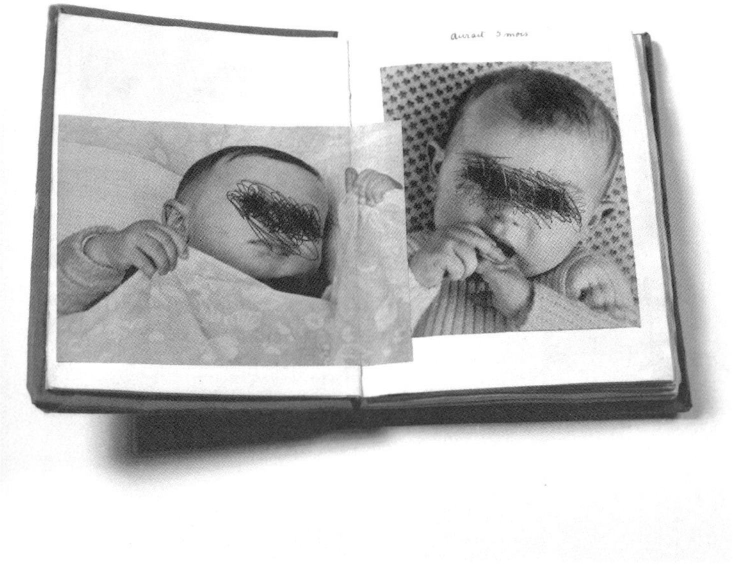

25 Annette Messager, *Les enfants aux yeux rayés*, 1971–2, installation, drawings and black-and-white photographs with 2 album collections under display case.

question of what the 'it' is that confronts the subject today. And what are its forms?

The Traumatic Object

An answer to these questions can be found in the shift from the object as a personal and cultural site of emotions to the art-object as a critical counterpart. From its early appearances the art-object has challenged representation through the creation of recognizable and yet provocatively transformed artefacts that are duplicitous and subversive. Recognition is interwoven with ambivalence and incongruence. This subversion is nonetheless polymorphic, like the artefacts it generates, and exploits the cultural and emotive connotations with which things are imbued. Things are made, acquired, kept, handled, broken, forgotten or lost.

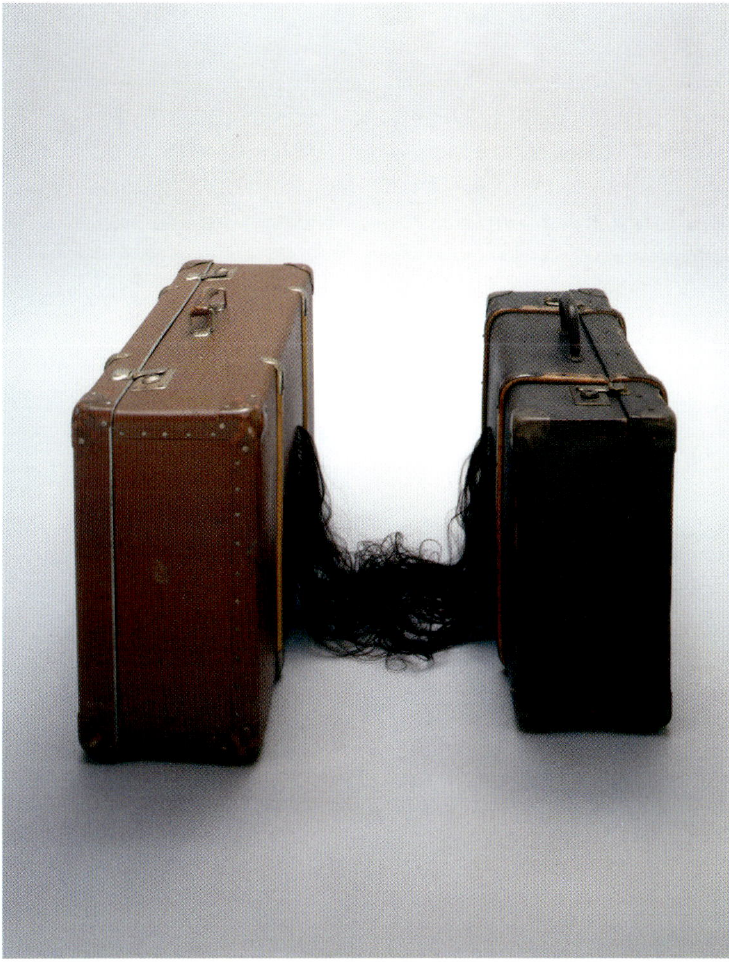

26 Mona Hatoum, *Traffic* II, 2002, compressed card, leather, metal, human hair and beeswax.

They belong or are given and received. They are part of social and personal practices that endow them with meanings that often supersede the object's original function. Personal objects, including clothes, photographs and other mementos, utensils and tools are loaded with emotional significance for the individual and can easily turn into shared cultural icons. Everyday life and museum practices collide: the home and the gallery are similarly furnished with objects as tangible proofs of the past and recognizable referents of a life or cultural tradition. Think of the memento from a trip abroad, the photograph in a frame, a family heirloom, but also of the aura surrounding the display of a dress that Madonna wore or that of Napoleon's writing kit.[29] Artists have used this potency of objects to evoke feelings in various ways. Mostly they have drawn upon the physicality of things to elicit sensory and emotional responses, further involving the viewer critically.

The emotive response to things, whether a domestic gadget or an artwork, is inherent to the sensorial apprehension of the physical qualities of the thing itself. We encounter the material world through the senses. We see, touch and smell it. We bend over things, move around them, grasp them and look at them. We feel an object with pleasure, excitement, attention, anxiety and even disgust. Physical sensations build up a range of conscious and non-conscious responses triggered by sensory stimuli across the body and in the brain that further solicit cognitive and emotional states. This affective encounter with things stirs thought, memory and feeling. By intervening in the physical appearance of objects, artists affectively manipulate artefacts and replicate a perceptive blurring of reality and imagination that is aesthetically akin to the uncanny and to its cultural role of exposing contemporary experiences of inadequacy, estrangement, disorientation and uncertainty.[30]

The motif of everyday things, of the mundane furnishing of domestic life, as a means to convey political and social alienation, recurs in the work of the Palestinian artist Mona Hatoum. Informed by her experience of exile, Hatoum uses metaphors of entrapment and dislocation to articulate socio-political concerns of disempowerment. Dysfunctional beds, soaps skewered with pins, pointed metal carpets, oversized domestic tools and kitchen utensils, a wheelchair that cannot move, are instances of tension between the homely and unhomely that subverts the emotional endowment of ordinary things, turning them into dangerous artefacts that elicit feelings of alienation and estrangement. The immediate visceral response solicited by these objects is, however, also layered with meanings. If what we are presented with is strange, dissonant and equivocal, the strategies of distortion and assemblages of different material including discarded bodily material, such as hair, blood, nails and skin – part of a process of anthropomorphizing pieces of furniture – are integral to an artistic practice in which the manipulation of the object is either menacing or a beguiling evocation of absence (illus. 26).[31] In her work, Hatoum confronts the viewer with unpredictability, making the surfaces of sculptures treacherous, entrapping and alienating. The unreliability of the material, its physical alteration, belies a hidden malevolence that cannot be domesticated or reconciled.

Hatoum maps out the precariousness of a condition whose menace is depersonalized and depersonalizing, interrogating the imperative of political, social and economic integration. The divide that her art and artefacts insinuate by substantiating the precariousness of spaces

27 Mona Hatoum, *Webbed*, 2002, steel, rubber and wood.

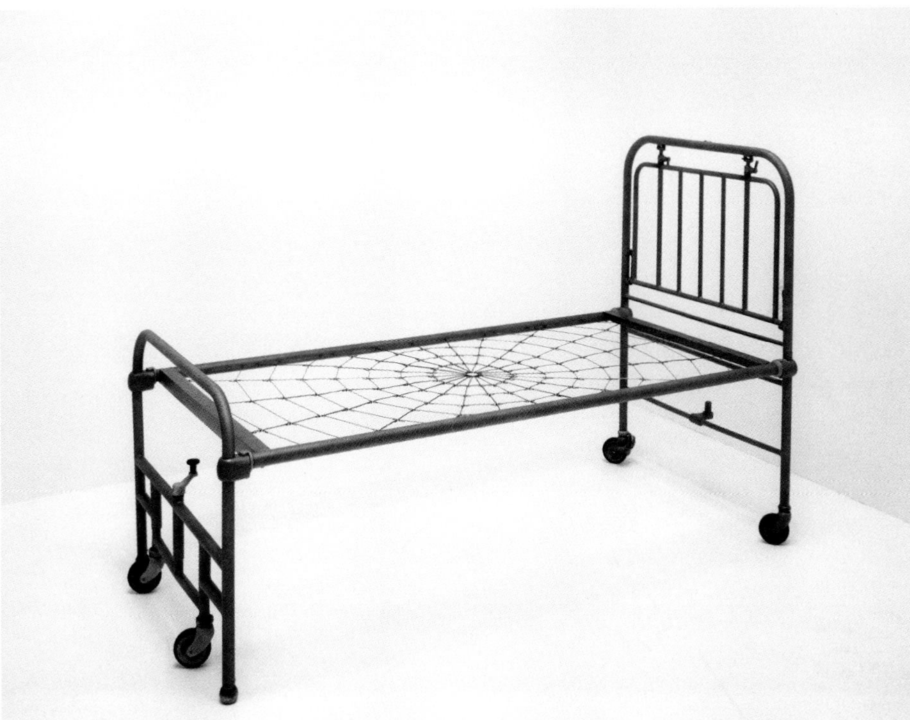

and the imperviousness of boundaries, whether in the shape of an oversize grater (*Grater Divide*, 2002), of a treacherous mat (*Prayer Mat*, 1995) or bed (*Webbed*, 2002), resonates with the post-colonial enquiry into the positioning of the migrant in Western societies (illus. 27). Hatoum explores the unsolved ambivalence that characterizes experiences of displacement, and the exposure of dynamics of inclusion and exclusion within groups and countries, as well as more general issues concerning the economic and political relations between centre and periphery. Her work goes beyond an alignment with theory to contend with the emotional actuality of homelessness and social and political exclusion.[32] The visual metaphors and paradoxes are exaggerated to provoke the viewer, tangibly creating distance and probing borders, affective and otherwise.

Dislocation, exile and horror are also central themes for the Iranian artist Parastou Forouhar, who lives and works in Germany. The daughter of intellectuals who were politically persecuted under Shah Reza Pahlavi and later murdered in 1998 under the Islamic Republic, Forouhar revisits the motifs of traditional Persian calligraphy and decorative arts to reflect upon the totalitarian situation in her homeland and the tragic toll of torture, death and terror. Printed fabrics, as in *Eslimi* (2003–10), street signs, as in *Signs* (2004–10), and wallpaper, in *A Thousand and One Days* (2003–10), are artworks in which the geometrically harmonious and delicately sensual beauty of the decorative patterns is deceptive (illus. 28 and 29). The jolt of recognition is the more powerful and ominously disconcerting as the concealed figures of cruelty gradually become apparent. Weapons, scenes of torture and unnerving images of horror are the shapes that slowly emerge and cohere from the sinuous, beautiful lines of the patterns. Thus, the object and its decor turn treacherous. As the artist observes, the work bears within it the ambivalence of beauty and its 'disintegration', which is the more subversive since: 'the beauty is not lost in the process . . . At first glance you see the beautiful patterns and think that you have understood it. And then you get closer and realise it is completely different. The viewer is thrown back on himself and is forced to re-evaluate his perception.'[33] This 'throwing back' and 're-evaluation of

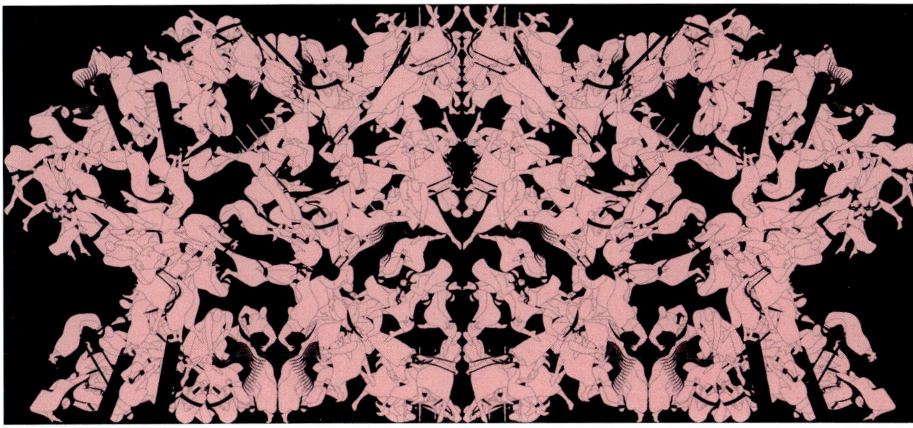

28 Parastou Forouhar, *A Thousand and One Days*, 2003–10, wallpaper.

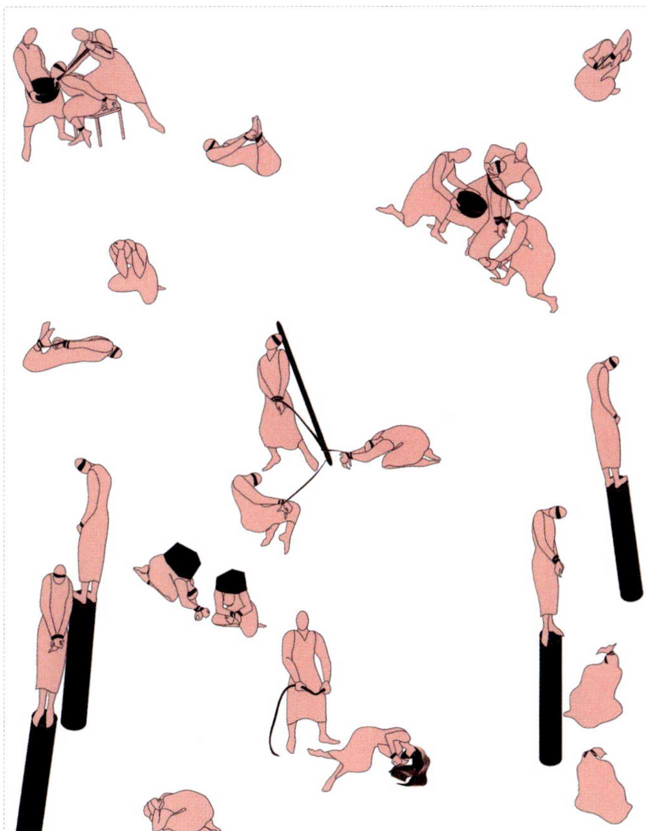

29 Parastou Forouhar, *A Thousand and One Days*, 2003–10, wallpaper.

perception' defines the uncanny recognition of the sinister and unhomely, deflecting certainties of vision that concern the Western viewer in relation to a country whose politics are thought of as overtly threatening, but towards which we seem to stand as impotent witness. Violence towards women is consistently reworked as testimony against injustice but also as a metaphor for the affective interaction of fear and aggression, paranoia and hostility that are active both in Iran itself and in Western perceptions of the country. Ancient motifs, but also historical patterns of misperception and misinterpretation, are uncannily at play, and uncannily transpire in Forouhar's work. Indeed, Forouhar metaphorically entraps the viewer. As the artist and critic Lutz Becker comments, 'In her depiction of everyday mental and physical brutality, she creates images of aesthetic appeal but disturbing ambiguity.'[34] This modality of displacement of perceptive and aesthetic boundaries is a common denominator in the quest for a visual language capable of voicing the traumatic experience of horror.

This quest is also central to the work of the Colombian artist Doris Salcedo, who addresses issues of socio-economic displacement and disempowerment in relation to her native country. 'I myself feel displaced', she says of her position as an artist from a country considered peripheral, dangerous and already displaced from a supposed centre, and as an artist whose practice consistently engages with violence and horror.[35] Working closely with Colombian victims of war and extreme poverty, Salcedo uses discarded objects and waste, reconfiguring them in potent figures of loss, absence and trauma. As she observes:

> In the Third World, when you encounter five hundred homeless people and there is no 'paternal' State, you have to notice them. This presence becomes part of the environment, part of the air you breathe. It is always with you. You can't get it out of your mind; there is no way to avoid it. So, having been born in Colombia is what makes me look at the Other. I have no choice.[36]

The central motif of 'otherness' and of a tension between private fears, horror and trauma, and of public recognition is reiterated through many of Salcedo's works. Furniture and clothes, often sutured or encased together, are recurrent features. The solid world of the domestic interior is reassembled in distorted and abrasive configurations. In the series of *Casa Viuda* (*Widowed House*, 1992–4), unhinged doors stand aloof, violently pulled against a cracked cabinet, a camisole lurks embalmed and pinned with bone in another one, a zipper pierces a wooden desk.[37] The furniture is hard, resilient and yet it exudes intense vulnerability. One gets the feeling of the aloofness of estrangement and the violence of displacement in the collision and encapsulation of materials, the seamless opposition of the hard and soft textures of wood and cloth.

Similarly, the tables comprising *Unland: the Orphan's Tunic* (1997), whose title references the homonymous poem by the German writer Paul Celan (1920–1970), are ordinary, almost insignificant at first sight. Yet on closer inspection these common kitchen tables appear more equivocal. For one of the works, two tables of different size are forcefully jammed together, disproportionally squashed against each other. The surface of one of them is covered in frayed silk. Through small holes, hundreds of hairs are threaded through the wood and the cloth, interweaving the tough surface of the wood with the frail fabric. Absence permeates the physicality of the work, with the empirical traces of bodies and use, and of the scars of fear and pain. In an earlier work, *Atrabiliarios* (1991–2004), Salcedo used shoes of the *desaparecidos* ('the disappeared') to expose violence and death in her native country. Shoes are the item of clothing through which relatives of the deceased are able to recognize the loved ones in mass graves. Covered by a thin layer of animal skin sutured with surgical threads, the shoes are displayed side by side, single or in pairs, like reliquaries in protective niches (illus. 30). By focusing on the qualities of materiality, Salcedo conjures up the essentiality of horror, 'the key affect that', as the art historian Mieke Bal remarks, 'Salcedo inscribes without sentimentality' in her work.[38] The meticulous labouring of surfaces and contour turns ordinary things into 'impossible object, a boundary and a limit'.[39] The semi-transparent layer of skin of *Atrabiliarios* thus figuratively metamorphoses in the opaque wrapping wall in *Abyss* (2005), exhibited at the Triennal of Contemporary Art at the Museum of the Castello di Rivoli, near Turin.

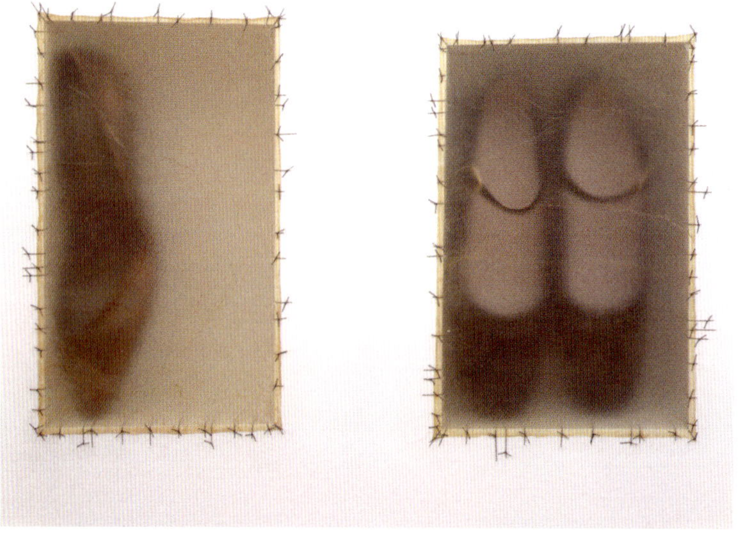

30 Doris Salcedo, *Atrabiliarios* (detail), 2004, shoes, animal fibre and surgical thread.

Here, Salcedo built a wall within the gallery space, enclosing it from inside (illus. 31). Walls are potent symbols of ideological and national demarcation, a signifier of right and wrong. They solicit a positioning of the body in relation to them as well as figuratively taking a side. Walls are meant to protect and limit; for the home as well as for the city they are emblems of safety. But they may also stand for the delimitation of freedom, imprisonment, or impossibility of movement. They may symbolize the unhomely edges of separation. The duplicity of the signifier thus encloses the ambiguities of the signified, raising the questions: what is within? What is beyond? The artist emphasizes the void that the walls produce and contain: an unnerving emptiness, a gap within, a distance that excludes. Salcedo's work aims to act as a testimony, but can things be the material referent of stories and histories? Can they document?

The fascination with objects and the well-established tradition of the display of personal possessions in exhibitions and house museums

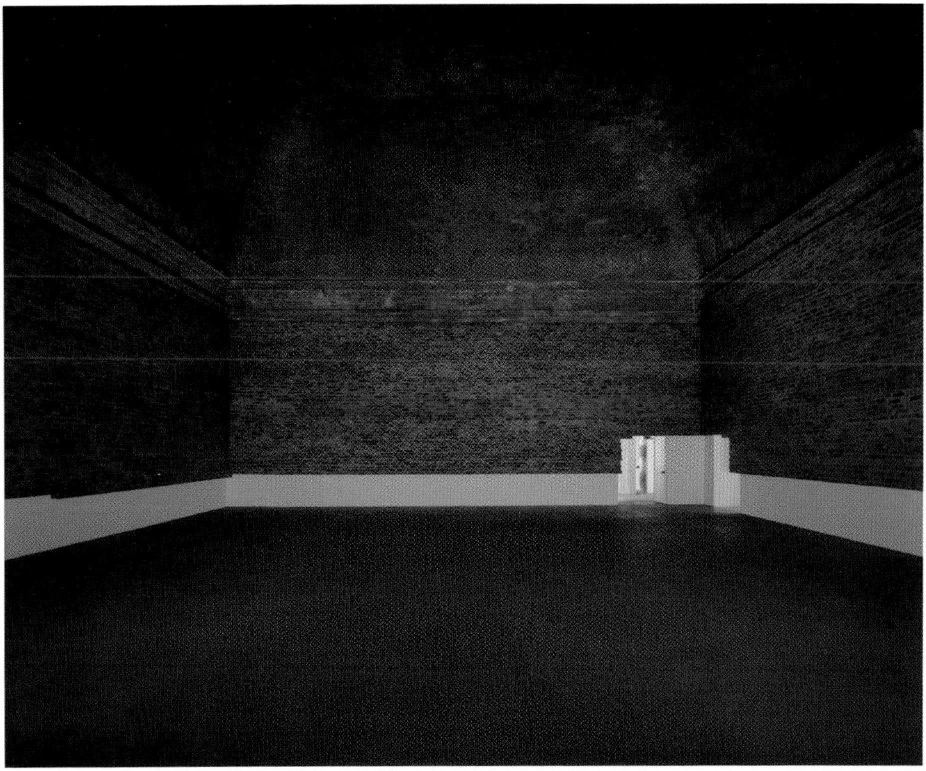

31 Doris Salcedo, *Abyss* (detail), 2005, brick, cement, steel and epoxy resin. Installation Castello di Rivoli, Turin.

presuppose that the cognitive response to objects is as important as the affective one, and that the psychological valences attributed to things turn them into complex cultural icons endorsed with diverse and even conflicting narratives. Chosen for aesthetic, commemorative, historical and anecdotal reasons, objects are displayed to testify and tangibly account for a story that is inherent to the museum context. Furniture, garments, glasses and shoes may be part of displays on the history of decoration and fashion, the evocation of the life of an illustrious person, the unravelling of histories. Emotion and narrative indeed coexist in our encounters with things. The role of things to document and act as tangible reminders of personal and collective events is, however, complicated by this convergence and by the possibility of plural readings that it entails, allowing for multiple stories and meanings. This is, for instance, the case of the display of a pile of shoes and suitcases belonging to victims of the concentration camps at the Auschwitz Museum (illus. 32). In this context, the object acts as an icon that transitions from individual trauma to collective history, from personal pain to public horror, entangling questions of remembrance and documentation with emotional susceptibility.

The French artist Christian Boltanski has variously probed the complexities of this transition by both exploiting and challenging the potential of objects to testify to the past and mutely to suggest stories through traces of use and belonging. Hence, Boltanski has appropriated museum display practices in a number of installations where he has shown personal belongings and mementos, including photographs, letters and locks of hair, of people whose lives cannot be recollected. His work attests both to an attainable presence hinted by the object and to the challenge of documenting the horror predicated by the thing. Boltanski takes the cultural fascination with personal and historical memorabilia and reverses it into an evocation of loss and of the impossibility of adequately remembering and recollecting stories: things only offer mute fragments and traces of the past. This lack of reassurance produces uncanny possibilities. The duplication of a cultural practice renders recognized icons the source of a troubling déjà vu, and asks for a confrontation with the cultural imagery that history invokes. It asks us to look at the density of the object as a sign and at the intricacy of the ways in which we relate and respond to things.

The horrifying effect of the piles of shoes and suitcases at the Auschwitz Museum is indirectly revisited in Boltanski's monumental installation *Personnes* (2010), made of thousands of garments neatly arranged as in a cemetery of fabric. At the centre of the installation, a crane relentlessly piles up a mountain of clothes. The garments stand for absence and presence, recognition and estrangement, life and death (illus. 33). The work is both overwhelming and intimate. The title plays on the double meaning of the French word that means both 'people' and 'no one'.[40] The pile can be read as a metaphor of persecution and extermination, but also of consumerism, economic exploitation and

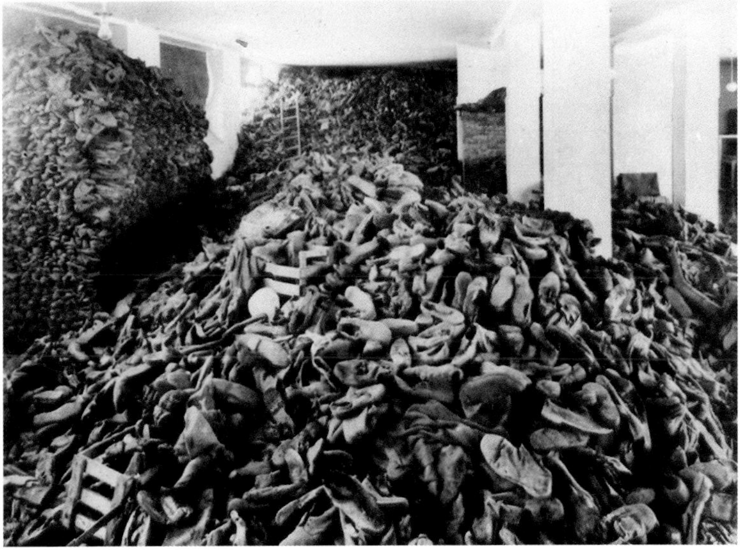

32 Piles of shoes or suitcases from the archival collection of the State Museum Auschwitz-Birkenau, Oświęcim.

waste, which still locates a discrepancy and dislocation between developed and underdeveloped countries, between those who have the power to acquire and those who stand at the impoverished end of the sweatshop. Meanings layer. Past and present overlap and collapse. The garments evoke horrors but are also akin to the currency of extreme poverty, violence and dispossession of post-industrial relations. The thing thus stands in mutuality with the subject, with the artist and the visitor, at the encounter of the 'I' with the 'it', at a point of integration as well as of resistance, of recognition and of alienation: at the moment when the homely may turn into its opposite.

overleaf:
33 Christian Boltanski, *Personnes*, 2010, installation view at Monumenta 2010, Grand Palais, Paris, France.

The Contentious Object

When we think of things, we cannot disregard the processes of transformation that an object undergoes in its making, through use and finally in its discarding and eventual decay, corrosion and rotting. They are part of practices of production but also of neglect and destruction

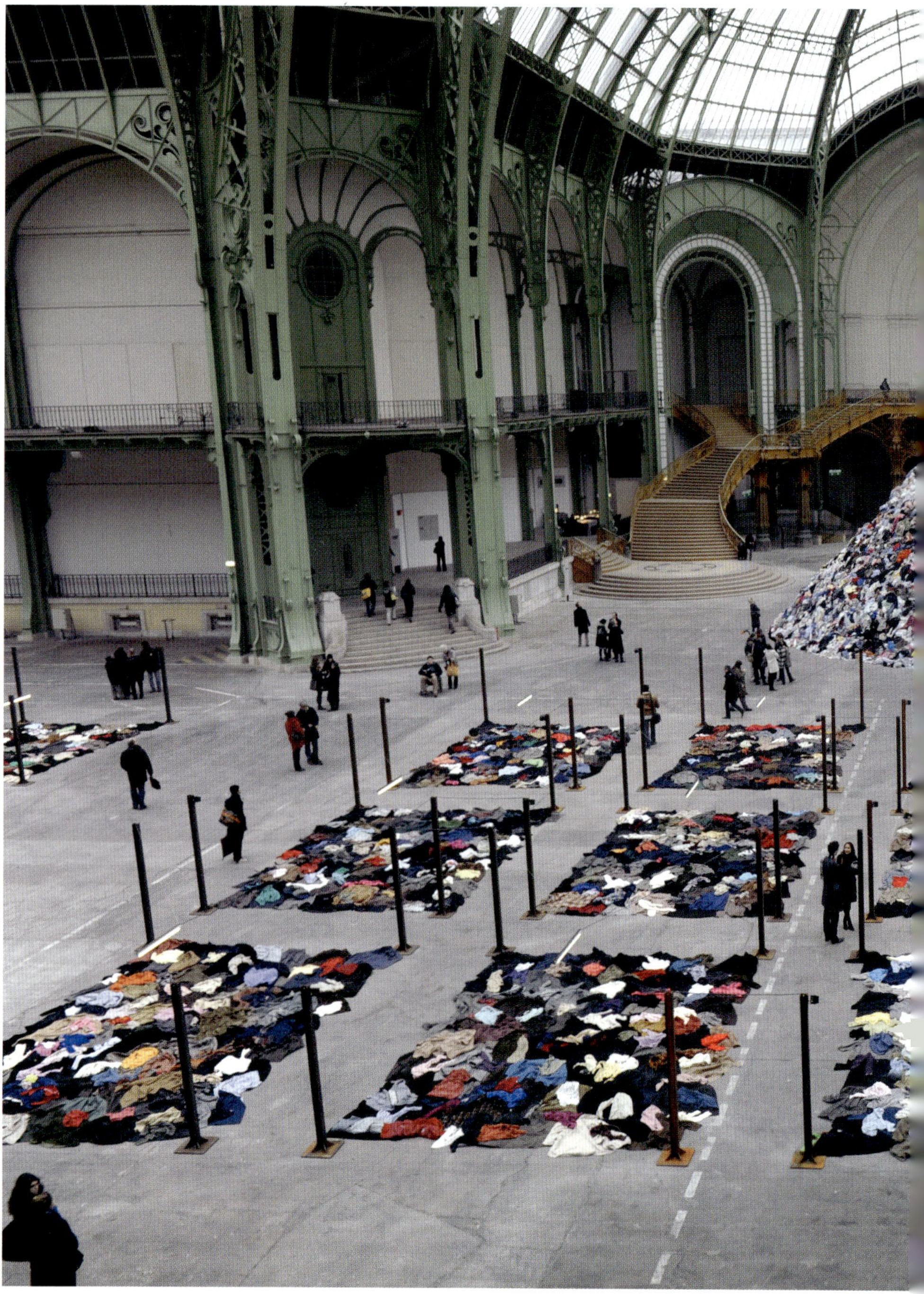

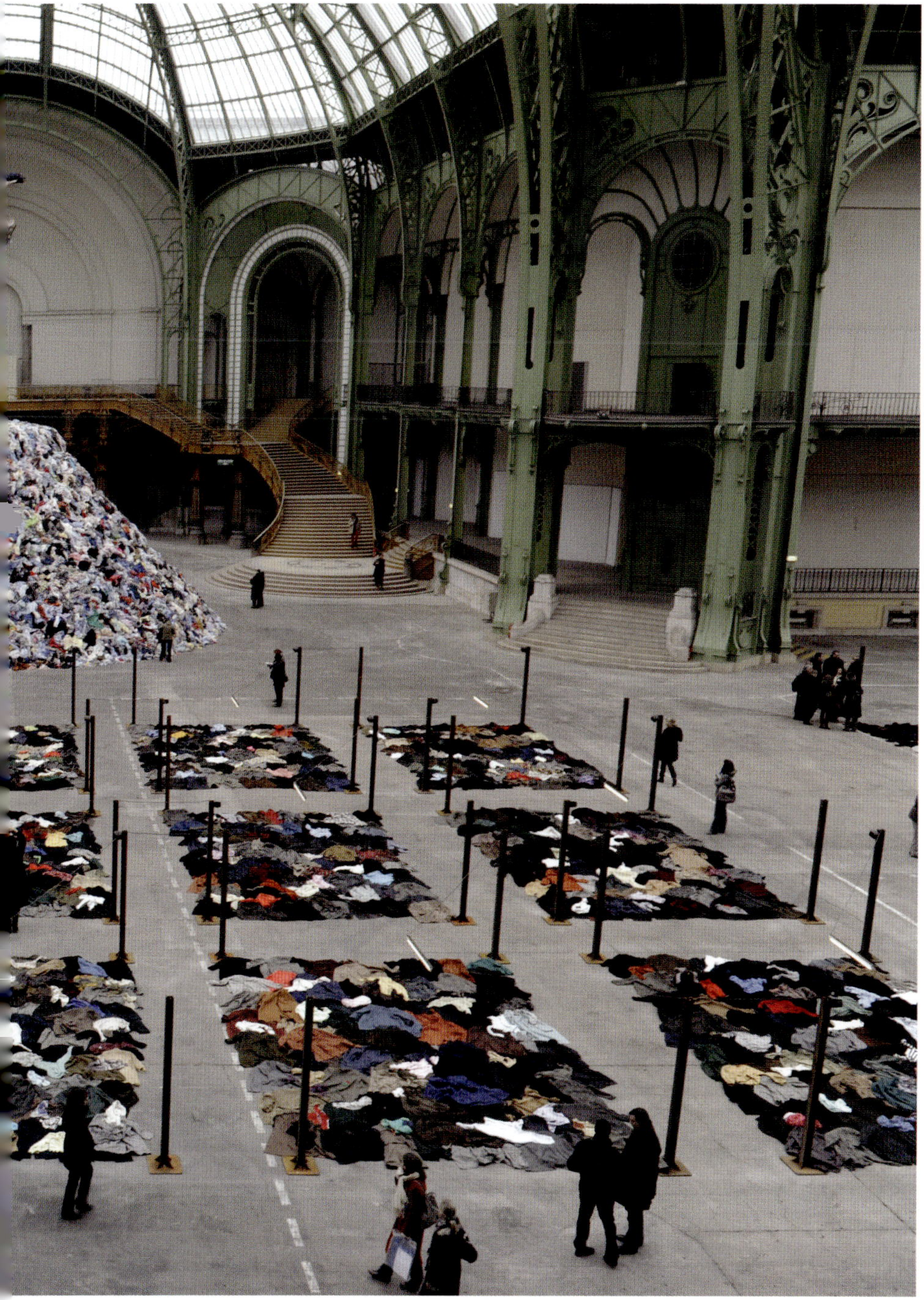

that are integral to the cultural constitution and appropriation of the object. If the signs of use and belonging potently elicit personal and collective memories that induce emotional responses, these signs can become unsettling when they linger with impasse or annihilation. The desolation of debris intensifies the affective charge of the object, ironically informing its cultural presence. Hence, while the object has long been used as a means to address the contentious legacy of history and its implication for the present, the ruin embodies, for the contemporary sensibility, the most potent material rendering of the uncanny. The ruin is already disturbing, already the product of violent impasse or of the effects of time and transformation. As an object, debris resists cultural practices in its relegation to the category of waste, where it lies damaged, ruined and desecrated. Yet this resistance makes it, in various forms, particularly relevant in contemporary art practice, and beyond. The historical preoccupation with the physical world, which produced the uncanny in the first instance as a side effect of technological and scientific advancements, reappears to contend with today's concerns with the effects of industrialization and economic exploitation, politically and environmentally.

Joseph Beuys is the acknowledged maverick of the post-war exploitation of the sinister 'functions' of the unknown buried in the material world. For Beuys, the wounds and scars of history corrode, tarnish and deteriorate the surfaces of matter to reveal undeletable signs. Beuys inscribes his work within the alchemical processes of transformation, tracing within the inherent relation of matter and form the singularity of the object. In his cabinets he mixes and meshes organic products and inorganic materials, bodily matter and the ready-made. Clods of earth, lumps of fat, a slice of hardened sausage, wax casts, metal blades, household appliances, waste: these assemblages upset taxonomies, making everything count through process, everything singular and singled out from the indistinct multiplicity of industrialization and commodification. Beuys inserts objects within a personal and cultural mythology of symbols to reinstate the lost value of the 'sacred', and of the 'bewitchment' of things. Soiled, stained, corroded, dried, these objects are irreparably blemished and flawed, debris that testify to loss and pain. If the alchemical rites of such art substitute and duplicate the order of reality, they do so to haunt and destabilize, turning the prosaic materiality of the everyday into the abject, corroded and corrosive reminders of history.[41]

Beuys relies on the cultural formation of the ruin and of debris as metaphors of modernity and industrialization, of the historical alienation of the subject from both nature and systems of production. The gesture harks back to the Romantic pursuit to realign the self with a natural if not cosmological order that was already an exposure of an embedded dichotomy. It endorses a metafiction that regards history as well as nature. The historical moment that gave rise to the uncanny revelled on the archaeological fragment and the ruin, at the binary relation with time that it opened up, on the residue of unknown that it retained. This ruin is a relic of historical polarity rather than natural decay, of a tension between past and present, between the aspiration and the failure of knowledge to encompass both nature and history, of the rational endeavour to erase the 'shadows of fear'. The post-modern rescue of debris is no less dense with 'epistemological value as it undermines the vestiges of certainty and so forges a new criterion for knowledge', making the ruin a problematic and yet sought-after referent, if not the very icon of our present.[42]

However, can the ruin and debris be called upon to testify an event? This question is the more salient as the ruin is invoked to testify to collective experience and memory as indicated by the collection of remains such as the debris of the buildings and of personal possessions from the attack on the Twin Towers and of the Pentagon in Washington, of which the Smithsonian National Museum of American History is the official repository. Forty-seven of these objects went on display across the United States as part of the exhibition *September 11: Bearing Witness to History* (2002–3). The collection confirms the susceptibility of ordinary things to attend to the construction of meaning and the creation of cultural heritage. Among the 'powerful' objects conserved and exhibited are 'twisted steel from the World Trade Center, damaged items from the Pentagon, memorials from the crash site in Pennsylvania, clothing worn by survivors, and objects used by

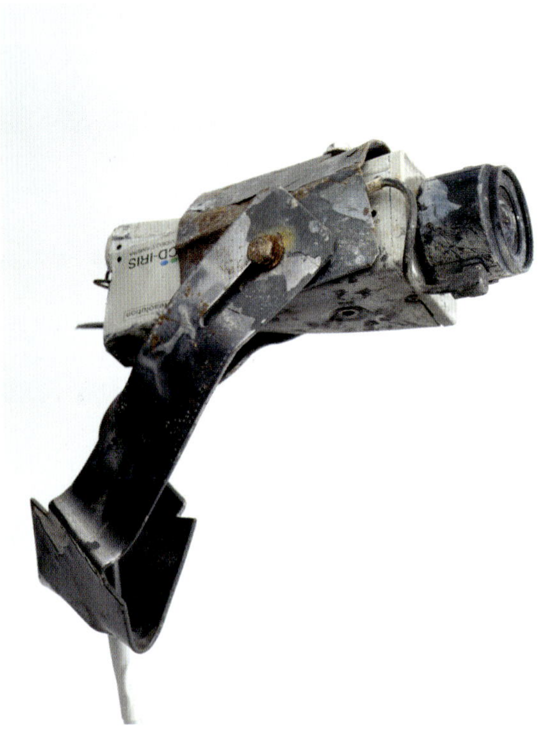

34 Sony video surveillance camera recovered from the debris of the World Trade Center.

rescue workers and public officials' (illus. 34).[43] As the museum website further underlines:

> The collection also includes several everyday items that have now taken on extraordinary significance because of their association with the Sept. 11 events. One of the newly exhibited objects is a filing cabinet from a Ben & Jerry's ice cream shop in the World Trade Center's shopping concourse. The crushed and twisted metal holds file folders in its mangled form.[44]

Far from being inert residues of an event, these objects are conferred a specific cultural function. They have 'taken on extraordinary significance' and entered a 'bewitched' and bewildering mythology that closely resembles the shifts from the ordinary to the 'extraordinary' signalled in Beuys's work. The crushed everyday items symbolize an event forever marked in its materiality, a collision that is ideologically contaminated. The work of British artist Cornelia Parker and of the South African artist Kendell Geers is useful to examine the problematic nature of these objects and exhibits, and further link the role of the object as an uncanny means of exposing the latent fear of terrorism, violence and destruction.

Parker's work often consists of smashed objects or objects that are at an intermediate phase of production or whose normal state has been altered by the artist. For instance, she uses domestic items that have been thrown from the eroded coastline of Dover, molten silver dollars drawn into a coil of wire the length of the Statue of Liberty, Colt .45 guns in the earliest phase of production, incisions inflicted by cutting implements belonging to renowned people, a doll, a loaf of bread, a newspaper, a pack of cards and a tie cut with the guillotine that beheaded Marie Antoinette, a hat burnt by a meteorite, a pile of burnt cocaine, a man's suit perforated by pearls shot from a gun (illus. 35). The list could continue. Spoilt, transformed, adulterated, attacked, reassembled, recontextualized or decontextualized, Parker's artefacts are invariably acted upon and contested.

Using this manipulation, the artist explores the meaning of objects through their materiality and conversely their materiality through their meaning. Both are far from permanent, eroded by time and use, recast by history and narratives, and performed by physical and cultural processes. The actions of time are, for Parker, integral to matter and materials. They are imbued in the objects and in the meanings we attribute to them. As for Kelley and Messager, the self is not detached from the material world, but partial and connected to the lingering on of things. Yet these objects always also present an otherness in the dissonance between past and present, between one physical form and another. As a result, Parker leaves the gaps of meaning open, allowing things to destabilize the contours of perception and visibility, of the familiar and unfamiliar, without resolving the dualities that transpire in the dynamics of processes and transformation, and in the impalpable shifts of reality and imagination. The traces that she 'inflicts' lead to a

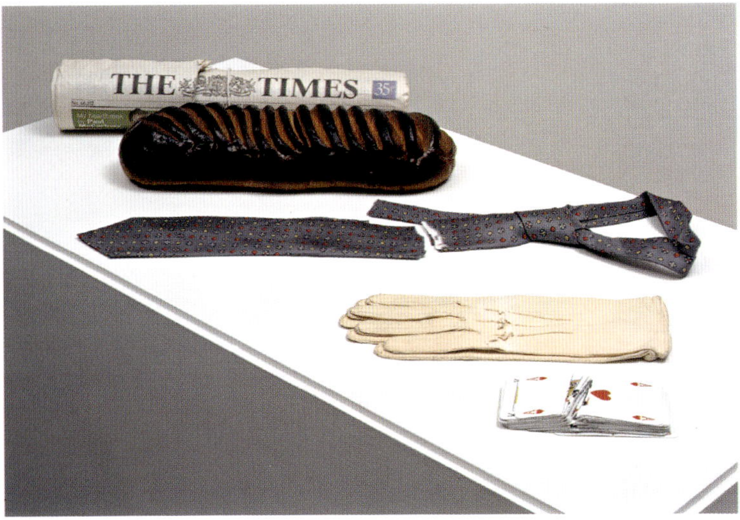

35 Cornelia Parker, *Shared Fate*, 1998, objects cut by the guillotine that beheaded Marie Antoinette (newspaper, loaf of bread, tie, gloves and cards).

disturbance of signification by producing a puzzle of relations between the subject and the world, the object and the subject.[45] In the process she interrogates the role of objects as relic, fetish, testimony and memento, suggesting that traces are at best ambiguous, never univocal, never fully reliable, always ideologically contaminated.

For Kendell Geers ordinary objects can instead become signs able to carry the charge of the corrosive potential inscribed in the well-being of society. A match on a white plinth, a brick and the top half of a broken bottle metonymically stand for the unpredictability of terror (illus. 36). A cluster of entangled loudspeakers addresses its unspeakability. A suitcase containing red and blue safety lights or hundreds of tied locks professes an exacerbating pursuit of security. Throughout his career Geers has provocatively questioned the ideological safety net that envelops contemporary Western societies, from issues of property to national protection. Deeply aware of the discursive entanglement of power relations, exemplified in a neon installation in a self-contained bunker-like space that plays on the phonic relations of (T)ERROR (DIS) ORDER (D)ANGER, Geers argues that artworks are physically and conceptually located in the specificity of a moment in time. As such they can

36 Kendell Geers, *The Terrorist's Apprentice*, 2002, installation consisting of a single match on a pedestal. The artist's instructions stipulate that no other work may be exhibited in the same room.

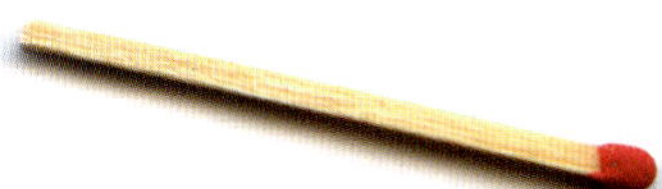

contend with contrasting meanings and act as a catalyst for ideological dislocation and provocation. For Geers, a work of art is meant to shake the 'moral prejudices of the viewer' to 'become the checker board on which the delicate game of ideological chess is played out'.[46] The frisson is ambiguous and critically embedded in the tangible properties of the material world from which it seems to emanate.

Considering himself a contemporary alchemist, Geers ideologically extracts the potentials of matter, exploiting the cultural tension between the disowned 'sacred' of modernity and its uncanny presence within contemporary value systems, whether in the form of capitalism, the dogmas of politics or in the art world itself. A declared supporter of TerrorREALISM, Geers reworks the provocation of modernism across layers of signification. His work revels in the ideological toxicity that endangers order, certainty and righteousness – the clean surfaces of meaning – to expose the threatening magnetism of the unknown and the repressed, contagious energy of subversion.

Seen in relation to the ruinous cabinets of Beuys, the in-between artefacts of Parker's *Wunderkammer* and the contentious presence of Geers's objects, the Smithsonian collection of debris from Ground Zero is more intrusive and disturbing than suspected, since its testimony to history is one of terror, not only in terms of destruction but also of rebellion, not only of remembrance but also of provocation. As these artists remind us, the ruin stands ambiguously in time and in-between time: it is liminal and hence ambivalent. It intrudes subversively in the fabric of memory, since its traces are duplicitous and polymorphic. Such debris unsettles, and uncannily so, since it can sabotage the meaning it is meant to signify and thus be ideologically corrosive.

The ruin attests, for the contemporary imagination, to another form of terror, namely ecological disaster and the debates surrounding climate change. The work of Cornelia Parker is also indicative of the current dialectics of destruction pervading nature and culture alike. The burnt remnants of a devastated forest in *Heart of Darkness* (2004) literally evoke through debris the lingering presence of the event, the marks of 'a terrifying piece of reality'[47] (illus. 37). Suspended in mid-air, pieces of charcoal form a shadowy forest of fragments, compellingly conjuring an absence. The fire that burned down the forest in Florida whose timber makes *Heart of Darkness* was started as a standard 'controlled burn' by the local Forestry Department. Fuelled by the wind, the fire raged out of control.[48] The artist captures the inherent drama of cataclysmic events – whether sudden or in slow motion – rendering both their spatial and temporal dimension through deformed materiality, repositioning the tension from which the historical uncanny originated at the boundaries of nature and technology. The ruinous violence of nature erupts from volcanoes, but also in the tectonic movements and slow erosion of geological strata. *Edge of England* (1999), *White Abstract* (2001) and *Red Abstract* (2001) witness the accumulation of small avalanches that are causing the gradual erosion of the cliffs of Dover. The chalk and brick dust from a house that fell from the cliffs tangibly reminds us of the harshness of destruction. Parker's works critically implicate the debris, the remnant and ruin, to probe the immanence of human and natural catastrophes.

Rather than the uncontaminated realm pursued by the Romantic imagination, nature re-emerges for contemporary culture as an 'object' continuously tinkered with by human intervention, existing at the interface of science and technology whether through exploitation, manipulation, enquiry or documentation. Nature thus appears as a residue of practical and theoretical knowledge constituted by geopolitics and economics, by scientific and technological advancements, by social and cultural differences. For the Peruvian artist and former UN diplomat Jota Castro, these themes interlace as the subtext of sculptures and installations that critically stigmatize the vulnerability and exploitation of financial and natural resources. In artworks such as *Mortgage* (2009), an installation consisting of suspended ropes made of US dollar bills, or *Amazonas aka Merdolino* (2009), an installation of wooden poles stacked up with rolls of toilet paper, Castro comments on the financial crisis and the deforestation of the Amazonian forest, suggesting a continuity of causes and effects, of uses and misuses, of consumerism and capitalism (illus. 38). Both faeces and money involve absorption and liquidation across semantic systems of signification that move from domestic hygiene and policies of sanitation to the

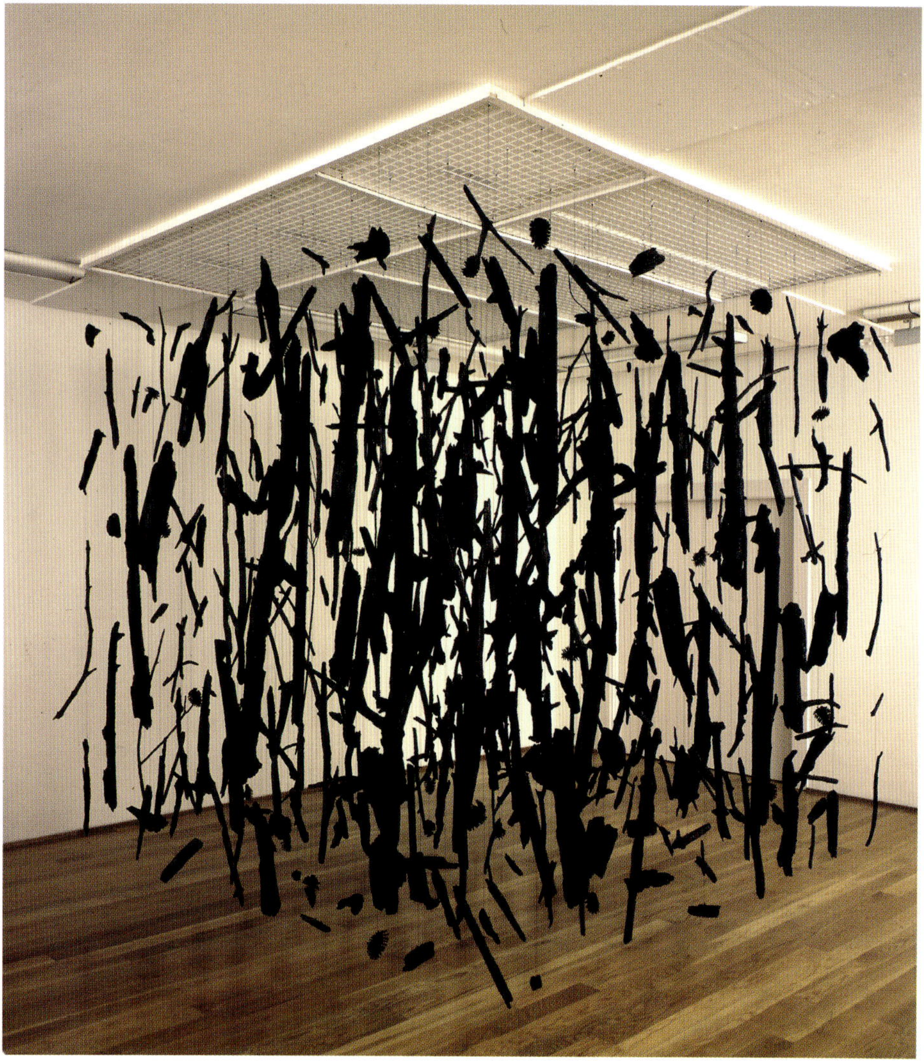

38 Jota Castro, *Mortgage*, 2009, dollar bills, 6 ropes, each 3 metres long, dimensions variable.

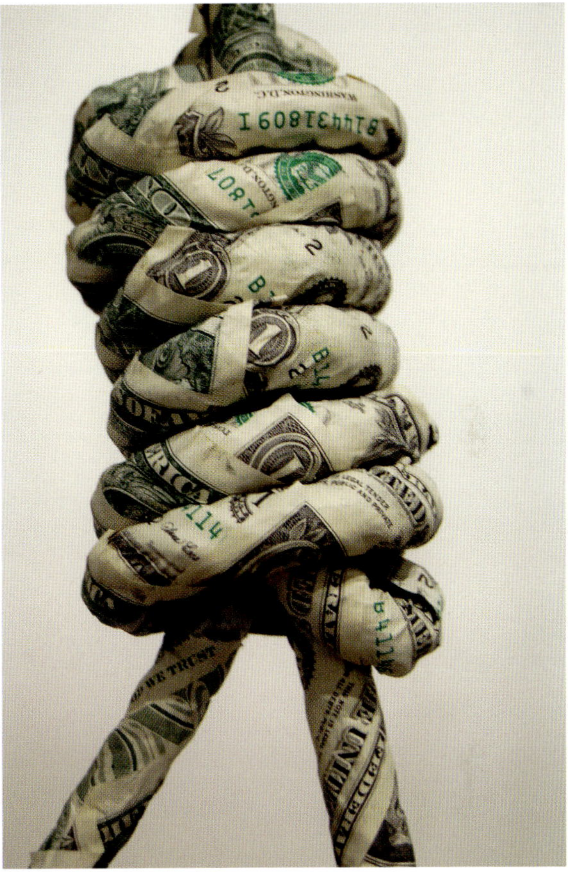

market economy and the politics of production and consumption, from the private to the public and the global.[49] Still resonant within the free-market liberal ethos, this unresolved duality points to the imbalance between regional and global economies and to the underpinning exploitation and inequality of labour as an example of the abject issuing from within capitalism. Similarly, *Tricky* (2009), consisting of two balls – one large and one small – armoured in barbed wire orbits, points to the disparity of two encased and isolated worlds. The artwork implicitly refers to the orbits of the earth and the moon to suggest the

37 Cornelia Parker, *Heart of Darkness*, 2004, charcoal from a Florida wildfire (prescribed forest burn that got out of control).

reciprocity and dependability that dominate global relations as both dangerously suspicious and aggressively defensive.

Indeed, today's shadows of fears are increasingly situated in the boundless territory and hegemonic frontier of cyberspace as one of the most contested and eerily impinging spaces of political and economic supremacy. The menacing assault to this frontier lies within the familiar, in the risk of the unknown hacking of the daily transactions of millions from home computers. Subversively, Internet networks also threaten to undermine the hegemony of authoritarian regimes worldwide, from China to the Middle East. More generally, in the last two decades of the twentieth century these technologies have produced new ways of conceptualizing communication, information and modes of interaction that have been variously aligned with the uncanny. The tension has shifted at the interface of reality and simulation.

The unhomely, predicated on contemporary consumer culture, is epitomized by the Internet as a site of globalization. The Italian artist Carlo Zanni, whose practice explores the form and materiality of the digital, translates icons into painting and constructs digital environments constituted by the web's uninterrupted flux of data. He creates a blueprint of web-works that mostly use what the artist refers to as 'OFF key board interaction'.[50] Rather than a direct interface, the spectator's behaviour and social choices influence the works on a daily basis, which are further translated into the data feeding the web and which then affect the artist's digital worlds. Zanni's *Flying False Colors (The Sixth Day)* (2009) interrogates this dynamic by visually rendering the contamination and erosion of 'an environment' due to the consumption of resources, the economies of exchange and politics of control. The international ecology flag showing the Ancient Greek letter theta, an allusion to danger and death, symbolically represents the space in question. In the work, the colour of the flag is black, rather than orange, and it flakes making the icon disappear under the effect of wind generated by the minute by minute incoming of online data related to the number of barrels of oil requested by any particular country, matched with those of the weather conditions of the country's capital. Under this accumulation of data, Zanni's flag

39 Carlo Zanni, *Flying False Colors (The Sixth Day)*, 2009, installation view at Marsèlleria, Milan. Customized hardware and software, real-time Internet data.

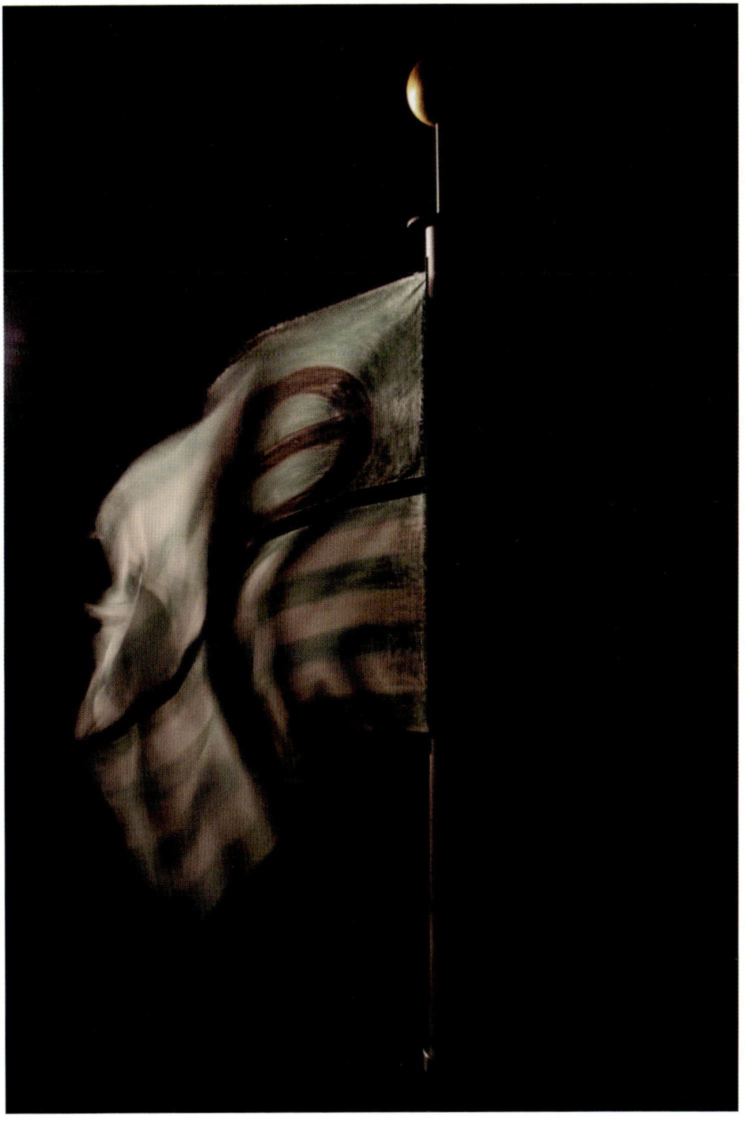

metamorphoses in the affected blank icon of surrender, exhaustion and erosion (illus. 39).

Loosely based on Sydney Pollack's film *Three Days of the Condor* (1975), which connected US military policies in the Middle East to the control of oil resources, the work is part of a trilogy aimed at exploring the collision of the real and hyper-real in the shape of digital information, in other words in the collection and transmission of data that is determined by praxis, in this case, the importing of oil. The constant flow of data acts as a quantification of the real that interferes with the environment of the work by affecting it visibly. As the title indicates, this practice of contamination and erosion is one of politics.[51] The erased flag thus becomes an icon of a corrosive chain of forces: a blank sign both depleted and charged with significance, at the interface of digital information, trade and consumption. The object embodies its own disintegration; it sinisterly displays the corrosion of the homely at the boundaries of environmental and digital interference. With late modernity the aesthetics of the uncanny mirrors back to its origins and reflects within new technologies old fears that tread at the boundaries of the real.

THREE

NARRATIVES

Willie Doherty's video installation *Ghost Story* (2007) shows a slow-moving extended shot of a country road meandering towards the horizon. The voice-over recollects walking along a 'deserted path' and the ghostly presences that people it:

> I looked over my shoulder and saw that the trees behind me were filled with shadow-like figures. Looks of terror and bewilderment filled their eyes and they silently screamed, as if already aware of their fate . . .
>
> A few, in their panic, ran towards a wire fence, further trapping themselves.
>
> As they scaled the fence a military vehicle drove through it tossing them into frosty air.
>
> Troops spewed from the back of the vehicle as it screeched to a sudden halt. They raised their rifles and fired indiscriminately into the fleeing crowd . . .
>
> He was waiting for me as I always feared he would, emerging from a scorched corner where broken glass sparkled on the blackened ground.[1]

Who is 'I'? Who are 'he' and 'they'? Where is the path? What are the events being referred to? When did they happen? What is the relationship between the images and the voice-over's account? To ask these questions is to engage with the narrative structure of the video, to interrogate the visual and verbal palimpsest that constitutes it. The title alludes to the Gothic tradition. The ghosts evoked are those of violence – arguably political violence – whose cultural references include the Northern Ireland conflict, earlier Irish unrest that resembled civil wars in many other countries, and acts of ethnic, political or religious persecution. But can horror be narrated?

To narrate, as the etymology of the term suggests, is to know. To tell is to give shape to the real and the imaginary alike. Literary criticism has made us aware of the complexities of stories, or rather 'texts', 'contexts' and 'sub-inter-texts', as well as the implications of narratives as ways of knowing. Not only *what* but also *how* we narrate matters. The modalities of narration, in the broadest sense, involve the bringing together of heterogeneous elements and their framing into a coherent structure to create meaning. They are constitutive of the ways in which the subject constructs itself and the world. This includes verbal as well as visual forms of narratives, and indeed the visual has been increasingly called upon to document and testify to the self and experience. Painting, but also photography, film and other art practices, such as art video games, are some of the media that attest to the elaboration of cultural narratives and to the affective relations that they unfold, making both the real and the subject the narrative product.

This chapter is concerned with ways of narrating fear, and hence with the ways in which we frame our knowledge of horror, from the thrill of entertainment to trauma, from the visual tales of fright to the harrowing silence that engulfs any attempt to convey the most traumatic experiences of suffering. It looks at the affective unfolding of stories and investigates the supposed relation between the real and the image, the mind and the screen, to answer the question whether it is possible to narrate horror.

Narratives of the Real

Of what images is fear made? How do we represent to ourselves the ghost that lurks within? How do we tell our own and others' horror? If knowledge depends on ways of telling, visual and otherwise, these questions regard the potential and failures to account for, and hence know, 'fear'. For centuries artists have addressed the question of whether it is possible to narrate horror visually. Henri Fuseli's nightmarish visions and Francisco Goya's grotesque spectres acknowledge the presence of the disturbing, irrational forces that mar the Enlightenment. As Marina Warner observes: 'The dreams of reason, as dreamed by modern imaginations since the eighteenth century, as evoked by Goya in his art, conduct us into painful subjectivities, where disturbing fantasies provoke powerfully mixed feelings.'[2] Here Warner alludes to feelings such as thrill, amusement, ridicule, fright and terror. These feelings are not extraneous to contemporary sensibility, though their origin may be other than from the eighteenth century, and are part of different visual practices that infuse genres as diverse as painting, photography, video installation and computer simulation.

Inherent to this quest for visual narratives of horror is the affective force of images and their power to shock. The 're-presentation' of the real in its ugliness and most disquieting manifestations is complicit in modern attempts to narrate horror, since at the dawn of the modern era realism, as a visual mode of telling, emerged as a reaction to traditional mythological and religious painting. This 're-presentation' of the real concerns images, which are not necessarily a 'copy' of the real but a by-product of the imagination, in the realm of disturbing fantasies and fearful forces that are constitutive of individual and cultural subjectivities. Perhaps one of the most harrowing examples is Théodore Géricault's (1791–1824) painting *The Severed Heads* (1818–19), which features two heads of victims of the guillotine captured in the instant of decapitation (illus. 40). Not shown publicly, the painting is a private reflection upon the French Revolution and its aftermath. Like Géricault's paintings of slaughterhouses or of monomania, this picture captures the horror of the moment in the frightfully transfixed expression of the man at the impending guillotine. The dismembered heads are anonymous, and objectified. They conjure the ghost of the Revolution, the terror of the unleashing of obscure uncontrollable forces, whether linked to the irrational or to the brutal reasoning behind social

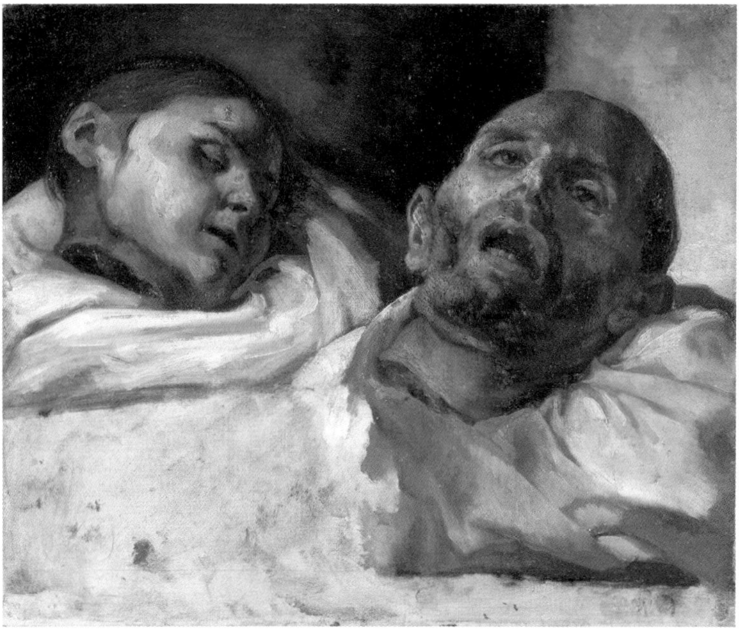

40 Théodore Géricault, *The Severed Heads*, 1818–19, oil on canvas.

upheaval.[3] Yet the painting also betrays an epochal aestheticizing of death that finds a literary equivalent in Thomas De Quincey's awe of murder as a form of art.[4]

The tension between the aesthetic fascination and horror of violence, between the thrill and the fright of the horrid, remains as a motif of narratives of fear and of the disturbing mix of feelings that reverberates across modernity and beyond. Photography, followed by film (as photojournalism and news reportage), have become well-established means of documentation that over the last century have probed the centrality of the visual in the cultural articulation of horror. From their beginnings these genres have entailed the consumption of images of atrocities, disasters, natural calamities and violence as part of a visual currency that, with degrees of goriness and harrowing details, filters through the media. The visual conventions that originally informed pictures of war and disaster shared pictorial and literary tropes with genres as diverse as epics and propaganda in dramatically staged visions. These images, however, gained immediacy and abiding 'realness' as the increasing portability of the equipment and sensitivity of the film enabled the immediate documentation of events. The photographic and moving image has thus acquired a special status in the apparatus of collective memory as a way of narrating that is endowed with the veracity of 'documentation'. Issues of censorship, circulation and dissemination are not secondary to those concerning the ethics surrounding the image itself, as the pursuit of captivating, often sensationalized, photographs whose aesthetics have been condemned as intrusive, exploitative and amoral.

Other concerns pertain to the viewer's assimilation of the images themselves. For Susan Sontag,

> Ever since, battles and massacres filmed as they unfold have been a routine ingredient of the ceaseless flow of domestic small-screen entertainment. Creating a perch for a particular conflict in the consciousness of viewers exposed to dramas from everywhere requires the daily diffusion and rediffusion of snippets of footage about the conflict. The understanding of war among people who have not experienced war is now chiefly a product of the impact of these images.[5]

Critics debate the emotional responsiveness to what is regarded as an overflow and over-exposure to images, and contest the rising consumption of, and indeed the demand for, disturbing pictures. At the same time, trauma is claimed to exceed representation, whether visual or otherwise, and to be unspeakable. Realism – as a mode of narrating that, as Barthes argues, is essentially normative – is at odds with the nature of an experience that effaces understanding.[6] Trauma thus disturbs like an unhealed wound in the body, its ineffability making the possibility of narrating horror a question of form as well as of content.

Rather than positioning horror and trauma outside or beyond narrative, we consider instead the inherent resistance of trauma to figuration within the contemporary currency of fear narratives as constitutive of an unravelling of dissonant, ambivalent and unsettling feelings that shape contemporary subjectivity. Through the spectrum of the narratives of fear, from thrill to horror, we question whether the unsettling of the visual practices that characterize these narratives imaginatively confronts the unrepresentability of trauma and exposes its affective disturbance. The frightful and horrid exploited by film, the shock effect of simulation, and the documentary use of photography and film are part of the cultural frameworks that articulate contemporary 'horror stories', within which the disturbance of trauma can be located. By destabilizing modes of visual narrative and making disturbance integral to the image, contemporary art still pursues methods of effectively 'narrating' horror.

Narratives of Fright

In discussing the video installation *Caribbean Pirates* (2005), the American artist Paul McCarthy comments:

> It's also about Hollywood. It's about horror films, the deception of violence, and the horror genre. It's about the horror of war. It's about the horror of children having their arms and legs cut off. It's about all that. It's about the consumption in Western society that contributes to violence in other parts of the world. It's a pirate story, Pirates of the Caribbean in Disneyland invading the village. It's about deception, representation, figuration, but it's also about something else.[7]

The inscription of violence within a fantasy scenario that echoes Hollywood and Disneyland is loaded with the presence of other horrors. The visual hyperbole of violence, sex and taboo is both a parody and indulgence of the horrid, evoking contrasting emotions as a site of both the comic and the sinister. The work, as the art critic John C. Welchman observers in the same interview, occupies 'an uncanny space between the real and the make-believe'.[8] Or in McCarthy's words, 'everything is filtered through the media, the camera effects, editing, camera angles, etc. The media is glamour. Films are similar to a dream, and they end up as some type of abstracted representation.'[9] McCarthy's video reworks the monstrous and the grotesque at the boundaries of horror movies and the artificial fantasy of Disneyland, critically adopting multiple camera perspectives and editing techniques to confront the 'something else' beyond representation. As the philosopher Slavoj Žižek notes, we grasp 'the gist of an epoch' by focusing 'not on the explicit features that define its social and ideological edifices but on the disavowed ghosts that haunt it, dwelling in a mysterious region of the nonexistent entities which none the less persist, continue to exert their efficacy'.[10] The visceral possibilities of the image are invoked to challenge institutionalized narratives and their collective meanings through a playful collision of references that is reminiscent of the 'allegorical moment' argued for horror film by Adam Lowenstein and central to a supposed 'aesthetics of fear'.

The horror glamorized by Hollywood, the search for special effects that push the possibility of the screen-thrill, TV drama versions of vampires, *The X-Files*, aliens and bio-enhanced heroes are all instances of the persistence within today's imaginary of figures, themes and motifs of decay and catastrophe, of the supernatural and the monstrous, of violence and evil that encode new and old fears. To tell these fears is to give form to what is believed to be sinister, horrid or monstrous. If fear and evil are inseparable aspects of experience, the question of asking 'what is evil?' is, according to Bauman, fraught with unintelligibility: '"Evil" is what defies and explodes that intelligibility which makes the world liveable.'[11] The excessiveness of evil, 'unintelligible, ineffable and inexplicable', also belongs to other aspects of horror.[12] At the interface of popular and high culture, the ambivalence between a taste for the horrid as a laughable hyperbole and a darker subtext has been a defining feature of the Gothic, from its early literary and visual manifestations in the second half of the eighteenth century to the present.

Reflecting on the destabilizing presence of eighteenth-century phantasmagoria, Terry Castle notices the epistemological shifts of the term 'horror' from an artificial spectacle to the subjective, phantasmic realm of the mind. She describes the absorption from the eighteenth century onwards of the artificial illusions of ghosts and spectres into a world of the mind filled with images that unravel figures and scenes as if on a screen.[13] From the earliest appearances of silent projections to contemporary special effects, film, as medium and perhaps most significantly as a cultural metaphor, has become the distinctive site for the surfacing of horror. Walter Benjamin saw in the moving image the medium of modernity, the one that best reflected its anxious sensibility. The hectic hustling of modern life caused, for Walter Benjamin, a nervous overcharge that ran under the skin, and which the cinematic image epitomized in its 'shock-effect'.[14] Already evident in early film adaptations of novels such as Mary Shelley's *Frankenstein,* Robert Louis Stevenson's *The Strange Case of Dr Jekyll and Mr Hyde* and Bram Stoker's *Dracula*, as well as Robert Wiene's *The Cabinet of Dr Caligari* (1920), F. W. Murnau's *Nosferatu* (1922) and Fritz Lang's *Metropolis* (1927), the double cultural implication of film as exposure and narrative simile has been exploited by household names including Alfred Hitchcock, David Lynch, Dario Argento and Quentin Tarantino as *auteurs* of *jouissance*.[15]

Once again the visual arts act as a reflective mirror into this exposure and simile, as artists rephrase and reframe the language of film into the specificity of video and beyond. The work of the Scottish artist Douglas Gordon has consistently moved across and between the cultural frisson of film as medium and narrative of horror, co-opting cultural and social references at the boundaries of memory and imagination, of the rational and irrational, of the real and the fictional, of high and popular culture, of original narratives and their cultural reconfigurations. *24 Hour Psycho* (1993) notoriously slowed the projection of Hitchcock's classic to 24 hours. The story as remembered disappears in a delayed shift of frames, as the spectator is caught in the in-between of watching a slowly changing presence. Projected without sound, the film is distilled to pure image that lingers in the present. Rather than in the suspense of the story, the spectator is caught in the eerie unravelling of narrative transitory junctions that disrupt and dissolve the morality of the original text into a reflective double, both the same and other. Gordon deflects the image from its usual chain of relations in ways that, according to the film theorist Gilles Deleuze, are already embedded in

Hitchcock's deliberate tension between actions, perceptions and affections, and the chain of relations that constitute the mental image of the film in the spectator's mind.[16]

Gordon's doubling, replication and juxtaposition of filmic references recur in a number of other works that confront the stereotypes of thrill, suspense and horror as elements of visual narration. For instance, *Between Darkness and Light (After William Blake)* (1997) projects, on the opposite side of the same screen, two films: respectively, Henry King's *The Song of Bernadette* (1943) and William Friedkin's *The Exorcist* (1973). The contrasting stories blur in this conflation of images. *Confessions of a Justified Sinner* (1995) is based on an excerpt from Rouben Mamoulian's *Dr Jekyll and Mr Hyde* (1931) and focuses on the moment of Jekyll's transformation, enlarging and slowing the metamorphosis of the head and hand (illus. 41). Stevenson's story is mediated through James Hogg's 1824 tale of sin and guilt that lends its title to Gordon's work, and merges religious and scientific anxieties.[17] At the dawn of modernity, Mary Shelley's *Frankenstein* (1818) exposed the monstrous as a product of humanity's tinkering at the limits of scientific imagination, rather than the eerie mishaps of nature. Robert Louis Stevenson's *The Strange Case of Dr Jekyll and Mr Hyde* (1886) similarly dwelled on the capacity of science and technology to act on nature. The

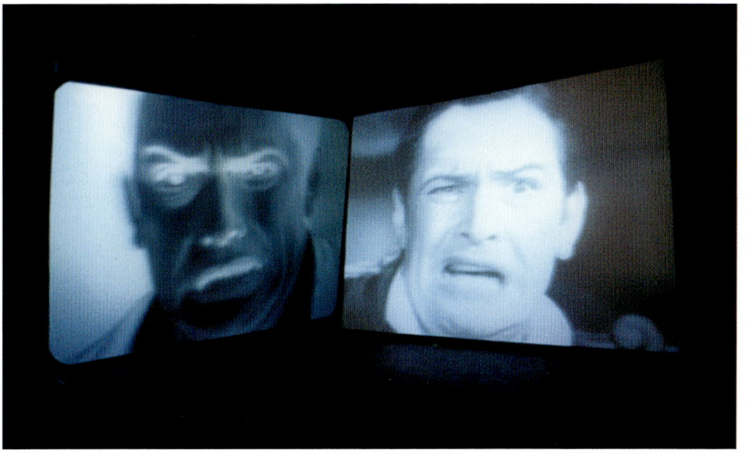

41 Douglas Gordon, *Confessions of a Justified Sinner*, 1995, video installation.

understanding of chemical transformations in Stevenson's story and the experimentation with electricity for Shelley are compelling and unsettling areas of scientific knowledge in which the moral and natural category of the 'monstrous' intersect. The face of fear returns in the narrative negotiation of opposing forces: good and evil, right and wrong, sinful and sinless, victim and perpetrator. Thus intimately embroiled, these blurred opposites engender confusion. The modern concept of monstrosity is in fact tied with scientific and technological advancements, but also situated, as Stevenson's novel already shows, within the dark territory of the mind. Decaying and phantasmic presences manifest as split selves, disturbed personalities that inhabit the treacherous spaces of urbanization. The sinister dwells within subjectivity and without in the amorphous body of the city.

The resonance of these concerns has continued throughout the nineteenth and twentieth centuries, with contemporary ramifications. Gordon revels in the confusion of the spectral that lies within or in-between material life and its imaginative surfacing. His work exposes the struggle of contrary moral and psychological forces as a mutating and yet pervasive narrative feature that returns to haunt culture. It also reflects on the circumstantial experience of watching, the very physicality of being a spectator. At stake is the physical and mental alignment predicated by the screen. In altering traditional ways of seeing and disrupting expectations, Gordon exposes the narrative mediations that shape the culturally horrific within the containment of frightening stories, which allow the surfacing of fears while also keeping at bay the troubling unintelligibility of evil. Once narrative containment is formally effaced, confusion ensues in ways that are potently sinister.

The content and form of horror film are, however, increasingly moving beyond the confines of fictional narrative to expose a further dimension of the sinister that exploits the very pervasiveness of the screen as a site of the imaginary. The move from the large cinematic screen to the homely television set has domesticated the encounter with these figments of the imagination, projecting the frisson within the familial space of the home and opening it up to the new possibilities of the computer screen. According to Fred Botting, 'Horror, it seems, has moved out of the realm of Gothic fiction and film and into the hyper-realism of everyday occurrence. And while endless objects are presented to arouse the visual consumer, none ever seem to fill the gap of a pervasive and unspecific anxiety.'[18] Hyperrealism creates an undefined space between the real and the imaginary that affects the forms and materials of seeing.

The September 11th attacks were a tragic 'live' spectacle, cinematographically compelling to the point of raising doubts in millions of remote observers as to its actuality. Its symbolism exploited the media's proclivity for, as well as the cultural idiom of, visual rapture, bringing the uncertain relations between the real, the simulated and the virtual into the foreground of the debate. The art-game or mod *9/11 Survivor* by Kinematic, which briefly circulated on the web after the attack, is an indication of such contentious slippage. An altered version of an existing game, *9/11 Survivor* presented players with the scenario of the collapsing towers and trapped them in the mayhem of corridors as they tried to escape by jumping from the building. With the incipient presence of digital technologies, the real has – borrowing Žižek's phrase – shifted into the disavowed ghosts of the present, slipping across the uncertain borders of the hyper-real, the virtual and the simulated. The material qualities of the tangible appear eroded to accommodate bio-interface, cyber spaces and virtual links. Reality threatens to dematerialize into images whose predominance, for some critics, informs today's definition and consumption of the factual. Marred by the ghost of virtuality, the real is absorbed by its simulacrum into the cyber contingency of the daily experience of digital technologies.[19]

The virtual windows of computer monitors and of iPhones are a locus of uncanny simultaneity, simulation and continuous circulation of information. Icons govern the interaction, modelled through digital codes, between the user and the virtual. This governance is the subject of another work by the Italian artist Carlo Zanni. In *Average Shoveler* (2004–) Zanni deploys the graphic layout of the famous game *Leisure Suit Larry 1* (1987) to investigate interactive narratives. The work mixes real-time images and stories taken from web channels including news, politics, entertainment and sports with an imaginary snowy landscape

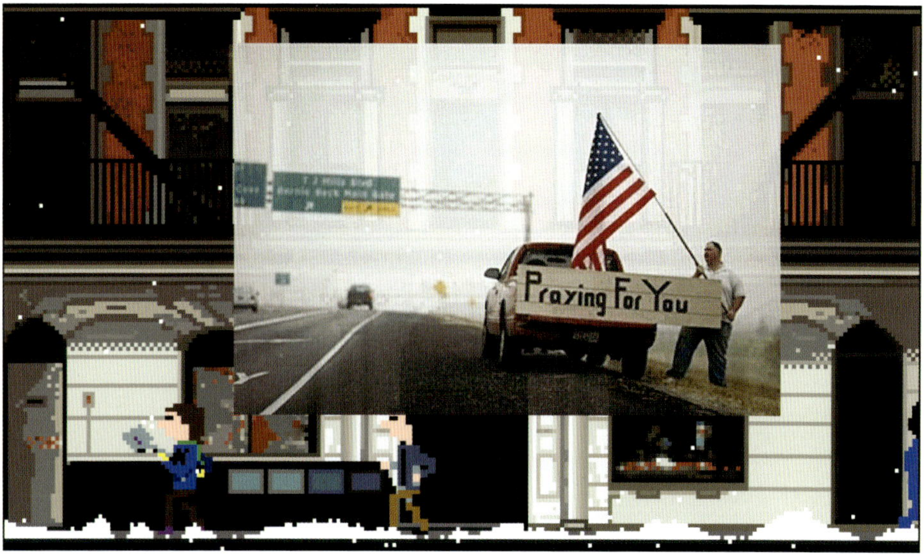

42 Carlo Zanni, *Average Shoveler*, 2004 ongoing. Rhizome.org commission, online game, customized software, Internet.

in New York's East Village. The game consists of shovelling the artificial snow of news in an environment that is neither fictional nor real, but rather a virtual combination of both. Hyper-real, the work rolls out 'digital news' in real-time (illus. 42). The viewer-player navigates the imploding content, encountering the inherent dichotomy of the game-artwork that has no winning end. The task is never-ending as if the player were trapped within a digital tangle of pointlessness: a contemporary Kafkaesque nightmare of ineffective struggle. Unlike traditional games, the piece also includes static moments where the player is inactive, watching as if in front of a grotesque interior painting or a screen-shot in a film, which replicates itself in an uncomfortable stagnation of the ever-moving virtual. Aesthetically, *Average Shoveler* differentiates between the incoming pixellated images of the web and the snow scenario to denote the increasing merging and reciprocity between reality and digital fiction. This interference is not dissimilar from the game slipping into a static mode. It suggests Zanni's critical reflection on the visual codes that typify both the web and interface environments, the experience of which, for want of a better word, is 'interactive'.[20]

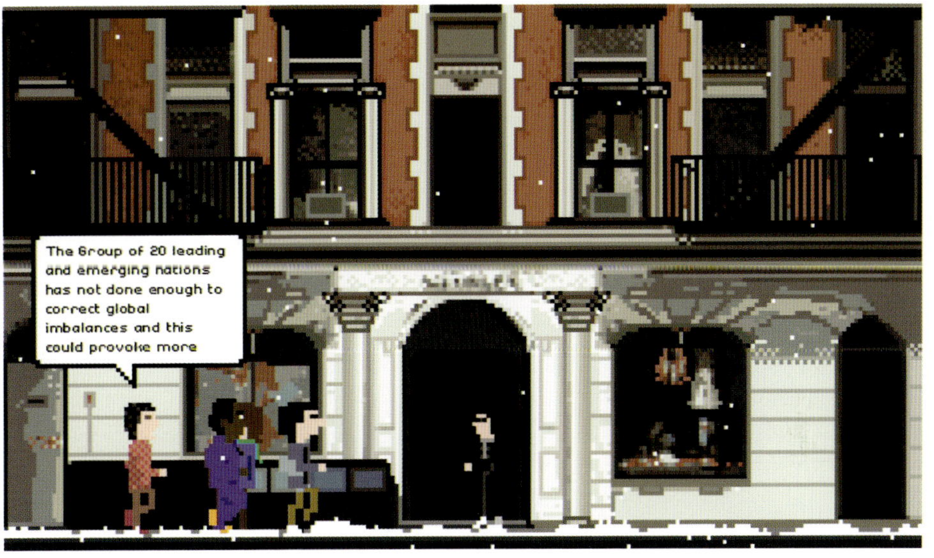

Recombination, layering, figural alteration of action and the manipulation of sensory inputs emerge as structural functions, not only of the game, but more broadly of the web, where the continuous circulation of data in relentless exhilaration and thrill betrays the indiscernible unfolding of real and non-real images: what Deleuze defines as the 'hallucinatory' quality of the virtual.[21]

Characteristically embedded within technological innovation, the horrific has found in the digital and, in particular, in the genre of computer and video games, its latest incarnation. According to Fred Botting, 'The hi-tech worlds of computer games are also places of destruction and decay, spectral fears and primitive energies, fictional worlds in which the future is as ruined as the past.'[22] As in the case of Gothic novels and *film noir* before them, complex affective narratives exploit the uncanny possibilities of the medium to build stories of fear.

Narratives of Virtual Fear

Drawing from and contaminating film in both form and content, video games have emerged with the development of computer and digital technologies, reframing the thrill and suspense of traditional fear narratives within the realm of the virtual. Avatars move across the screen as doubles or alter egos, entwining players in a parallel world that structurally involves them in the unfolding of the game's trajectories. The uncanny offers a critical standpoint from which to decipher the surreal environments of virtual simulation. Action is based on structural repetition and on the interface that ties the player and the avatar. Reiteration governs the unfolding of stories that the player partly constructs and controls. In this scenario, reality returns as a simulated and haunted territory of figurative and structural doubles, eerily familiar figures of a supplanted other: the real.[23]

Subjects encompass a broad range of topics, including crime and war. Fantasy scenarios propose anew the tropes of the Gothic, while 'real' settings are drawn from the Vietnam or Iraq wars as instances of the actuality of the games' 3D interactive worlds. Not unlike photography and film, these figurative or realistic scenarios are narrative constructs that allow for a 'moral' representation of war or crime. It is the specificity of these worlds, collapsing the actual participation of the player with the virtual situation of the game, that invokes the theoretical critique of the interference of the virtual in contemporary experience, expressed by Jean Baudrillard and others. Here the ghostliness of contemporary popular culture finds new forms of thrill, darkness and sinister manifestations. As a condition of the real characterized by interface and simulation, the virtual gives way to what we may call 'virtual fear'.

Games are, in fact, spaces governed by 'kinetic, affective and material dimensions around meaning and representation', through which the mimetic reality of the game is constructed.[24] Figurative conventions of cinema metamorphose in the interface of playing. For instance, the person-shooter games adopt the first-person point of view as central to the game's shooting action within a war or thriller scenario. In film, the first-person perspective – rendered by the first-person camera angle

– is traditionally associated with alienation, violence and fear. It produces a formally charged image that generally enables the viewer to see through the eyes of a criminal or a victim, to share a predatory or impotent gaze.[25] A convention in horror film, the first-person perspective is also a fairly standard means in games deployed to create a sensorial experience of motion by suggesting visual trajectories and by mimicking the physical perception of movement in space that conveys 'an intuitive sense of affective perspective'.[26] In the enactment or confrontation of violence the player experiences this active, mobile and emotionally involving quality of the first-person point of view by ways of doing, of manipulating relations, and of reorganizing sensory inputs, thus assuming a virtual presence within it.[27]

Drawing on Deleuze's definition of cinematic imagery as a 'sensory aggregate', games are caught in the mechanisms of perception and sensation at the boundaries of the actual and the virtual.[28] They are kinetic because they uniquely exist in the space of interactive movement.[29] Their narratives thus unfold at the crossover of the sensory-affective act of playing and the resulting linkages of imagery and sound. War veteran, game designer and artist Eddo Stern has pushed this actuality of the sensory-affective thrill further by giving players a mild electric shock through specially devised braces in correspondence to the avatar's injuries during a performance of the art-game *Tekken Torture Tournament* (2001) (illus. 43). This shock seems symptomatic of broader cultural references.

The etymology of the term 'shock' reveals the multiple associations that make it culturally relevant. Shock was first used in the sixteenth century to describe the encounter of armed forces. From physical collision, the term has subsequently come to mean, in physics, a blow inflicted on material bodies, and in medical terms signifies the act of imparting 'a physical shock to, to cause (a person or a part of the body) to suffer a nervous shock'. Hence, metaphorically, it is now used to suggest offence and scandal.[30] The etymological over-layering of military, scientific and medical connotations is revealing of the polymorphous absorption of 'shock' in the cultural fabric of modernity. Railway shock, whose diagnosis dates from the 1870s, epitomizes the

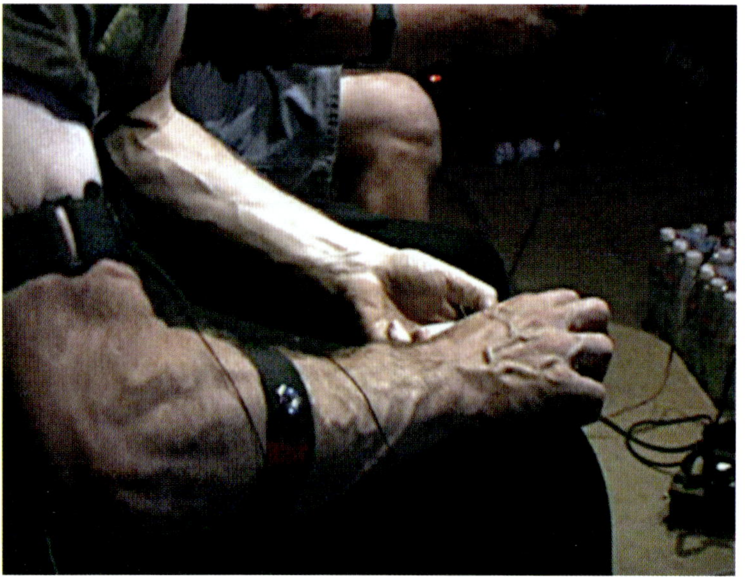

43 Eddo Stern, *Tekken Torture Tournament*, 2001, game performance/custom hardware.

impact of technology on the nervous system. The concussions of railway accidents betray unconscious wounds as well as physical injuries.[31] The concealed hurt inflicted by shock is indeed central to Freud's elaboration of traumatic neurosis, which theorizes the association between physical symptoms and unconscious traumatic memories. This predicts the diagnosis of war neurosis and its devastating effects. Shock denoted the experience of modern warfare in which technology reforged the collision of forces through the introduction of weapons and fighting strategies, including barbed wire trenches during the First World War. Not so much related to the fright of explosion, but rather to the strenuous state of fear and relentless dislocation experienced in the trenches, 'shell shock' is suggestive of emotional exhaustion. Across time, shell shock has partly mutated and partly been absorbed by the aetiology of war neuroses, and is known today as Post Traumatic Stress Disorder (PTSD).[32]

Within the framework of digital games, the cultural references of shock acquire new actuality. Stern's unexpected electric shocks reframe

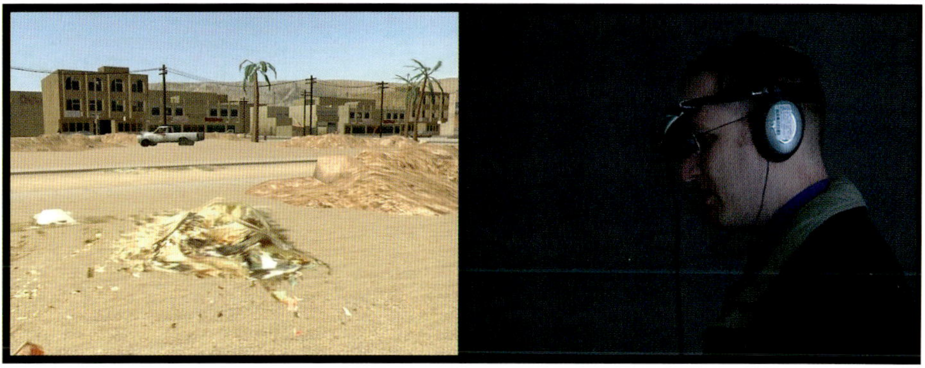

44 Harun Farocki, *Serious Games 3, Immersion*, 2009, double-screen installation, digital simulation and film.

and collapse the collision of forces, implied in the original meaning of the word, in the physical concussion of overstimulation due to a surplus of information, violent stimuli and acceleration. The real shock breaks the boundaries of the virtual not by its realness, but as a reflection and repetition of the simulated injury inflicted in the virtual. Its effect is to seek another form of surplus, another means to 'shock' so as to avoid the numbness of the senses and produce fright. In his practice, Eddo Stern revisits the shock effect that manifests in contemporary computer culture as the abrasive spectral presence of the real. Mixing installation and gaming, Stern explores the context and meanings of video games, mobilizing the rhetoric embedded in the contemporary remaking of war battles and video crime violence. In particular, he exploits the omniscient narrator that, like the first person, is characteristic of realism, the narrative form typically invoked for video games. Stern exposes the status of virtual violence by tearing apart and recomposing the codes that define its implications within the present culture of fear, where the virtual emerges again as a condition of the real. The US Army notoriously deploys adapted versions of games to train soldiers, on the assumption that, since synthetic experiences induce actual reactions and responses, playing fosters tactical teamwork. Yet, often removed from these game-actions is the representation of the fictitious death of the player. Benjamin's assertion of a 'complex kind of training' exerted by technology returns in the era of the digital, sinisterly moving under the skin anew.[33]

At the same time, digital games also endorse fantasies of desire, violence and terror, reasserting the porous limits of the real. If, as James Der Derian comments in his discussion of video games, reality has always been a product of the virtual, the hybrid experience of simulated combat devoid of the consequences of death sets a further obstacle to the comprehension of the lurking horror involved in the action when it shifts from the virtual to the real.[34] Perhaps it is significant that *Special Force* (2003), released by the Hezbollah Central Internet Bureau and based on similar existing militaristic shooter games, though with Israeli planes as targets, is condemned in the West for fostering terrorism. For young Palestinians, however, it is a way of mediating the actual experience of violence.[35] The sensory manipulation that defines the simulated environment of games is thus affectively 'shocking' in ways that go beyond the digitally simulated images of gaming, emphasizing the ideological collision of the politics of fear.

The shock effect of the virtual also mobilizes its 'interactive' potential in the modified versions of war games deployed in the treatment of soldiers diagnosed with PTSD. *Immersion* (2009) by filmmaker and artist Harun Farocki was filmed during a demonstration carried out by the Institute of Creative Technology for the US Army. The double-screen projection shows simultaneously the virtual world of a village, reminiscent of a war zone in Iraq or Afghanistan, and a soldier reliving a traumatic experience. With the help of a psychologist he is directed through a virtual landscape that painfully matches his traumatic recollection (illus. 44). The visual slippage of the screening is potently effective and uncertain, as it ambiguously duplicates the real with disturbing significance.[36] The suspense of the narrative is heightened by the increasing discomfort of the soldier that borders on sickness, reaching extreme physical and mental stress as the unfolding of the action and the emotional turmoil of the recollection merge. The digital simulation is paired to the role-playing upon which the whole situation is built and which becomes evident at the end of the video. Though fraught, the emotional intensity of the work compellingly suspends disbelief, moving between the harrowing reality of trauma and the affective interaction of the game. The digital evocation is thus the more unsettling as reality diverges into simulation. The thrill of entertainment reverts in the painful legacy of violence and trauma. Virtual fear is our contemporary version of modernity's shock effect, and one that reveals an emotional breach wherein narrative fragments and tangles in the uncertainty of the limits to which it is exposed, thus propelling it towards the 'excess of horror'.[37]

Narratives of Frightful Memories

In 2008 SXS Enterprise (Zacharias, Heather, de Boer) conceived *Fear-Lab* as a response to the rhetoric of fear heightened by the outbreak of the war in Iraq. An interactive performance, the work exploited the visual and sound idioms of reality TV and horror film, theatrical illusions and quotations from George W. Bush's speeches, to explore the mechanisms that underpin the narrative construction of fear. The work asked 'what makes us decide to be afraid as an individual and as a society?'[38] Through live projections of city- and landscapes, and using model train sets, *Fear-Lab* manufactured unsettling ambiences of light and shadow. Overtly fictional and artificial, the scenarios betrayed a shared recognition of what is culturally ascribed as scary, delving into common interpretations and imaginative connections. This sensorial mimesis of the performance was sinisterly intermeshed with the political rhetoric and the uncanny appeal of terror that has marked the last two decades of Anglo-American politics.

In the second half of the performance, the audience was faced with a blank screen and invited to imagine their worst fears by mentally projecting the narrative unfolding of this emotion. Through headphones a voice provided guiding directions, asking where one stood in the imagined scenario, where the light came from, where the shadows were cast, what noise one heard. Being standard guidance in psychological visualization techniques, the questions acted as clues of narrative structuring. They deployed a common vocabulary of sounds and images, of oral and visual associations to forge frightful mental imagery of internal and personal landscapes of fear, in which the spectator acted. *Fear-Lab* addresses the construction of narratives and their emotional valences, exploring the visual features that denote narratives of fear in daily life and in our culture, suggesting mutuality between the pictures of the mind and those that move across the screen. This mutuality is the more productive as we consider the nature of narrative, and explore the cultural and psychological consequences of the comparison of mental processes to the images that inform them.

Imagery, as the result of sensorial stimuli, is integral to the working of the brain and contributes to the formation of subjectivity. Visually we not only narrate real or fictional events as if they were snapshots or film sequences; we also 'narrate' the self by structuring experiences and thought within a consistent framework that edits and links mental pictures. These imageries are better understood as a compound of sensorial perceptions. In this sense they are not a picture of a lived moment, but a reconstructed interpretation of it and of the sensations and emotions that it arouses, all at the moment of interface of verbal and other mental formations of thought, memory, feeling and fantasy. Within brain systems a complex interaction happens between what psychology refers to as autobiographical memories and autobiographical knowledge. Considered primarily visual, autobiographical memory is constituted by transitory, sensory-related memories that then enter long-term memory. There they are framed within the enduring structures that add to individual informative frameworks of knowledge, acquiring a 'story-like quality'.[39] The sensory (including visual ones) stimulae that produce these memories – central to both autobiographical knowledge and autobiographical memory – are imbued with the emotional experience of the real event, such as fear. When we retrieve a memory, we also gain access and evoke the feelings contained in such a memory. While psychologists and neuroscientists interrogate the neuronal and physiological basis of mental visual repertories, we may consider the cultural cues that inform them and ask if the mind's stories are shaped by abiding and contemporaneous imaginaries. In particular, we consider the nature of visual biographical telling through the work of artists Nan Goldin, Tracey Moffatt and Marko Mäetamm.

In her work, the U.S. artist Nan Goldin explores the aesthetic potential and visual rhetoric of the snapshot, rendering the apparently fortuitous photographs of family and friends as a means of tracing the irretrievable and disjointed fragments that constitute life stories. Goldin lingers on the prosaic to reveal the anecdotic vividness of details: a body tattoo, discarded clothing, a motorbike, a room interior. She appropriates traditional means of characterization proper to portraiture, as well as the motifs typical of magazine reportage, and transposes them within the contemporary visual currency of the confessional. This currency is made ever more accessible by digital photographic and video cameras, and further enhanced by web-networks such as YouTube, Facebook and MySpace. Her pictures of micro-moments and events accumulate to generate fleeting stories that bear similarities to our selective mental gathering of (auto)biographical memories, acting as tangible counterparts of instantaneous mental pictures that ground the internal narratives through which the subject constructs itself. Similar processes of selection, editing, blending and compounding equally comprise the making of mental and photographic images, as do the structural features of the shot itself, such as camera angle, light and frame. Indeed the sensorial qualities of these features hold the emotional charge of the picture.

Goldin points to the narrative significance of these components, but also to their artificiality, to the inevitable incompleteness of the narrative that they unravel. The shot is partial to the gaze beyond the camera, to the subject's attempt (or not) to stick to an internal, coherent story, to employ external and internal ways of seeing and perceiving. In so doing, the artist uncovers the ambiguity and irony of the visual tenets that endorse subjectivity and, more broadly, of the cultural notions of identity. The latter bridge across the private and the public, the personal and the anecdotic, the intimate and the voyeuristic, representing feelings as diverse as tenderness, self-confidence, expectation, sadness, distress, shame and angst. Every picture both adds to and changes the process of telling in which it participates, nuancing the narrative of a life-story from within and without.

The Australian artist Tracey Moffatt also powerfully exploits the confessional tendency exposed by the pervasive use of images across media and social networks. Throughout her work, Moffatt uses visual features of popular culture to contest issues of identity in relation to the social construction of race, as in works such as *Up in the Sky* (1998). Moreover, she questions the individual and social moments of horror, as in the photographic series *Scarred for Life* (1994 and 1999) and the video work *Doomed* (2007), which, respectively, captures a frightful event that is pivotal to the course of a life-story, and weaves a collage of fictional disaster and collective scenes of panic.

In *Scarred for Life*, Moffatt adopts a photographic style reminiscent of that of *Life* magazine in the 1960s and '70s, and replicates domestic tableaux, each of which has an identifying caption. The frisson between the image and the text conveys the distressing nature of the episodes that the camera freezes. Titles, such as *Heart Attack, 1970*, *Mother's Day, 1975*, *Doll Birth, 1972*, *Mother's Reply, 1976* and *Scissor Cut, 1980* disguise harrowing feelings under the fortuitous banality of cataloguing labels, as if the episode has stayed forever indexed in the memory (illus. 45 and 46). Intrusive, painfully personal and provocative, these captioned pictures condense ideas about the vividness of traumatic memories and their potential falsification. Overtly staged and brashly coloured, the series supposedly 'captures' the fearful event. However, as Roger Luckhurst writes: 'The care of re-staging does not authenticate but rather exaggerates falsification, dramatizing the interplay of traumatic fixity and narrative mobility that constitutes the trauma subject. In doing so, Moffatt's series plays

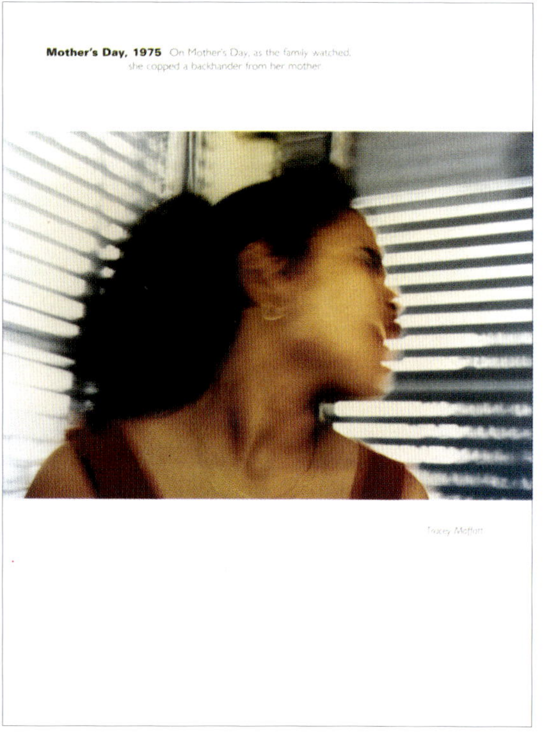

45 Tracey Moffatt, *Mother's Day, 1975*, 1994, series of 9 images, offset print.

with but also exposes the allure that originary plenitude promised by the imprint of the intrusive traumatic image.'[40] Indeed, Moffatt professes the encapsulation of a 'life-story' in the determination of an image, and asks the viewer to position herself within the dynamics of the gaze that the picture foregrounds. But in so doing, the artist also destabilizes the reassuring posture of the confessional to evoke the puzzlement of guilt and shame.

The video *Doomed* (2007) uses by comparison linear episodic sequences to build an apocalyptic crescendo of disastrous, fictitious fright scenes taken from film. The visual hyperbole is completely devoid of contextual narrative or rather it becomes a narrative in its own right. The seamless flow of the sequences makes us ever more aware of the inflated constructedness of the pictures, typical of Hollywood's indulgence in spectacular effects. In this sense, Moffatt reminds us of the coalescing of fantasy and violence in the filmic glamorization of thrill and fright. The focus is on the media dramatization of and alluring fascination with disaster. This is rendered through the gasping tension built into the camera angles that lead to the climactic moment, as well as the insinuating mood conveyed by the music, and the use of close-up and first-person camera angle, aimed to intensify the identification of the viewer and affectively charge the prelude to catastrophic climax. *Doomed*'s voyeuristic humour underpins the narrative rhetoric that defines scary scenarios in popular culture, the 'aesthetic' fascination with the ruin, and the visual enticement that

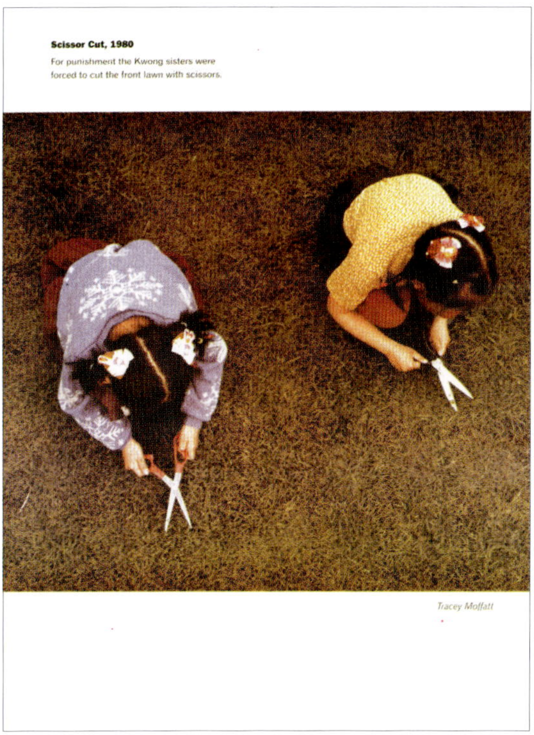

46 Tracey Moffatt, *Scissor Cut, 1980*, 1999, series of 10 images, offset print.

makes the thrill of disaster lucrative entertainment. Moffatt confronts us with the spectacle of devastation, and more specifically with its cinematic representation in Hollywood film, thereby complicating its cultural resonance. As a narrative trope, destruction is indeed contingent on private fears and anxieties that both necessitate and resist representation. As the film critic Mathias Nilges argues: 'Unlike Cold-War era representations of destruction that mediated a dominant fear of annihilation, contemporary representations of destruction are beautiful because destruction is in fact an antidote to a world that produces the fears we seek to escape'.[41] Moffatt both traces a visual trajectory of sequences of devastation from the 1950s to the present and conflates them with hyperbole, interrogating the aesthetic (as sensory potency) of the moving image vis-à-vis the cultural context of America's response to 9/11 and the War on Terror. This effect is not achieved through direct reference, but instead the artist formally emphasizes the cultural process of editing through sequence-cutting and repetition, typical of the media's construction of collective memories of atrocities. *Doomed* idiosyncratically collides filmic illusion and reality in its repetition and consumption of images. The jarring effect is an apocalyptic vision, intensely funny and disconcertedly daunting.

Alert to the reciprocity of private and public, Moffatt merges fictional and biographical elements through compositional condensation and editing, which reflects the processes through which memories and knowledge are shaped. As in the case of Goldin, she captures the inherent ambivalence of aesthetic images as the counterpart of mental pictures. Ever nuanced, never fully reliable, the pictures are visual compounds that betray cultural trends and attitudes, modes of seeing, perceiving, feeling and organizing self-knowledge, all in relation to an internal as well as external gaze. Moffatt draws attention, as does *FearLab*, to the mutuality of the visual strategies that inform the individual and cultural construction of images of fright and horror. These, as SXS Enterprise suggests, belong to the rhetoric of fear that equally exploits verbal and visual narratives. Continuity is evinced between autobiographical visual chronicles, as memory shots of a life-story, and the narrative disruption generated by pictures of fear, horror, trauma and shame. These pictures bear a contextual reference to an event – the traumatic event – that impinges on and freezes the narrative flow of a life-story with its emotional charge. Where can we then situate trauma in relation to narrative?

The act of confessing as a palimpsest of words and images, of fearful memories and macabre fantasies, of fictional and factual anecdotes of daily tragedy, is ironically used as a metaphor for the present by the Estonian artist Marko Mäetamm. The artist's ominous, grotesque world harbours menace and violence within the safe confines of domesticity. The microcosm of the home and of the 'artist's life' translates into the broader spectrum of anxieties about power relations, abuse and disavowal. Nursery rhymes stir up fear and frightening imagery of death. Graphic stories of abuse twist macabre conventions to uncanny effect. In *Family* (2007) the artist deploys cartoons to build repetitive stories of domestic violence with hyperbolic crescendos of horror (illus. 47 and 48). The video-work *No Title* (2007) consists of a circular story, the text of which scrolls on a black screen, centred around a pseudo-confession of dispossession, violence and guilt:

1. I have a wife, a 6-year-old daughter and a 2-year-old son too. As my income as an artist was irregular, I accepted the position of dean at the Estonian Academy of Arts a couple of years back.
2. To get a bank loan and provide a flat for my family.
3. Now I have a 25-year bank loan and a nice little apartment in central Tallinn.
4. Working as a dean is interesting but draining and takes up practically all of my time.
5. There's constantly less and less time to do art – a few hours in the morning before going to work and in the evening after 17.00, when I should actually go home and spend time with my children.
6. So I feel guilty the whole time I'm working in my studio. They're waiting for me at home but I get there after they've gone to sleep.

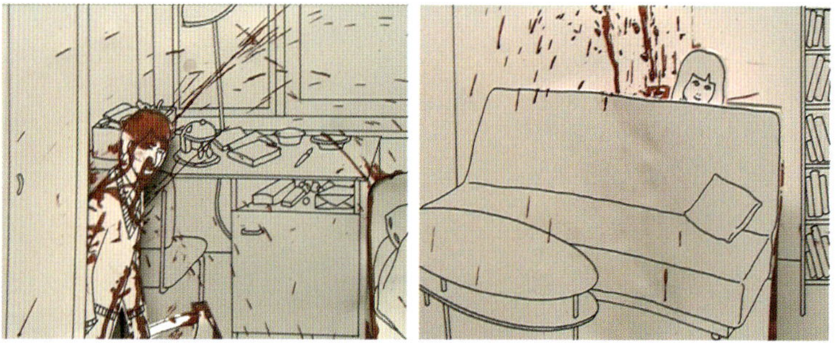

47, 48 Marko Mäetamm, *Family*, 2007, animation DVD, colour, 4'9".

7. And I go back to the studio in the morning before they get up.
8. And I cannot change any of this for the next 25 years because I have a bank loan.
9. I'll no doubt spend the best years of my life like this instead of pursuing creative projects.
10. And this torments me.
11. All the time.
12. It's like I'm in some kind of vicious circle. I'm doing everything I can to be able to pursue my art, but doing what I must do takes so much energy, that I'm not able to create.
13. I recently had a small exhibition in Budapest and happened to get acquainted with a scientist. I told him about my problem.
14. The scientist told me he knows what I must do and that he knows someone in Tallinn who can help me.
15. When I got back home I called the number I'd received from the scientist. I was given an address and asked to bring my wife and children along.
16. It was some kind of physics lab. My wife and children were directed into a room containing nothing but a funny bench.
17. A kind of white, square bench and in the middle of its backrest was a little pull-down shelf. On the shelf were some worn-out looking toys like you usually find in the waiting rooms of clinics. And some funny looking straps hung from the bench.

18. I was directed into another room right beside the one with the bench and asked to wait.
19. After some time a man came in and told me that he knew what the problem was and that it could be solved by killing my wife and children. This shocked me completely.
20. When I had somewhat pulled myself together I went and peeked in the door to see what my wife and children were doing in the next room. They were sitting next to each other and playing. I watched them for some time with confused feelings and snuck back the way I'd come.
21. The man was still there, waiting. I'll briefly sum up our conversation.
22. ME: Is there really no other way?
    THE MAN: No. You are the one who wants this. It's necessary.
23. ME: (after a pause) But . . . how then . . .?
    THE MAN: With electricity. That bench is an electric chair. Or put them into the meat chopper. We'll see.
24. ME: (after a long pause) No I can't . . . This is . . .
    THE MAN: Do not worry about that. You are going home now and we are taking care of this at night. You don't need to think about it anymore.
25. ME: (after a very long pause) And you're telling me that . . . it must be done? . . .
    THE MAN: Yes. It must.
26. I burst into tears. I was led out of the building through the back door and I went home.
27. That was the worst night of my life.
28. I can't even tell why but the next morning I went back to the lab.
29. I carefully peeked into the room, where I left my wife and children the previous night. The room was empty.
30. They had already been taken away.
31. Only the same weird bench in the corner.
32. And the same worn-out looking toys on the pull-down shelf. And the straps.

33. I was overcome with unbearable anguish.
34. Actually it is like this:
    1. I have a wife, a 6-year-old daughter and a 2-year-old son too. As my income as an artist was irregular, I accepted the position of dean at the Estonian Academy of Arts a couple of years back.
    2. To get a bank loan and provide a flat for my family.
    3. Now I have a 25-year bank loan and a nice little apartment in central Tallinn.[42]

The narrative of the video of Mäetamm's *No Title* is the more disquieting as the viewer is both moved and repulsed by the unfolding and looping of this sinisterly humorous and shameful confession. Self-deprecating and ironic, the artwork reveals the entertainment value of the act of self-exposure implicit in the confessional as a dominating form of narrative in contemporary culture. Indeed, shame and shaming concurs with the emotional currency of much of today's reality television shows and other kinds of entertainment that exploit self-exposure.[43] The viewer is complicit in a testimony that is doomed to narrative circularity and to the perpetration of a story of disempowerment and shame.

Guilt and shame are emotional counterparts of trauma and horror. While guilt entails a responsibility towards one's actions, shame relates to one's identity and inadequacies in relation to an internal or external gaze. Indeed, shame has gained prominence as 'the emotional reference' most intimately associated with the disruption of horror in contemporary culture.[44] This seems to further locate trauma within the contemporary tendency towards the confessional and autobiographical, and hence within the production and consumption of images. The analogy of the mind as a screen acquires new significance, as exposure becomes a trope of the narrative strategies of subjective knowledge and the dynamics of the gaze foreshadow fear in its utmost expression. Similarly, the analogies that tie, in their sensory and visual density, the snapshot or film sequence to autobiographical memories, as the sequences on which the subject unfolds its own narrative, have consequences for the cultural valences of images and for the failure of representation that denotes trauma in contemporary discourses.

Narratives of Trauma

The strong visual and generally sensory quality of traumatic memories is accompanied by narrative fragmentation. Neuropsychology locates the formation of these memories, not through the pathways of the hippocampus, where they would be voluntary and verbally accessible, but rather through the alternative neuronal pathways of the amygdala, the brain area related to fear. This theory explains the loose temporal connotation of these memories as well as their vivid sensorial, visual-spatial qualities. Unconscious or repressed, these memories interfere with other autobiographical memories and disrupt the narrative processing through which the subject articulates and confers meaning to experience. Characterized by what psychology refers to as 'flashback' (a term shared with cinema), traumatic memories are dominated by vivid visual impressions and recur, often triggered by involuntary cues, as disjointed and fragmentary.[45] A ground-level witness of 9/11 who developed PTSD, for instance, had the destabilizing memory of seeing himself floating in the sky with the plane flying beneath him as it was approaching its target. Such dissociative symptoms show a breakdown of the continuous processes of perception and of the unifying temporal construction of the self in the discursive flow of subjectivity.[46] The fractured presentation of thoughts and feelings related to traumatic memories is a constant symptom in the diagnosis of PTSD, which may be overcome in therapy when trauma memories are 'organized' within a narrative framework.[47]

The research and definition of PTSD, which has undergone a number of revisions since the 1960s, marks a shift from earlier aetiologies of shell shock and war neurosis and concerns experiences as diverse as the Vietnam War, the Holocaust and other genocides, sexual abuse, forms of victimization and harassment and other forms of violence. Controversy has raged around the reliability of traumatic memories.

The validity of the concept of trauma from its early formalization in the 1870s has also proved unstable and susceptible to cultural and historical interpretations. Contingent on the development of the concept of trauma has been the question of its mental 'representability', and this has raised the question of the reliability of traumatic memories. Hence, imagery as the non-conscious, fragmentary and intrusive visual trace of horror is the contested referent of a concept that has become a potent metaphor for the articulation of suffering in contemporary culture.[48]

Doomed by 'unspeakability', trauma culturally finds in the realm of imagery an equally contested and yet powerful complement to that which can speak without saying, testify without showing, and which, if we turn back to the moving image, appears throughout modernity as a site of hallucinatory fantasy and documentary memory.[49] Endlessly repeatable, the moving image is the locus of the cultural flashback, an image that can move backwards and forwards between temporal and spatial narratives. Placing the image at the centre of contemporary investigation on trauma, Roger Luckhurst proposes cinema to be central to the constitution of the PTSD subject, and to the shaping of both the 'psychological and general cultural discourse of trauma' from the 1980s to the present.[50] Beyond cinema per se and its close association to the flashback, we may consider the affective charge of the moving image and its contextualization in the discourse of trauma, both embedded in practice, through the use of film in psychological experiments, and as a means of documentation. Rather than turning directly to these practices here, we will focus instead on their mediated appropriation in the work of Douglas Gordon and his use of historical footage, and on a video installation by Shona Illingworth developed collaboratively with the neuro-cognitive psychologist and memory researcher Martin A. Conway. These artworks enable us to penetrate the cultural fabric of the narratives that surround the painful experience of trauma, as the artists interpolate and interfere with the sensorial texture of the images, neither to tell nor to represent trauma, but to exploit the cultural metaphor of mind and screen by which the narratives of fear and horror can be contextualized.

Looping, editing, collating and manipulating are the means of this visual recounting that prefers the essential dynamic shot of film to the fix-framing of photography. Deleuze argues that the cinematic image is intrinsically sensorial and affective, as it results from an assemblage of visual, oral and haptic perceptions and engenders sensible impressions in the viewer, who is affectively looped into the unravelling of the image.[51] Figuratively, trauma memories are also part of processes of mental editing, collating and alteration during memory retrieval of the sensory (both visual and acoustic) perceptive details that contain the emotional charge of the traumatic experience. Some of these details, as suggested, remain inaccessible although their emotional content may indirectly affect what we see or remember. Others of these details can, on the contrary, be associated with other non-traumatic ordinary imagery, such as that of an everyday object. These non-traumatic details become then the vehicle through which the intrusive and overwhelming feelings of fear interfere with the unfolding of memories and thoughts, the mental film in our minds.[52] The analogy between mental and moving images has profoundly infiltrated the common imagination, and it is hard to distinguish their reciprocity and influences.[53] 'Monstrously prosthetic', as 'the contents of sensation', the moving image designates a convergence between the subject and the text in the continuum of film, in its immediate affective sensations.[54] Discreet, malleable and time-based, the moving image ideally reminds us of the sensory-perceptual continuum of mental imagery and of the structural editing, looping and shuffling of spatial and temporal relations that are supposedly integral to the production of autobiographical memories and other forms of knowledge, and to the troubling interference of trauma. Hence, rather than the literalness of the flashback, the moving image itself, when manipulated or distorted, can be conducive to disturbing feelings.

Slow motion and multiple screening are strategies that Gordon adopts for presenting original footage of shell-shocked patients in *10 MS* (1994) and *Trigger Finger* (1994). Dating from 1918 and made by two army doctors, Arthur H. Hurst (1879–1944) and James Llewellyn Montfort Symns (b. 1885), the films portray these patients' symptomatology and their treatment with hypnosis and physiotherapy. Hurst and Symns believed in the hysterical causes of the traumatic symptoms that included ataxic, paralyses, paraplegia, jerk reflections, amnesia, blindness and deafness. The films document a narrative trajectory from illness to rapid recovery.[55] A man's frustrated attempt to get up from an institutional bed, wearing only his underpants, falling over and struggling to pull himself up again, or the tremulous clenching of a fist mimicking a gun, the videos collapse the original visual narrative in the impotence of a gesture (illus. 49). The body is trapped in contracted impossibility, and the emotive tension is signified in the fight between paralysis and action. Whether experiencing an impossible desire to help or the sadistic pleasure of watching, the spectator stands at a distance, also the prey of impotence.

Gordon's video installation *Film Noir* (1995) is based on footage of a man undergoing an insulin-induced coma. First experimented with in 1933 by the Austrian neurologist Manfred Sakel (1900–1957) for the treatment of schizophrenia, insulin-induced coma was largely used during the Second World War, and well into the 1950s, for trauma-related and psychotic conditions. Gordon presents discrete sequences,

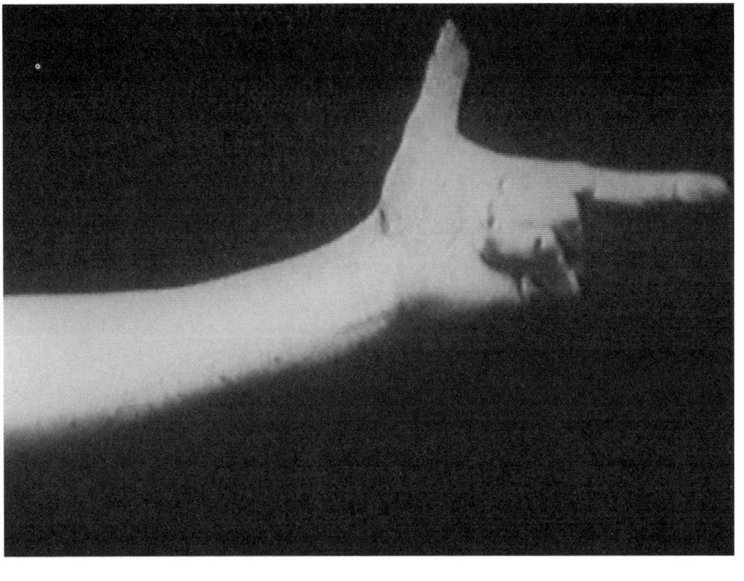

49 Douglas Gordon, *Trigger Finger*, 1994, video installation.

on different screens, of the original medical film documentation. The patient is anonymous, the cause of trauma unknown. The multiple-screen installation formally suggests the fragmented and dissociative experience of trauma. This results in a visual palimpsest of separate and intertwined works that shows close-ups of the man's disturbed face (*Film Noir (Fear)*), an eyelid covered in sweat (*Film Noir (Perspire)*), and a twitching hand (*Film Noir (Hand)*) (illus. 50 and 51). The scientific footage is intentionally dismembered and enlarged, rendered emphatically intrusive and disturbing. As viewers, we are asked to recompose the picture and to reintegrate this burst narrative of hallucinated coma that the film captures in physical signs of pain, exhaustion and stress.

In these artworks, by distancing the original footage from the historical medical context in which they originated, Gordon contends with the fascination and repulsion of trauma that ambiguously coexist as critical features of both art and science. He implicitly subverts the use of film in the study of trauma as objective record and exploits the so-called emotive imagery that relates to it. Gordon does so by figuratively 'bursting' the transparent celluloid. He disturbs the medical narrative that seeks to disavow the 'traumatic' symptoms, visually dissolving, altering and dismembering the original footage to suggest the tense, unresolved and fretful disturbances between thought, action and emotion, internal and external realities, between the observing and the enacting subjects. Rather than the historical question of trauma, and the specificity of its diagnosis at any given time, by asking us to look at the most minute movements and contractions, Gordon directs us into the realm of obsessive repetition, of dissociation and of the fractured components of trauma. The medical footage loses its documentary relevance and entraps the viewer in the physical and emotional upheaval of the paralyses, trembling, sweat and jerks of warped bodies. If the eyes of the spectator identify with the scientific gaze, the body is cast in direct relation to these images, at the fissure of eruption, in the gap of signification, in the emotional somatoforms engulfing subjectivity and culture alike.

In Shona Illingworth's sound and video installation *The Watch Man* (2007), repetition and fragmentation similarly interfere with the

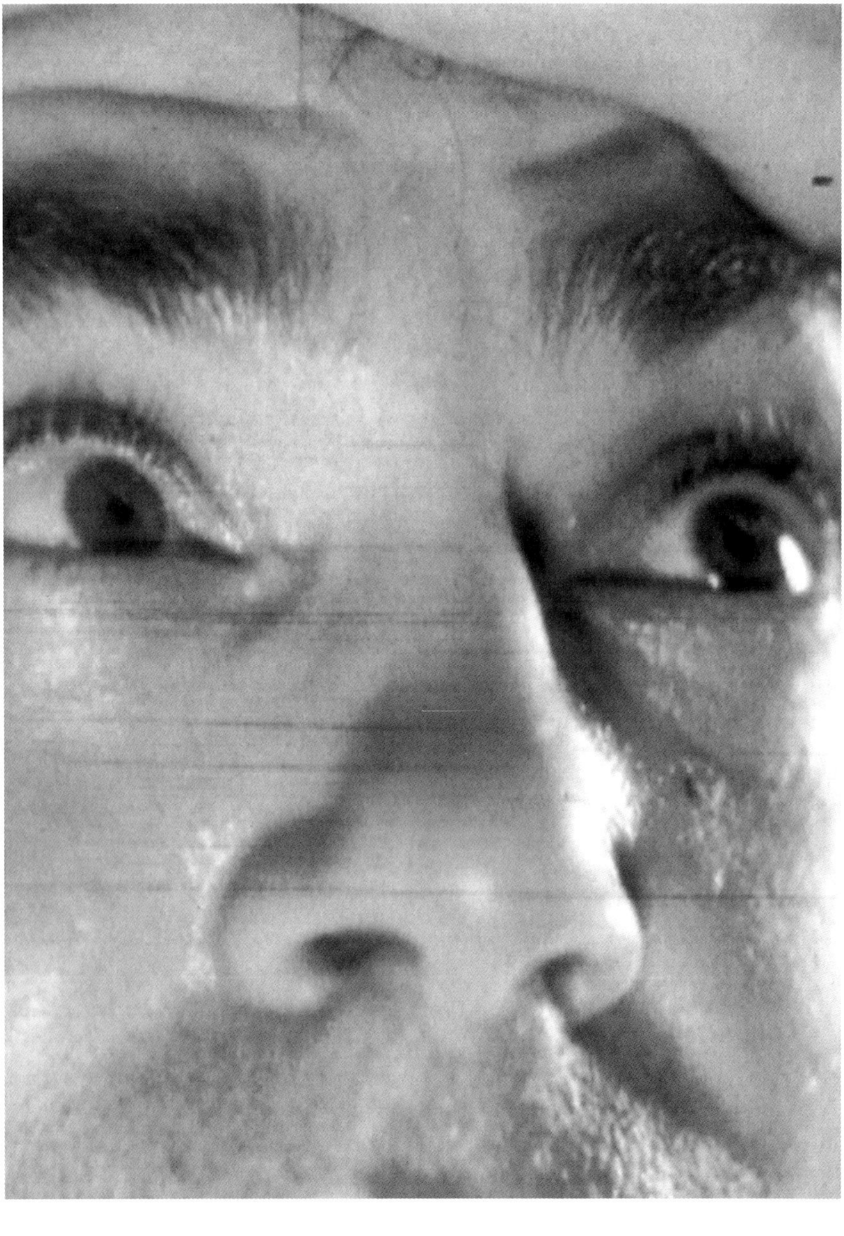

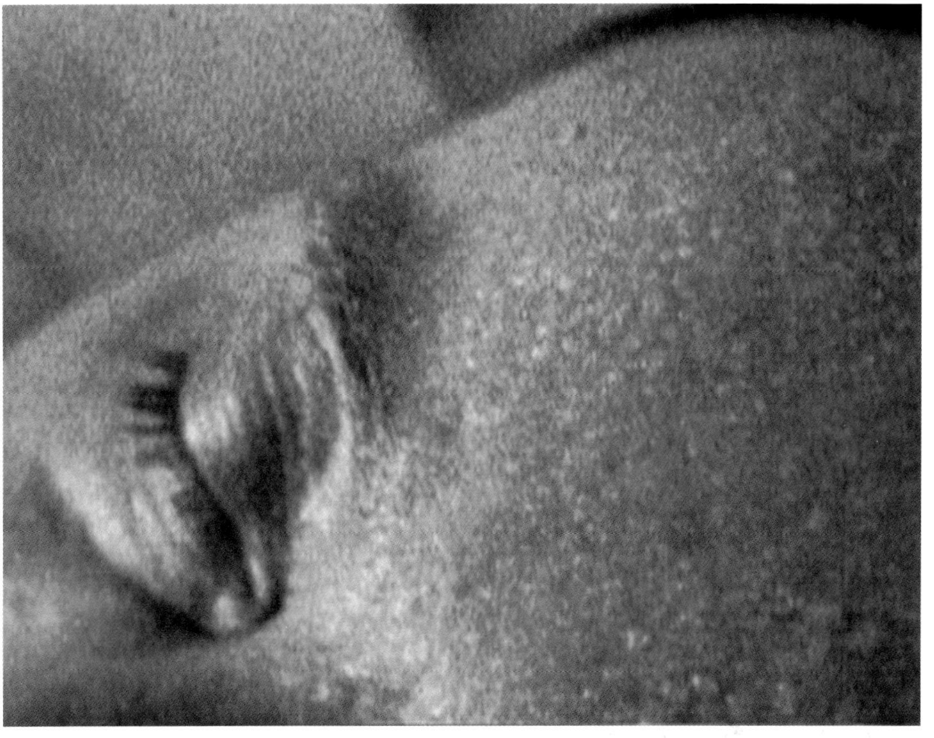

51 Douglas Gordon, *Film Noir (Perspire)*, 1995, video installation.

50 Douglas Gordon, *Film Noir (Fear)*, 1995, video installation.

pulsing of time and the recollections of the elderly man: 'They didn't want to hear . . . Four o'clock. Just a minute past four . . . all around were these people – figures . . . They were not walking, they were not walking, very slowly moving, slowly moving . . . shrouded figures . . . they were not looking . . . shuffling, shuffling along . . .'[56] The memories refer to Belsen concentration camp at the time of the liberation by the British Army and belong to a young 'sea boy', the youngest of his group, who was an unprepared witness of the Holocaust. Muted for years because nobody wanted to listen, allowed no space for testimony or confession, the memories re-emerge as obsessively frightening and vividly present, as an altered blend of what was seen and experienced.

Illingworth portrays the elderly man in the quietness of his daily routine, as he showers, prepares his meal, and repairs watches and

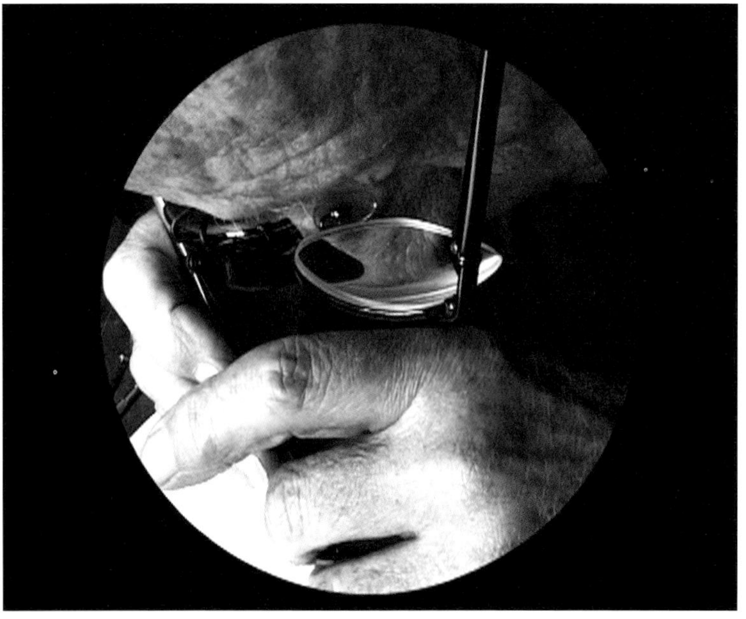

52 Shona Illingworth, *The Watch Man*, 2007, video and sound installation, digital video still.

clocks (illus. 52). Narratively distorted, time tangibly lingers, unavoidably present. Projected through a round screen that duplicates the lens through which the man repairs the mechanisms of time, the video unfolds. It breaks and recaptures the mundane flow of daily tasks through shifting colour shots of fluttering tree branches that interrupt the black and white streaming of the camera. Rather than picturesque, the phantom landscape of a wood is spectral and disturbing. It suggests the compound recollection of a place that merges different memories to produce a bearable story of events whose images the mind has blurred to protect itself. The close-ups of the elderly man's skin, of his movements, and of the things around him (tools, a mug of tea, a knife, a piece of soap and so on) are painfully ethereal as the apparent realism of the film fades in the shadowy contour of actual reality. The artist traces the ebb of disjointed memories that haunts the elderly man by focusing, almost over-focusing, on the continuum of imagery of the real. The enveloping and pulsating soundtrack that engulfs the viewer in auditory sensations vibrantly resonates, intensifying the emotive immersion of the video. Time, as the measured dimension of clocks that governs narrative linearity, acts as a superimposed frame in the work (illus. 53). Beyond the precise, meticulous order of daily gestures, the achronic temporality of memory is visually affected and affective.

Like a jigsaw without solution, Gordon's and Illingworth's artworks are essential in their almost reticent evocation of a latent, harrowing story that is always presupposed to be present in the films themselves. The spectator is made aware of the structures that distort and underpin the implicit narrative, without ever knowing its full content. In the case of Illingworth the spectre of the past returns in the 'atmospheric' force of everyday things, to use Walter Benjamin's phrase, and the image is inscribed with temporality, with the latency of what is delayed and obsessively recurrent.[57] The visual narration of the self collapses in discontinuous shots that bear the traces of different episodes in a palimpsest that rewrites itself as a déjà vécu. Gordon, by comparison, isolates and fragments his historical documentation, unsettling the

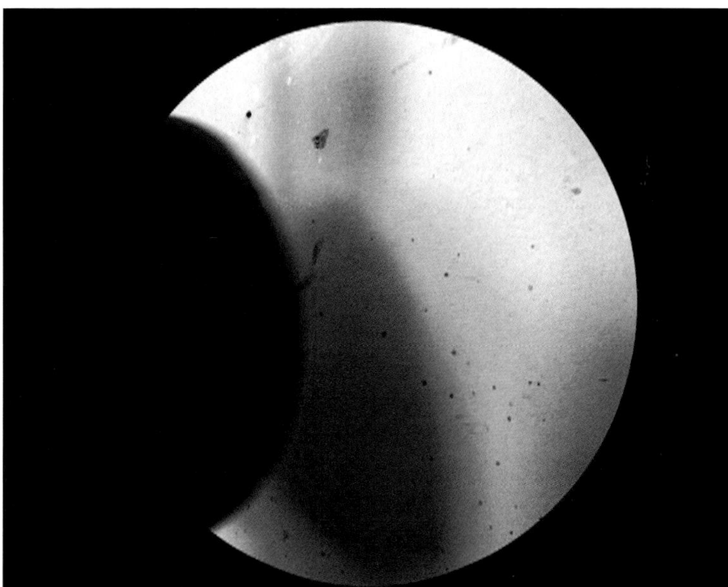

53 Shona Illingworth, *The Watch Man*, 2007, video and sound installation, digital video still.

position of the viewer. He challenges the assertiveness of stories by foregrounding the narrative context that trauma disrupts, and from which it emerges as a dissonant, disturbing slippage in the fabric of knowledge. Both artists thus exploit the sensory potency of imagery to affect and contend with the unspeakability of trauma and the contested narratives of horror. They confront the silence of untold stories, the muted despair of physical and mental pain making us look and hear, and most of all asking us to feel by disrupting the safe boundaries of narrative and hence of knowledge.

Narratives of Guilt and Shame

When we ask if horror can be narrated we irrevocably address notions of memory and the processes of remembering and forgetting. These notions are especially relevant when we account for collective stories of trauma. Paintings such as Théodore Géricault's *The Raft of the Medusa* (1818–19), based on the survivors' story of the shipwreck of the eponymous frigate, and Pablo Picasso's *Guernica* (1937), based on written accounts of the bombing of the Basque town during the Spanish Civil War, shocked contemporary audiences. They suggest that if it is not possible to tell horror, it is possible to implicate the viewer emotionally. Géricault's artwork, the epitome of narrative painting, captures the imagination of the viewer through a figurative world that tells of sea and adventure, of desire and terror, of life and death (illus. 54). Far from being 'naturalistic', the image is a product of the painter's imagination condensing a range of features, some real and some fictional, either derived directly from the survivors' accounts (which in themselves draw upon the tropes of travel writing and memoir) or from other stories and images. Uncertainty, delirium and expectation mingle in the tension that vibrates through the canvas.[58] *Guernica* is also an affective vision of horror: we are not presented with an infernal image of a bombing or collapsing buildings. Instead, the artist achieves an excruciating disintegration of visual forms, producing emotionally devastating effects. By stretching the medium of painting towards new possibilities, and

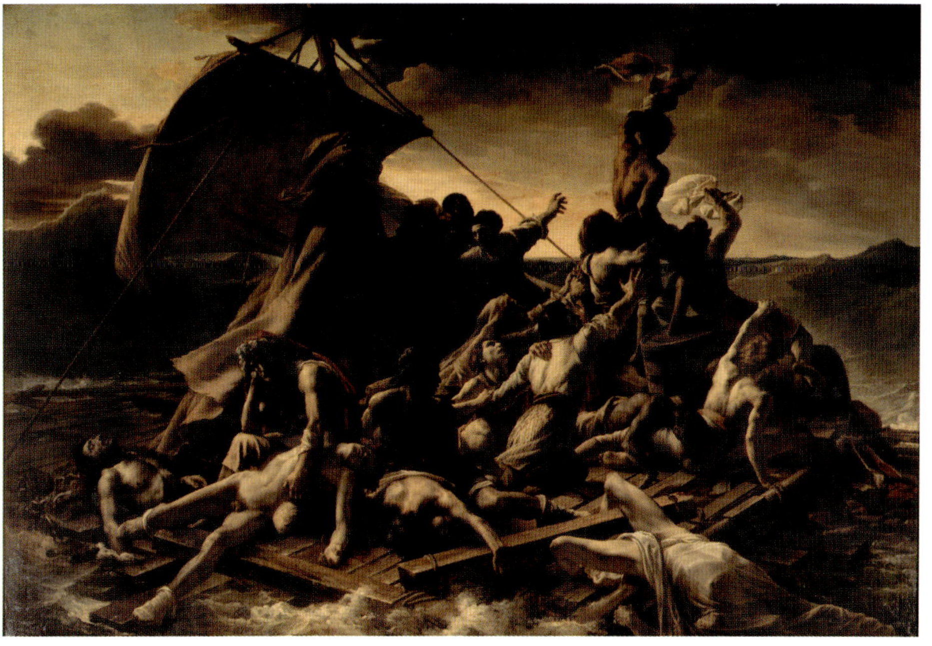

54 Théodore Géricault, *The Raft of the Medusa*, 1818–19, oil on canvas.

opening up a frisson from within, these artworks initiate a formal attempt to articulate horror visually that is still relevant. Indeed, our contemporary focus is on the cultural construction of collective memories of trauma, and the emotional charge of guilt and shame, which questions the very role of narratives and, in particular, of the visual. Through the work of artists as diverse as Anselm Kiefer, William Kentridge and Alfredo Jaar, we focus on the narrative contexts that, respectively, validate the legacy of the Holocaust in post-war Germany, the affective complexity that informs the South African Truth and Reconciliation Commission, and the Western perception of massacres, in countries such as Rwanda, as instances of current, contested sites of horror, pointing to the affective dynamics that circulate across these narratives.

In contemporary European and American culture the Third Reich's extermination of millions of Jews epitomizes trauma. Although other genocides have occurred from the 1940s to the present, none has been endowed with equal universality of horror. Because of this cultural significance, the narrative formulations and the emotional legacy of the Holocaust are conspicuously, almost paradoxically, at stake. In her reading of the 1961 Eichmann trial, Shoshana Felman draws attention to the function that the trial played in today's understanding of the Holocaust. The trial drew attention to the Jewish victims of the concentration camps and made them central to the legal prosecution that unravelled a collective narrative out of the survivors' individual testimonies of horror. Seen in relation to the Nuremberg trials of 1945–6 and to their paradigmatic role in establishing a precedent for the prosecution of crimes against humanity, the Eichmann trial was pivotal in establishing a link between trauma and law, shifting the emphasis from the private and individual to public and collective narratives. According to Felman, 'Prior to the Eichmann trial, what we call the Holocaust did not exist as a collective story. It did not exist as a semantically authoritative story.'[59] In entering the realm of the semantic, the Holocaust also entered the realm of potential representation and narrative, of space and duration.

Beyond the critical and historical debates over the formalization of the concept of the Holocaust and its memorialization, the cultural processes in which it is embedded are framed within the constitution of affective narratives that visually or otherwise are confronted with the emotional charge of the events. Directly bearing the conflicting traces of persecution and trauma, of the erasure of memory and the responsibility to remember, German culture has had to contend with the difficult questions posed by the international authorization of the Holocaust as a horrific event. Various artists, including Joseph Beuys, Gerhard Richter, Georg Baselitz and Hans Haacke, have dealt with the Nazi legacy in post-war Germany. Among them, Anselm Kiefer is especially interesting in relation to the appropriation and subversion of the possibilities of narrative highlighted by Felman, particularly in terms of the issues of guilt and responsibility that are central to Germany's affective response to the Holocaust.

Kiefer's large canvases present the viewer with a vision of nature that is disturbed by history, with an apparent emptiness that is literally layered with traces and material. The painting is a ruin, a sort of 'botanical and geological horror'.[60] By negating the landscape's visual expansion, everything coagulates in 'the density of texture and montage of disparate elements that the painter shapes and carves like a sculptor, inviting the observer to step inside of it'.[61] The organic sampling of straw, ashes, clay, sand and wood is dry and dead. The metal surfaces layered on the canvases are unwelcoming; they metaphorically hurt and wound. Inspired among others by the poetry of Paul Celan, Kiefer's paintings can be seen as a painstaking act of remembrance: ruins and ruined landscapes are the epitome of post-war Germany, whose present is marred by history. The inclusion in a series of paintings of the edifices designed by Albert Speer and Wilhelm Kreis (the architects of the regime) is telling of Kiefer's effort to contend with the legacy of the Third Reich. Lisa Saltzman reads this evocation of Nazi architectural structures as 'psychic places of repressed memory' from which the trauma of history is shadowed.[62] For Saltzman, 'The trauma of the historical catastrophe that was Nazism is configured, walled off and walled in, by the very concretized structures of Nazism itself'.[63] The artist himself comments, 'I completely transform architecture. The architecture I use in my paintings is already in pieces, completely destroyed'.[64] Kiefer's burning and charring of the material of his works and the construction of ruinous structures of debris infuse the practices of layering and sedimentation with aesthetic and symbolic connotations that disrupt standard ideas of the work of art as both object and image. He revisits the contemporary symbolism of the debris, of the adulterate trace and the ruin, exploiting their characteristics of space and duration, substantiality and fragmentation to interrogate the narratives that construct post-war German identity vis-à-vis the Nazi legacy and the related questions of responsibility, apathy and collaboration. As Saltzman observes, 'Kiefer's post-modern project moves towards the necessarily compromised recovery of a repressed history, be it repressed history of modernity, of modern Germany (Hitler, the Holocaust, barbarism, totalitarism), or the repressed history of modern painting'.[65]

This dialectics of memory and forgetting, covering and uncovering, signifying and silencing is symptomatic of broader formulations of historical trauma through cultural narrative, exposing contradiction, uncertainty and ambivalence, often tainted with guilt, that troubles the historical legacy of traumatic events. The South Africa Truth and Reconciliation Commission Public Hearings and Report is indicative of an attempt to acknowledge all parties, both perpetrators and victims of discrimination and violence during Apartheid, in order to testify to both the actions and the suffering that they caused. The accountability of a state of persecution and fear to the violence perpetrated and the complicity to the injustice of the regime of Apartheid are framed within the latency of remembering and the repression of trauma. In other words, they inhere in the tension between articulation and silence and the affective exposures of guilt and shame. As suggested, the psychological and psychoanalytical understanding of guilt and shame depends on concerns for one's actions versus those for one's identity. Shame in particular is understood in terms of an exposure of one's worthlessness and inadequacy to an internal or external gaze. If guilt is about moral responsibility, shame is culturally expressed in terms of visibility, one that is situated where the shaming gaze and the shamed subject meet, despite how transitory or unsettling such a meeting might be.[66]

The South African artist William Kentridge presents us with a different kind of erasure and internal temporality of the image. He testifies to shame's visibility by creating images that bear the signs of their own past and of the processes of making, in an attempt to explore the complexity of the latency of memories and query the affective dynamics of shame. Kentridge revisits the tradition of silhouettes and moving shadows, as well as merging drawing and animation, in order to deal with South Africa's recent history and, more generally, with the colonial legacy of the country. Central to his work is the permanence and disappearance of traces in the making and remaking of images. Kentridge uses only a few charcoal drawings whose features are reworked and erased in the time-based construction of the final animation. Smudges, smears and shadows all highlight the traces of what remains partly erased and partly visible. *History of the Main Complaint* (1996) uses the story of a car accident, coma and recovery as metaphors of a process of amnesia and recollection in which both the individual and history are implicated (illus. 55).[67] The film bears scar-like signs of its making, as Kentridge allows for that which was erased to interfere. He layers drawing on drawing, moment on moment, event on event. The resulting images are murky and stained. Like visual memories they are a composite, a condensation of other images, of what has been retained and what has been erased (illus. 56). The work unsettles memory and representation as coherent modes of narration. Kentridge's elusive visual palimpsest points to the process of telling as being one of working through, editing out, reconfiguring single instances that are haunted by internal contradictions, confusions, overlaps, into an acceptable narrative. It is ultimately unresolved whether what is lost in the process is irredeemably significant, and whether what remains is ostensibly reliable. Thus, Kentridge complicates the affective dynamics of shame, since exposure and concealment are equally equivocal and illusionary. The story is partial to its telling, and to the other narratives that coexist within and without it.

By undermining the relation between the visible and its opposite, whether in terms of consciousness, memory or cultural acceptability, the figuration, condensation and displacement that are at work 'disturb',

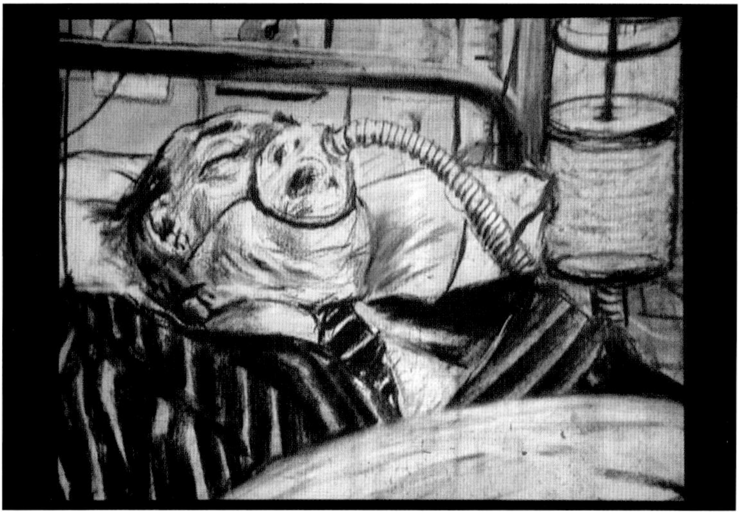

55 William Kentridge, still from *History of the Main Complaint*, 1996, 35mm film transferred to video and laser disc, 5 minutes 50 seconds.

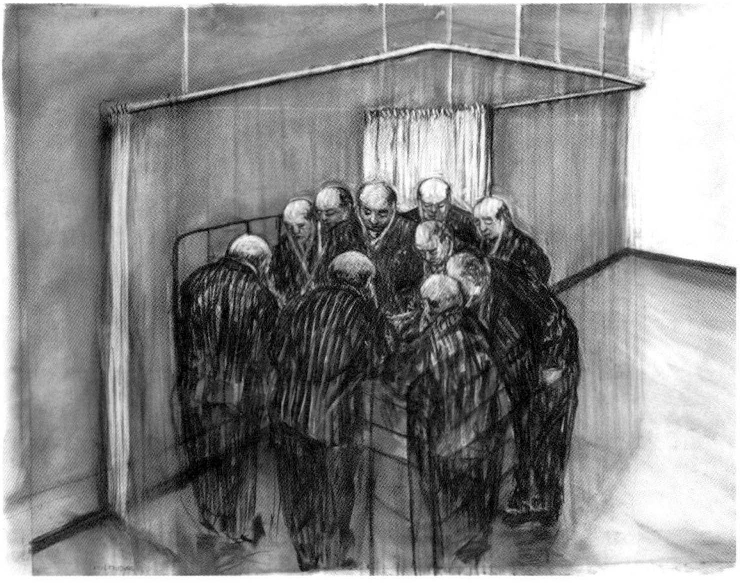

56 William Kentridge, drawing from *History of the Main Complaint*, 1996, charcoal and pastel on paper.

according to the influential French philosopher Jacques Rancière, 'the ordinary regime of connections employed in an official system of information'.[68] This raises questions on the documentary value and the emotional connotations of images as part of the contemporary currency of visual consumption. What do images tell us of horror? What do they tell us of the feelings of guilt and shame that horror engenders? The insidious interaction of the gaze that underpins shame is central to the work of the Chilean artist Alfredo Jaar, who investigates the politics of the documentary image and of the obsessive consumption of the visual. Central to Jaar's artistic practice is the reworking of media's presentation of atrocities. He reframes the relation between the image, the photo-journalist and the spectator, unsettling the narrative perspective that ideologically frames the manipulation and editing of images, thus calling into question the authenticity of the photographic image as a document and 'visual testimony'. Jaar focuses on the witness of atrocities rather than the victims, on the observer rather than the observed, a position that is also shared by the photographer as well as the distance audience. Thus, his work makes palpable the eye that defines the image and the emotional relation that the gaze establishes.

In works such as *Real Pictures* (1995) and *The Eyes of Gutete Emerita* (1996), rather than directly questioning the numbing effect of shocking pictures, which has been part of the critique of contemporary visual consumption, Jaar enters the process of their making to address the affective position of the viewer. *Real Pictures* shows 100 archival photo storage boxes, each describing Caritas, a woman who survived the Rwanda massacre in 1994. Ironically, there is no picture. The text is not substantiated by the image and vice versa (illus. 57). The work asks us to contextualize the story, to query the practices of authentication and the modalities through which we tell horror. We are asked to look beyond the words, to envisage what is not told as well as to critically question the emotional reactions with which we invest text and images alike. In *The Eyes of Gutete Emerita*, a gaze encounters the viewer's gaze, the picture being of a woman's eyes. In the installation, the eyes multiply. They are the image endlessly reproduced (illus. 58). As the accompanying text explains, Gutete Emerita witnessed the massacre of her family. Jaar's eye does not focus on what Gutete Emerita saw, but rather on the eyes of the witness and we are made to look at those eyes and, indirectly, through them, but at what? The politics of the Rwandan massacre involves the Western indifference to the events, and hence, as gaze meets gaze, the work establishes reciprocity between the image and the viewer. Who is witnessing what? Who is indifferent to what? Who is shamed and who ashamed? Who speaks and who remains silent? What is spoken and what unspoken? What is exposed and what concealed? Jaar displaces the position of the spectator within the internal frame of the image and, as the art critic Olivier Chow argues, catches and traps her within the woven structure of the 'document'.[69] Jaar invites us to be present in the sufferance of others by acknowledging the processes of trauma through images that question the possibilities of accounting for horror and the stories that make it. The eyes do not substitute the spectacle of horror that they witnessed; rather they remind us that an image belongs to a context of other images and texts. As Rancière writes, 'An image never stands alone. It belongs to a system of visibility that

58 Alfredo Jaar, *The Eyes of Gutete Emerita*, 1996, mixed media installation.

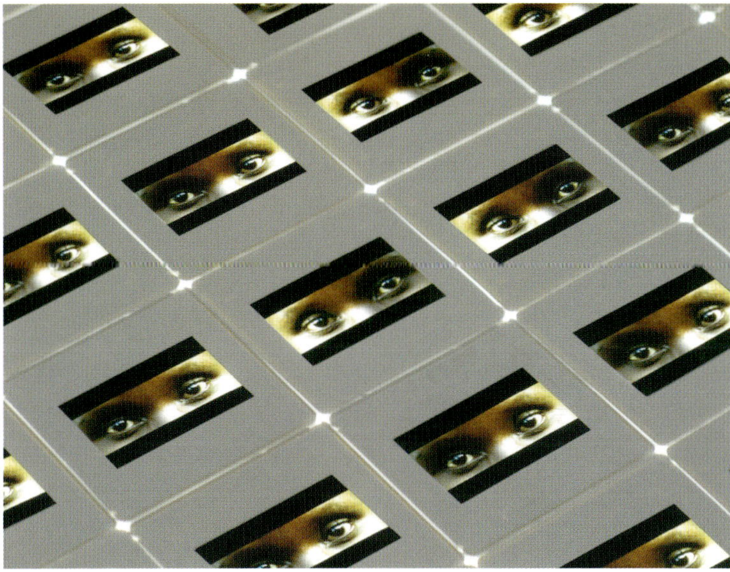

governs the status of bodies represented and the kind of attention they merit.'[70] Jaar repeatedly invites us to consider the rhetoric that underlies visual or verbal texts as a means of generating and directing affective responses. Narratives of fear are part of this ideological production that also affects the cultural articulation of the disturbance of horror. If horror resists narrative, it does so through the slippages, displacement and jarring of the normative systems of telling.

57 Alfredo Jaar, *Real Pictures*, 1995, mixed media installation.

FOUR

SPACES

Antony Gormley's suspended cast figures are an intimation of the anamorphic relation of body and space that has consistently informed the artist's work. Gormley embraces the corporeality of the physical (he notoriously uses casts of his own body) and the existential instability of dwelling. He intentionally sabotages the apparent transparency of this body-space relation in installations such as *Blind Light* (2007), which, as the title suggests, takes the viewer into a bright, clean and structurally symmetric space that is, at the same time, blinding and disorientating. Rather than entering the traditional 'spaces' of terror – areas that are dark, meandering, narrowly oppressive or disproportionately enormous – Gormley uses the pure forms of modernism to explore the instability of being-in-space and, as he claims, of 'losing the bonds of certainty about where or who we are'.[1] In so doing Gormley undermines the security of location and movement, questioning straightforward distinctions between interior and exterior, between space and place, between spatial and social relations. As a result, *Blind Light* engenders 'a profound disorientation, an unnerving feeling of almost losing *yourself*, of not being able to map out the contours of your own body, or being precisely aware where your body ends and someone else's suddenly begins'.[2] The body both defines and is defined by the spatial conditions of the installation, in the haptic ambiguity of finding one's own bearing.

Blind Light implicitly gestures towards a notion of vertigo that is deeply implicated in contemporary feelings of disorientation and dislocation that pervade the perception of space. Natural and social environments are imbued with insecurity and uncertainty. Inhabiting space, as inherent to being, is troublesome. The 'unnerving feeling' of losing oneself denotes an ambiguity that causes the subject to emotionally and conceptually falter, whether in her consideration of natural environments, urban landscapes or dwelling. Focusing on disorientation and dislocation as the valences of the affective relation to space and place that dominate our time, the following chapter considers the visual exploration of contemporary spatial vertigo through the concept of the Sublime and the traditional spatial phobias of agoraphobia and claustrophobia.

Scary Spaces

We are in space. The existential condition of 'being' is intrinsically situated and conditioned by being in space as well as in history, the fate of falling into a here and now that Heidegger terms *Dasein*. Through the senses the body navigates and maps space, continuously reorientating the subject within spatial parameters that, as Merleau-Ponty demonstrates, are centred on the body and on its sensory-affective capabilities of inhabiting a spatial environment. Emotions colour this essential condition of being and interfere with even the most basic ways in which, physically as well as psychologically, we position ourselves in space, such as body posture and balance. This is addressed for instance in neuro-psychological research that studies the interaction between emotion, movement and balance control. Experiments carried out to assess the relation between fear of falling and postural control intimates that fear and anxiety influence human posture whenever we are exposed to height, even if no real danger is involved. Characteristic postural strategies are in fact adopted when changes in level of fear are experienced independently from visual and other sensorial cues.[3] As it were, the body viscerally oscillates and dreads. In coalescing the disorientating sensation of being and moving in space, vertigo intimates a spatial malaise that characterizes modernity and beyond in its cultural metamorphoses. Gormley's work comes again to mind with the series of installations *Breathing Room* (2005–10). Particularly significant is *Breathing Room III* (2010), a structure of fifteen luminescent frames that replicates the volume of the gallery and creates a sculptural space in which to walk. Like the skeleton of a building – a space that, as in the case of *Blind Light*, is eminently contemporary and reminiscent of digital architectural models in its 'immaterial' three-dimensionality – the perfect geometry of *Breathing Room III* enhances a visual matrix of physical orientation (illus. 59). And yet the unexpected illumination of the frames upsets the experience. The visitor is jolted. The change is comparable to a vertiginous shivering that makes the body falter and feel disorientated, metaphorically throwing it out of balance.

Compressed by information technologies and acceleration, space is, in the words of Jean-Luc Nancy, 'imploding'.[4] The 'cognitive maps' of the body are inadequate, according to the American literary critic and political theorist Fredric Jameson, to chart the hyperspace of postmodernity and the built environments of our age. If neuroscience helps us to understand the psycho-physiological dynamics and conditioning of positioning, orientating and moving in space, the cultural posturing and postures of dwelling have been critically reconfigured within the compass of theory and the affective stance that postulates 'disorientation' as the spatial angst of our time.[5] Articulated within the distinction of space and place, this state of disorientation produces a gap between the sensorial perception of space and the social situation of late modernity, which manifests in a spatial conundrum. This is, for instance, evoked in the manipulation of road maps and street plans that characterizes the work of the Argentinian artist Guillermo Kuitca. In Kuitca's map paintings, the commonplace means of navigation are transformed through disorientating duplication. In one example, the painting shows a section of road map in which the names of all the towns are the same; in another painting the names of the cities in one country are substituted by those of cities in other nations; in another, names of rivers are replaced with personal names (illus. 60). The taxonomical method of cartography is substituted with an equally rigorous process of displacement and adulteration. The map becomes useless, orientation is

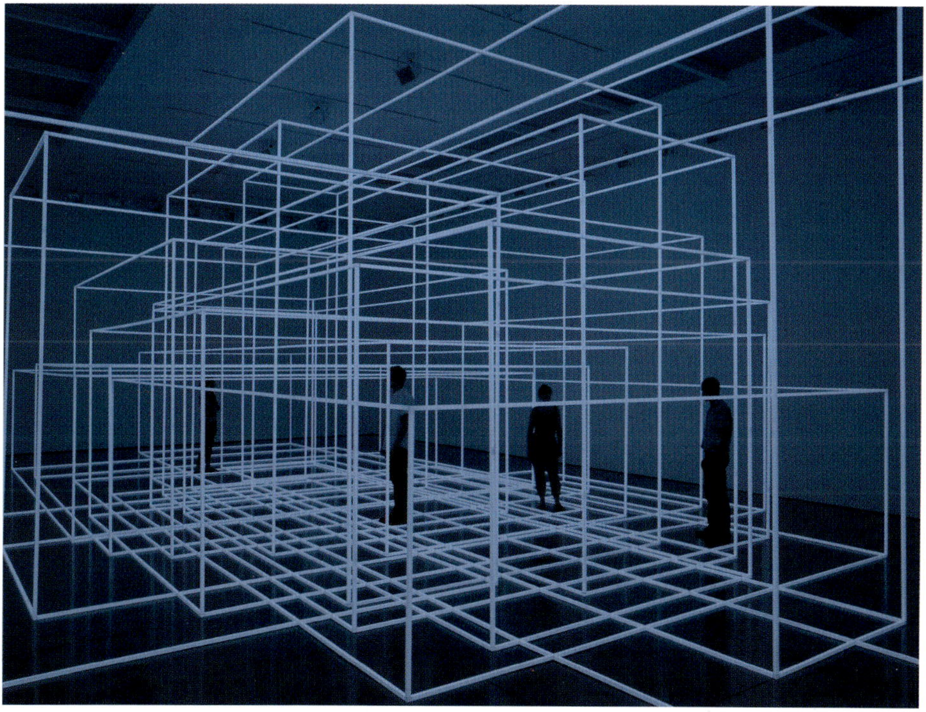

59 Antony Gormley, *Breathing Room III*, 2010, aluminium tube, phosphor H15 and plastic spigots.

deflected in a pointless and alienating search in which all places become one. In Kuitca's maps one sees reflected the contemporary nomadic experience of dwelling (some of his paintings are depicted on mattresses) and its inherent feelings of disorientation as an existential state of being-in-movement.[6] In this faltering environment, disorientation, dislocation and displacement are the theoretical starting points from which to interrogate contemporary phobic experiences of space.

The disproportion between the human body and the vastness of space that traditionally evoked a sense of the gigantic – whether in nature or in human-made edifices – and which the statesman and philosopher Edmund Burke (1729–1797) famously discussed in his concept of the Sublime, is reconfigured with modernity along the vectors of economics and technological advancement. Indeed, as the literary critic Susan Stewart argues: 'within the rise of industrial capitalism the gigantic

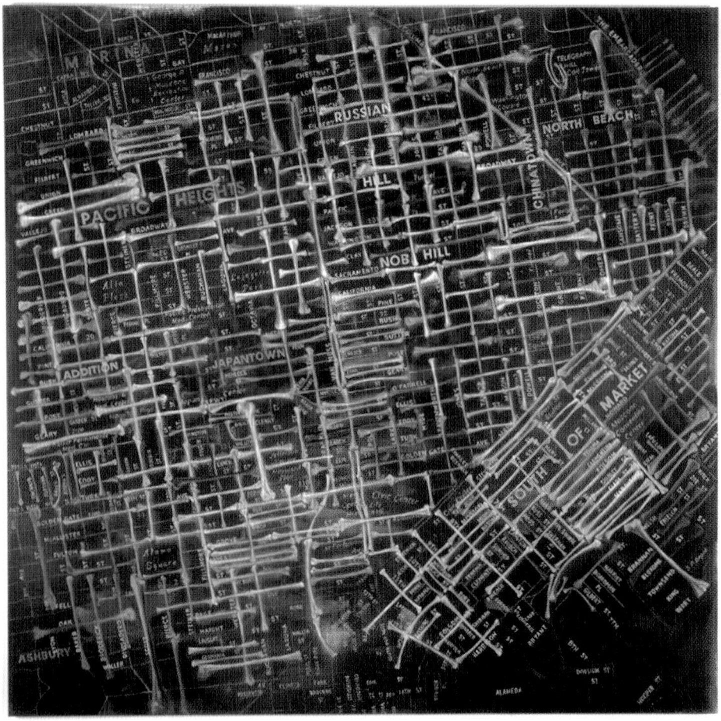

60 Guillermo Kuitca, *Untitled (San Francisco)*, 1995, oil and acrylic on canvas.

becomes located within the abstraction of exchange economy. The gigantic is moved from a pre-social world of the natural to a social world of material production.'[7] Hence, the threat of climate change stands as a new, contemporary fear, with no corresponding model in terms of scale and alleged consequences. The menace posed to particular living habitats, in the melting of the polar ice or the desertification of vast inhabited areas, is hardly confined locally, and predictions suggest devastating effects across the globe. If its objects evoke uncanny feelings, its commensurability is 'gigantic'. It is boundless in its terrifying enormity, and is therefore Sublime. The vastness of ecological disaster designates a space at the interface of systems of knowledge and policies of science, technology and economics, probing questions of legitimacy, salience and assessment at both national and transnational levels.[8]

The eighteenth-century awe for what is spatially incommensurable translates into an assessment, not of the relation between the body and the grandiose vastness of the environment, but rather of the commensurability of the means of capital production and communication. Here, space begins to 'implode', reconfiguring the gigantic into the global, a conflation of distances and of temporal instantaneity. From the last decades of the twentieth century to the present, the settings for this shift are eminently toxic. The residual imagery of the gigantic is an evocation of post-industrial desolation, of ecological contamination and of a past legacy of horror, calling to mind Robert Smithson's 1970s 'destructive' landscapes and his eerie futuristic scenarios, or Mike Nelson's apocalyptic installations of ominous devastation. Similarly, Edward Burtynsky's pictures of eroded landscapes from oil spillage expose toxic environments of economic and ecological contamination, while Paul Chan's photographs of natural devastation underscore human and environmental desolation as new forms of economic exploitation, for which disasters constitute a new market.

Whether considered in terms of nature or in terms of history, the contemporary notion of the Sublime invokes loss, silence and absence in ways that are comparable to the deconstruction of the object in unhomely configurations, and to the disruptive slippages registered in the narratives of fear. Formal abstraction has been interpreted in relation to the Sublime, particularly in the French philosopher Jean-François Lyotard's discussion of Barnett Newman's abstract painting through his rereading of Immanuel Kant's dissertations. However, the re-emergence of the concept of the Sublime is currently located within visual strategies of emptiness, in an imagery that exists beyond the gaze, beyond the physicality of the body, and that is therefore able to evoke the loss of a relation that presupposes a mode of being eminently dis-placed: an imagery of a ruinous and imploded place. Painting and photography are the visual indices of reality that are invoked to attest to emptiness.

The tension between space and place that, as suggested, is inherent to contemporary disorientation, is critically situated in the hyperspace of late modernity and, in Marc Augé's definition, in the 'non-places' of today's urbanization.[9] Their homogeneity manifests the 'imploding' of spatial and temporal coordination and the reframing of the gigantic within the dimension of the global, as a form of vast, determined uniformity. Arguably nothing more so than the city epitomizes our contemporary existential experience of disorientation. Since modernity, the city has been the site of nervous anxiety. Originally diagnosed as *vertigo hysterique*, *schwindel Angst* (dizziness) or *Platzschwindel*, agoraphobia (the fear of open or public spaces) referred to a specifically urban aetiology. This phobic condition had symptoms that included trembling, panic attacks and the inability to walk when the sufferer – mainly middle-class professional males – was faced with the vast boulevards and squares or the large bustling theatres of modern metropolises.[10] Indeed, because the cultural resonance of the spatial phobias produced 'by the new configurations of urban space' was, according to Anthony Vidler, 'irresistible to critics and sociologists alike', metropolises became critically contested places of anxiety.[11] Contemporary to the aetiology of agoraphobia is that of claustrophobia, first described in the 1870s as a 'morbid fear of enclosed spaces'.[12] Instead of the open boulevards and public places of the modern metropolis, the safe enclosure of the bourgeois household was the reversed referent for a phobic apprehension that pertained to the social as well as architectonic connotations of place.

If fear and anxiety have 'deformed' the aesthetic practices of modernism, redefining the spectrum of places of urban living, contemporary capsular architecture and design, which incorporate visual and structural systems of protection to exclude, isolate and resist, reposition agoraphobia within surveillance technologies as a paranoid apprehension of space at the interface of policies of monitoring and control.[13] At the opposite end of the spectrum of a phobic culture of space, claustrophobia intimates other forms of dislocation, related both to urbanization and migration, and partly related to the contemporary crisis of the home as a space of belonging and safety. The nomadic unrest of late modernity – propelled by economic globalization – is both a site of expansive dynamic change and a reconfiguration of social relations. This nomadism feeds into deeply felt anxieties that impart subjectivity and the cultural construction of the 'domestic' space of the nation state and of the home. Artists and designers have critically entered the debate by mapping contemporary places of fear through the same tools that visually denote them. The resulting videos and installations expose the affective dynamics that characterizes urban and domestic space, revealing the emotional anxieties of dwelling.

Sublime Spaces

Imagine the single isolated detail of a winter shrub, a ravished hut among wintry branches covered in snow, the morning light disclosing a mountain profile in the fog, the desolate infinity and emptiness of a seascape from which emerges a diminutive figure (illus. 61). This is 'Romantic' territory, filled with awe and the Sublime. For the first time in Western painting, artists questioned the appearance of place without an observer, asking if a place can exist beyond an observing gaze. Caspar David Friedrich (1774–1840) positions the subject, and with him the viewer, at the point of dissolution of the relation between perception and interpretation. Who sees and what is represented coexist in an unstable relation. As the art historian Joseph Leo Koerner observes, Friedrich is the first painter to represent emptiness.[14]

Situated within the Sublime tradition, Friedrich's depictions of unfathomable distance and condensed presences that exceed representation evoke Immanuel Kant's concept of the Sublime as a capacity of reason to acknowledge its power over nature, rather than Burke's extreme experience of the magnitude and power of nature observed 'at distance'.[15] Early nineteenth-century views on perception and the mapping of sensation as an affective web of impressions underpin the Kantian enterprise of comprehension. Burke's elating terror is superseded, if not redeemed, in the enunciation of a presence that implies a here and now that is susceptible to the judgement of reason rather than to the manifestations of the imagination. The Sublime for Kant is dictated not by the aesthetics of representation but by a rational confrontation of that which cannot be accounted for, and hence represented.

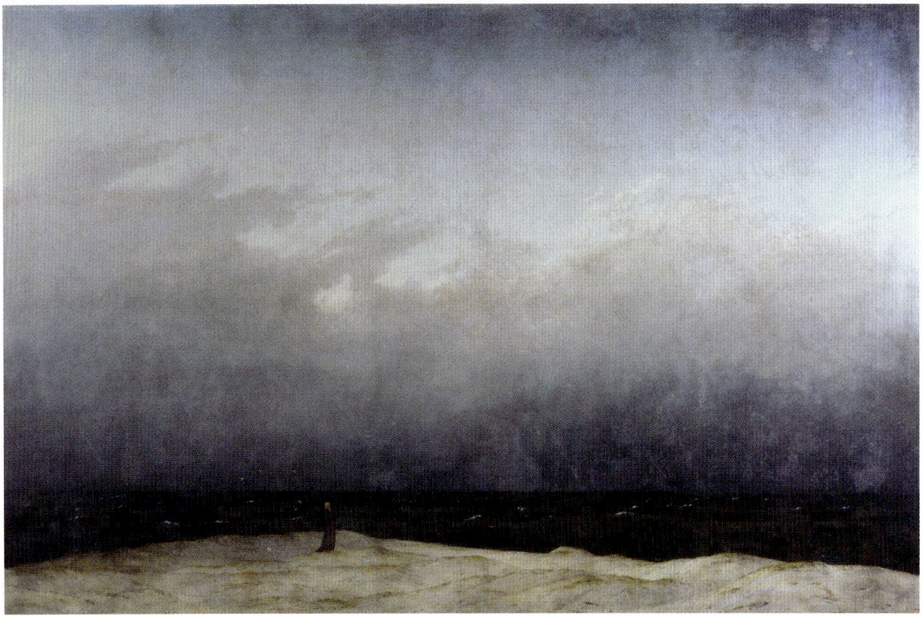

61 Caspar David Friedrich, *Monk by the Sea*, 1809, oil on canvas.

As Lyotard's critique of the concept further demonstrates, the Sublime inheres in the suspension of emptiness, on the traces of an event that remains latent at the boundaries of ethics as much as of aesthetics. Invoked by contemporary criticism, the Sublime has re-emerged as a category of the visual to account for the spectacle of terror, destruction and violence of contentiously disquieting and compelling images. Ideologically and politically charged, the Sublime stands both for the inhumanity that haunts late modernity, and as a site of resistance. It is marked by its own void, by the uncanny presence of an event that resists commonplace utterance.[16] This dual spectrum of the Sublime image is powerfully contested in media presentations of catastrophes, wars and violence that offer to the spectator the removed dismay of terror and horror. Nature and history – the sites of the historical Sublime – return within the context of contemporary environmental fears, natural disasters and devastation, as well as of terrorism and war through controlled strategies of framing, repetition and editing. The rhetorical manipulation of images whose horror lingers on a sublimated pleasure thus yields to the ideological framing of the initial shock within the heterogeneous consumption of images and information.[17]

The same strategies of rhetorical appropriation of the Sublime image can yet be revealing of disquieting silence and emptiness, of the unsettling enduring of the event, as political theorist François Debrix notes, 'a haunting mark, a scarring piece of reality that denotes something that refuses to hide the gaping wound left by the initial terrifying sight'.[18] In the eighteenth century, the historical rupture caused by the French Revolution, with its intense affective charge of horror, terror and exhilaration both substantiated and destabilized the category of the Sublime. The twentieth century's inhumanity has been predicated on the Holocaust as a comparable moment of rupture. The effects of this rupture are immanent and echo beyond the events themselves. Thus the Sublime image does not only contend with the vastness of space, but also with the immanence of history to reveal its haunting presence. Terror as a failure of comprehension is still at the core of contemporary intimations of the Sublime, which confronts us with the limitations of visual and ethical perspectives to assess fully and to rationally contain the affective dynamics of the real. Not unlike the uncanny object that exposes the politics of terror, the Sublime calls into question the ethics of such politics.

In direct pictorial dialogue with Caspar David Friedrich, the German painter Gerhard Richter revisits Romantic landscape painting in both its Sublime and picturesque incarnations. The results reveal the 'mesmerizing lifelessness – the total un-humanity – of the subject'.[19] Nature's response is a deadening silence to the contemporary eye. It is inhuman because it alienates the subject and, vice versa, the subject is empathically distant from it. As the artist comments, talking for himself as much as the viewer, 'What I lack is the spiritual basis which undergirded Romantic painting. We have lost the feeling of God's omnipresence in Nature. For us everything is empty.'[20] Richter depicts this loss of correspondence and the resulting lack and emptiness in the alienation of nature to the gaze that observes and rationally contains it (illus. 62).

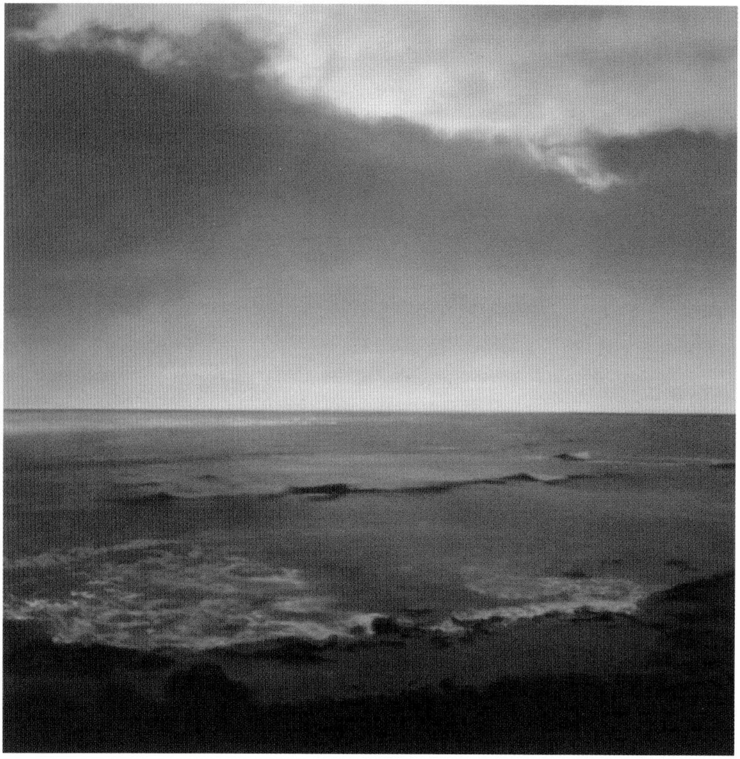

62 Gerhard Richter, *Seestück (Seascape)*, 1998, oil on canvas.

History is no less forgiving. The cycle *October 18, 1977* (1988) comprises fifteen paintings based on photographic images relating to the arrest of members of the Baader-Meinhof terrorist group, and to their presumed suicides in prison. Richter interrogates the documentary authenticity of the camera's record. The resulting paintings are three portraits of Ulrike Meinhof (two of which are of her corpse), whose features dissolve as if fading into the background; depictions of blurred scenes of the arrests and of the interior of the high security cells where the terrorists were found dead (*Hanged* refers to Gudrum Esslin's death), and of the funeral (illus. 63). Richter addresses the 'agony, desperation and helplessness' of the events and of their legacy through a medium that is traditionally associated with the account and celebration of

63 Gerhard Richter, *Hanged (Erhängte)*, from the cycle *October 18, 1977*, 1988, oil on canvas.

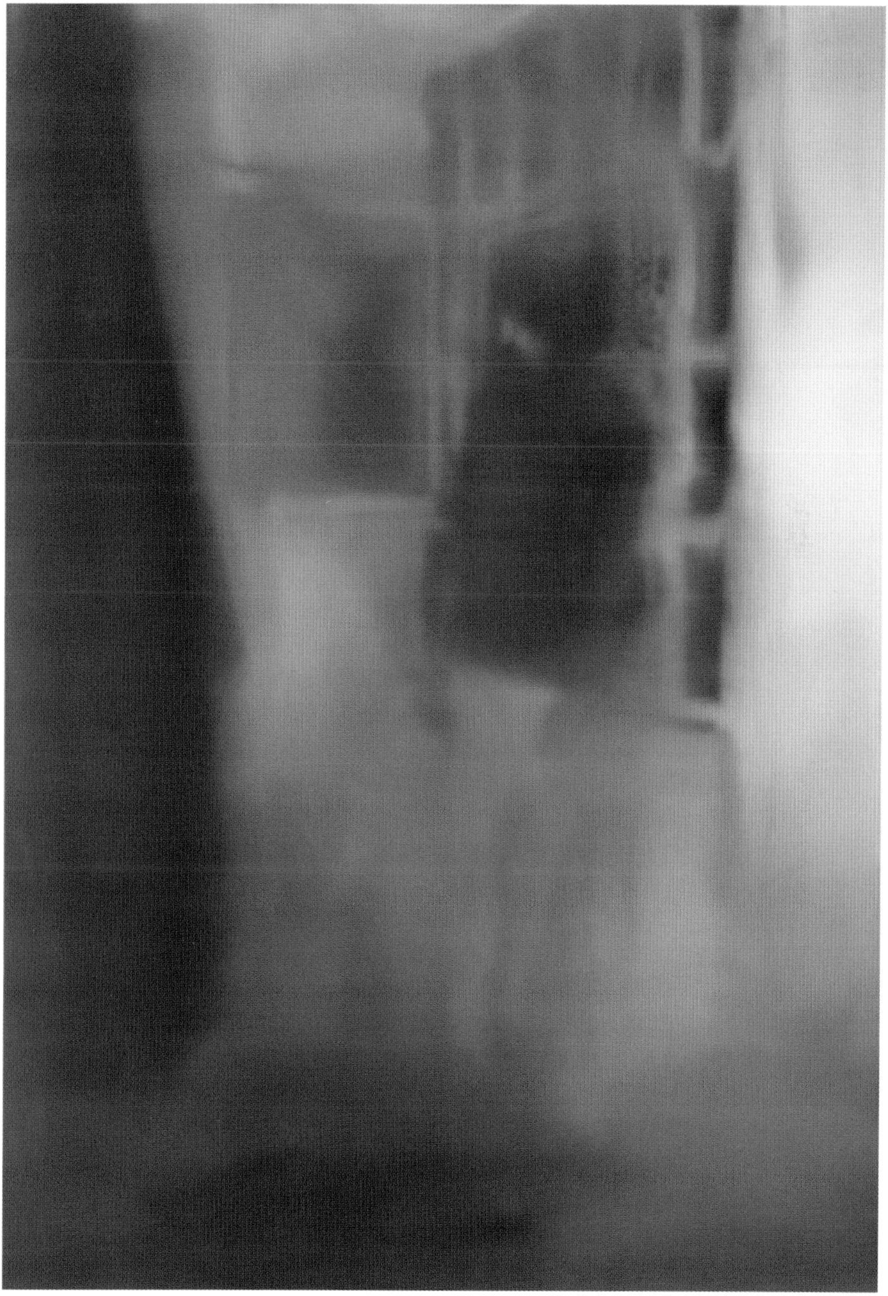

history, finding in painting a 'morally disquieting and profoundly moving artistic expression'.[21] Richter does so by evincing the gaps and silences that exude from official accounts. The paintings are in his words 'an expression of a speechless emotion'.[22] Silence, here, is the only condition of 'representation'. We can interrogate and search for answers but ultimately we are denied understanding.

Indeed, for Slavoj Žižek, comprehension is doomed to failure since the Sublime is unable to surmount the immediacy of the original shock. The image is always inadequate and unable to fill the gap engendered by trauma. Yet this very failure is also conducive to an experience of 'the true dimension of the Thing' – the repressed qualities, what exceeds words, images, monuments and stories.[23] Within this paradox, the notion of the void acts as an expression rather than negation of space, and rephrases the question of representing the un-representable as a quest for the uncanny, haunting sign of reality. Following from Žižek's interpretation of the Sublime, the void stands as a corporeal and impenetrable leftover of the real, whether we locate it in history, nature or in the global, rarefied realm of economics. The work of the American artists James Casebere and Robert Polidori relates an attempt to translate visually the ephemeral quality of emptiness through a medium – photography – that is culturally anchored in the 'real' and in the ideological appropriation of the Sublime. Both artists undermine the documentary quality of photography with images that reposition emptiness as a visual referent of contemporary decay.

At first sight, James Casebere's photographs of buildings and interiors are misleading in their apparent actuality. At a closer look, the contours of the architectural structures alluringly dissolve. The visual planes of the image seem to evaporate or liquefy. Casebere's territory is closer to the uncanny as an unconscious and disturbing return, rather than a faithful record of the real (illus. 64). As a template of his work, Casebere both uses and subverts standard tools of architecture, including model-making and photography, divesting them of realistic details to expose the dense construction of space.[24] In the process, the artist renders essential elements, such as surfaces, light and form intrinsic to the photographic space. The effect is visceral and disconcerting. The

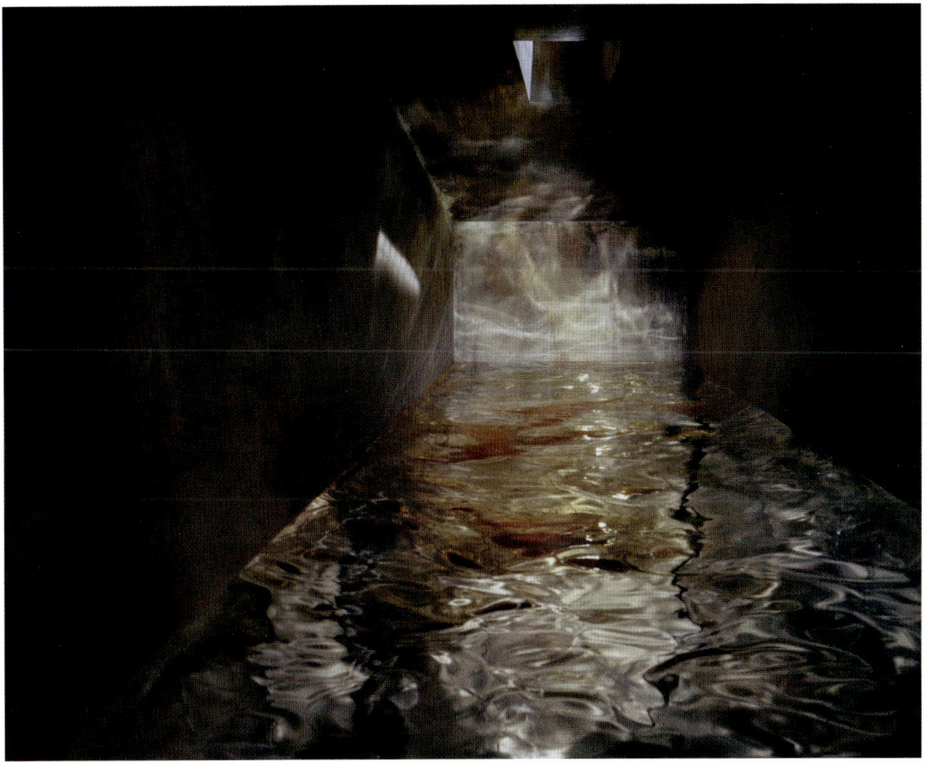

64 James Casebere, *Flooded Cell #2*, 2008, digital chromogenic print, edition of 5 with 2 artist proofs.

images draw the viewer within, producing a sense of entrapment in their enveloping void. Based on memory or faithful reproduction, the models act as duplications of the real, which the camera then further recreates. The places that Casebere chooses as the subjects of his work are often historical sites, charged with traumatic histories, from a slave port in the Caribbean to a slave fortress in West Africa, Adlon Bunker in Berlin, or renowned penitentiaries (illus. 65). His spaces are ambiguous, not easily decipherable. They are places of transit, implying a journey that remains uncertain 'without origin or destination'. They are perpetually nowhere.[25]

Robert Polidori's series of photographs of abandoned buildings in the towns of Pripyat and Chernobyl were taken seventeen years after the meltdown of the nuclear power station. They capture the devastation of the still radioactive area through the fathomable traces of past lives in the deserted schools, apartment blocks, and in the nuclear power station (illus. 66). Polidori evokes the invisible presence of radioactivity and of the related ecological disaster in the harrowing visibility of emptiness. The few human traces still recognizable act as desolate ruins, leftovers loaded with intangible contamination. Today's wilderness is shaped in abandonment and urban decay. The bleakness of the vision betrays a colliding of natural and man-made forces and the production of new forms of invisibility and bareness.

Emptiness and ruin are also the themes that dominate Polidori's series of photographs of the disastrous aftermath of hurricane Katrina,

65 James Casebere, *Samarra*, 2007, digital chromogenic print, edition of 5 with 2 artist proofs.

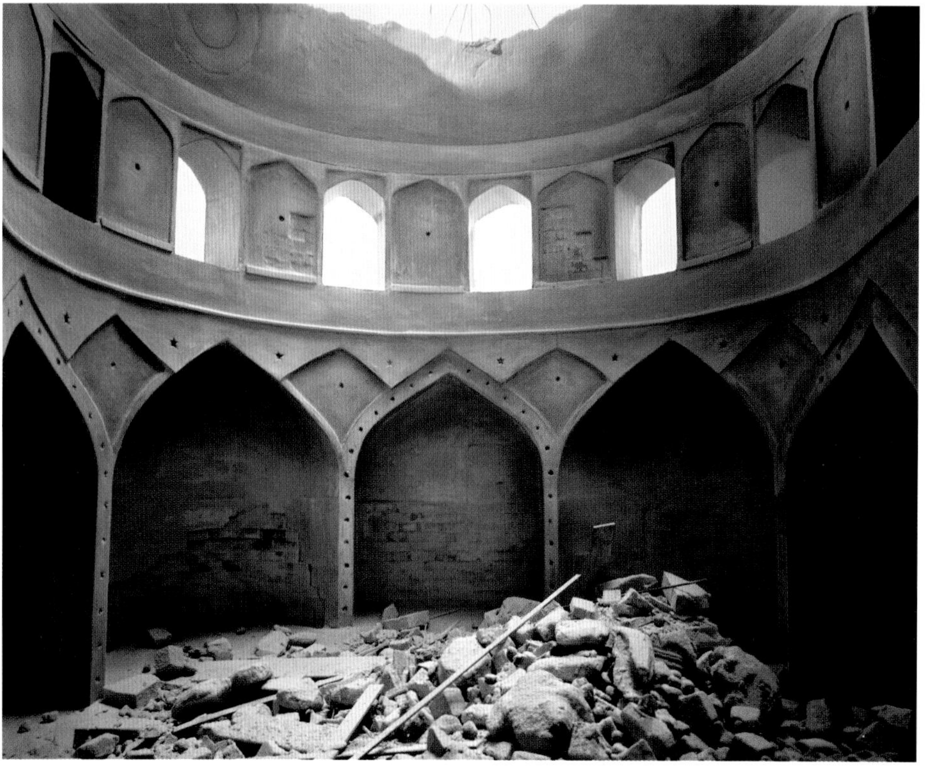

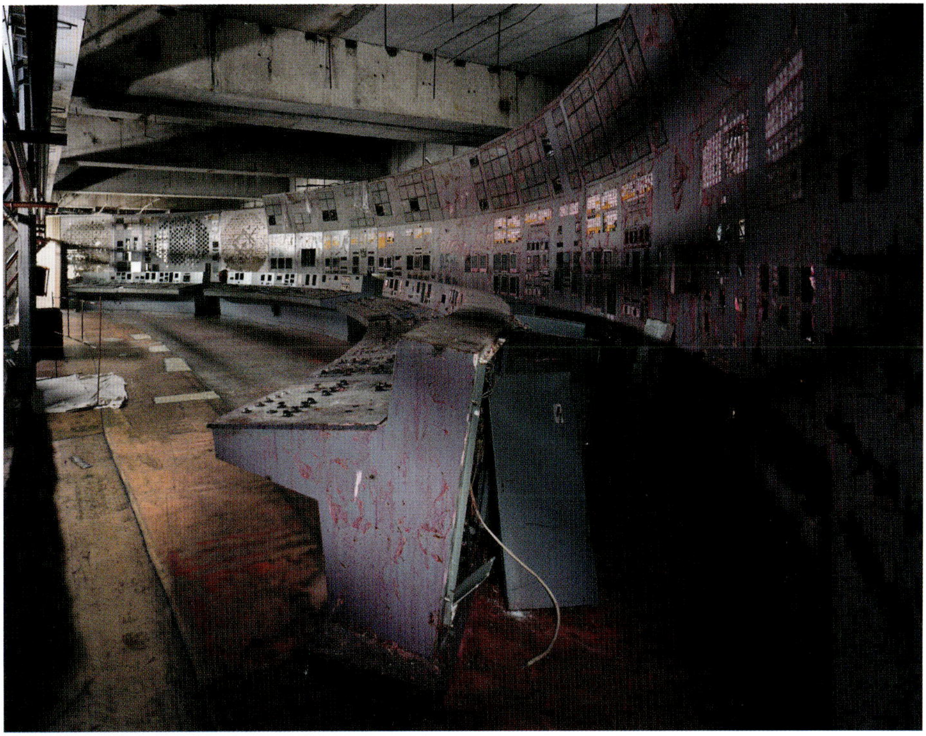

66 Robert Polidori, *Control Room, Reactor 4*, 2001, Fujicolour crystal archive print.

which devastated New Orleans on 29 August 2005. Polidori's camera lingers through long exposure in the interiors of the destroyed houses, whose rooms are pictured amid the precarious unbalance of overthrown furniture, collapsed ceilings and peeling walls that reveal growing layers of mould (illus. 67). He photographs the abandoned streets where lines of upturned cars, uprooted oaks and broken signs are still covered in floodwater. A pervading smell of mud seems to exude from the images. Polidori records the failure of policies and infrastructures, and exposes 'a black disaster' in what the art critic Jeff L. Rosenheim refers to as the 'widespread urban ruin' of a disintegrated community.[26]

Under Polidori's lens the event shifts from being merely news to representing the poignant silence of abandonment. The stillness throbs with the violence of an uncontrollable force. The series collectively

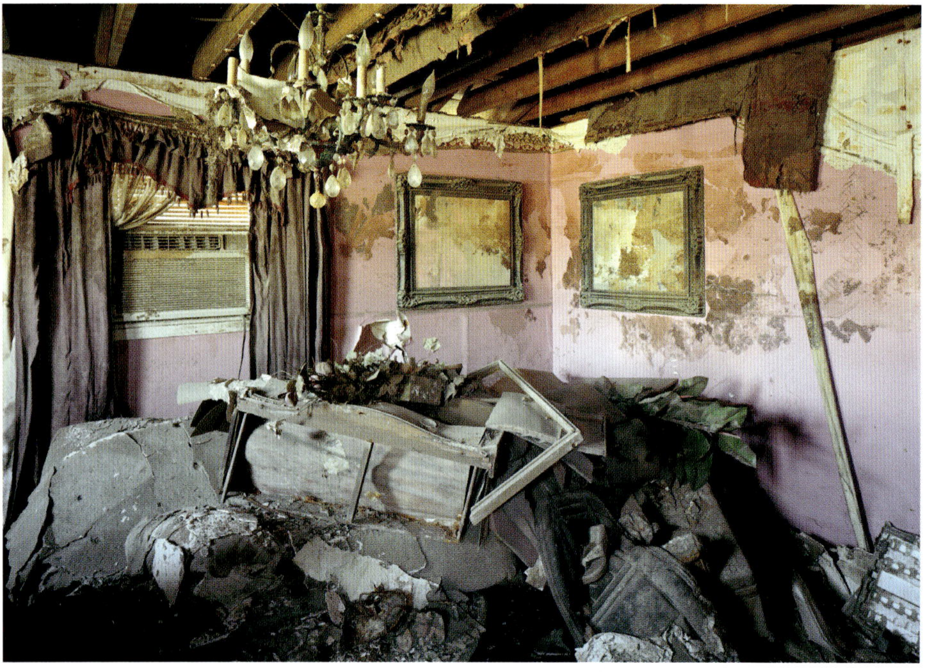

67 Robert Polidori, *2520 Deslondes, New Orleans*, March 2006, Fuji-colour crystal archive print.

creates a fragmented narrative of streets, houses and other buildings, places that are suspended in a moment in time as spaces of loss. Polidori's keen eye for architecture, for the texture of structures and for the nature of edifices, renders these spaces eloquent by conveying their tacit presence. The pictures are like portraits of buildings. This comparison is suggested by the artist himself, who uses the term 'habit' and 'violation of habits' to describe the subject of his work. For him, habitat is 'what societies do to the building', how space is affected by socio-economic, political and historical causes.[27]

Within this dialectics of space and encroaching destruction, Polidori's work questions the position of the viewer. The distance on which Burke's Sublime was predicated is exposed by the impossibility of participating in a drama that is confined and determined by the intersection of perception and interpretation, at the point of dissolution between presence and absence, between the moments of observation and representation.

The viewer may be moved, overwhelmed or captivated. As in the case of Friedrich's paintings, the image exceeds the mere documentary to testify to an imponderable incidence, to the possibility of an empty space that is independent of the gaze. The nuclear catastrophe of Chernobyl and the devastation of Hurricane Katrina are instances of impending ecological concerns. They suggest an imagery of the gigantic at the interface of technologies and ecologies (environmental, economic, political and social), making the Sublime a ruinous residue akin to a totalizing picture of destruction: empty spaces, relics of contamination and traumatized histories.

Anxious Spaces

As the sociologist David Altheide writes, in 'the pervasive presentation of the cultural meanings involving fear and dread in public discourse', we recognize the rhetorical framework that articulates events and forges their understandings.[28] Terrorism and the surveillance systems meant to control it sit within this framework of strategies and information, from which catastrophe and annihilation proliferate in the current imaginary, contesting ideologies and territories. Within this context the Sublime, as an aesthetic experience that is ethically affective, resonates as we enter the capsular realms of surveillance technologies. According to Jacques Rancière, 'Terrorism is precisely the name that trauma takes in political matters and it is one of the catchwords of our time'.[29] Though it designates 'a reality of crime and horror' that cannot be ignored, 'it is also a word that throws things into a state of indistinction'.[30] This notion is key to Rancière's reflection upon the current politics of terror. As he reminds us, the original meaning of 'ethics', from the ancient Greek *ethos*, is 'dwelling', and is thus associated with lifestyle. 'Ethics, then, is a kind of thinking in which an identity is established between an environment, a way of being and a principle of action.'[31] Today's ethics – as the kind of thinking that dominates our time – is nebulous and centred on terror as the supposed principle or strategy upon which our relations to physical and social environments are based. At the epicentre of this state of eradicated fear is the city as the focus of an 'experiment' that, according to Bauman, betrays the postmodern privatization of the fears of modernity.[32] Sites of global influx and connections, cities are perceived as both exuberant with possibility and intensely dangerous. Hence, 'enclosure, safety and control' dominate the constitution of capsular milieux, whether through architecture, surveillance technologies or the individual isolation brought about by wearing digital gadgets.[33] The safety of the atrium, of enclosed shopping areas and of building blocks with limited access contrasts with the expanse of suburban estates that are typically identified as 'at risk' zones, situated at the outskirts of today's metropolises, whether in Paris or Brasília. The arteries of transit and trade, including airports, undergrounds, railway stations or parking plots, are all contentious loci, the alleged targets of criminality and terrorism that require, as in the case of contagion, 'efficient repellents' through means of protection and control.[34]

Since the 1990s artists have critically investigated the commonplace presence and disciplinary function of CCTV cameras. They have questioned the conceptual and visual disjunction, inherent in a temporal and spatial gap, that these systems of visualization produce between the image, the location and the event. At the fore is the interface or relationship that ties back to the earlier discussion of surveillance technologies and the body. In particular, the Mexican artist Rafael Lozano-Hemmer explores the dynamics of contemporary public places through interactive installations that deploy tracking and other kinds of digital technologies often linked to intimidation, surveillance and the media. Using searchlights, sensory detecting systems, CCTV cameras and multi-projection, Lozano-Hemmer intervenes directly in the fabric of buildings and their underlying power structures, altering the ways in which people relate to public places in new personal ways. The artist regards the interactions between notions of 'placelessness' and 'multiplace' as integral to the artwork, which he merges with the architecture in which it is located. In this way, he suggests the continuity and complicity that can be created through connectivity to dispel the impinging anxieties associated with public places. If considered in relation to the current politics of terror, this kind of practice underlies the possibilities of an aesthetics of fear that both cajoles and unsettles the viewer within the affective circulation caused by the cultural 'implosion' of space. Since, following Rancière, aesthetics participates in the current ideological collapse of distinctions that characterizes the politics of fear, the attempt of art to convey the Sublime void engendered by terror, or to manipulate the visual dynamics of surveillance, partially reassesses the role of art as an 'ethical' discourse. For the French philosopher, in fact, in the changing panorama of capitalism, and of national and international policies, art is called upon to expose the pervasive discourse of fear and to be a witness 'at the service of the unrepresentable'.[35] Rancière's argument is useful, given both the potential and the limitations of an aesthetics of fear, to the discussion of artworks that explore the contemporary construction of places and the regime of surveillance that characterizes them.

The German artist Gregor Schneider, who uses space as his medium, translates the rhetoric of fear and its affective dynamics in unsettling installations through which the viewer is invited to walk. Once entered, Schneider's engulfing spaces have to be traversed to the end. Doors close behind you and do not reopen. Inside, odours may asphyxiate, freezing rooms become blindingly bright ones or pitch-black labyrinthine enclosures. In *Weisse Folter* (*White Torture*, 2007) the artist references downloaded images of Camp 5 in Guantanamo Bay and other policing institutions to create a deceptive and unnerving space of uniform corridors, cells and rooms. The pristine and blinding whiteness of the installation is both hyper-real and sinisterly disorientating (illus. 68). Visitors are admitted at an interval of one every five minutes, when the doors slide and close behind corridors from which there is no way back. As the art critic Dominic Eichler comments, 'Schneider's expert staging elevates the work beyond the ghostly theme-park attraction.'[36] The allusion to contemporary 'non-places' is evident, yet 'the signs and consumption-driven comfort zones have been removed', rendering them distressing, a blinding white vertigo.[37] It is as if Giambattista Piranesi's antique ruins, ominously labyrinthine and filled with menacing instruments of torture, have been institutionalized in new forms of dislocation. The perfect enclosure of the work recalls the

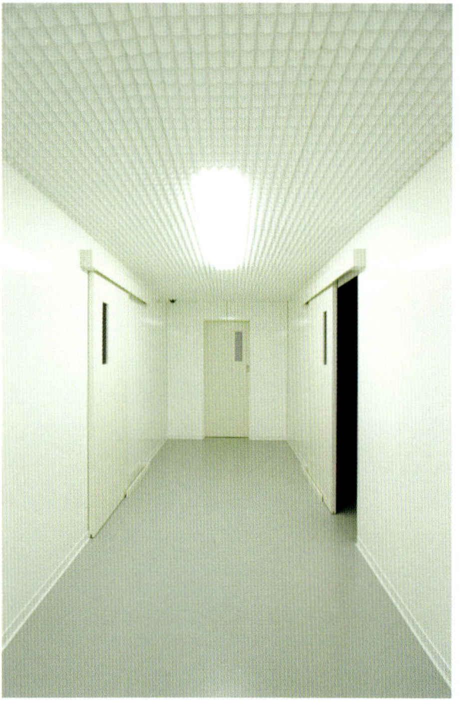

68 Gregor Schneider, *Weisse Folter/ Passageway No. 2*, 2005–7, mixed media installation.

protected environments that dominate the contemporary culture of fear and the regime of surveillance that constitutes its emotional charge. By building 'synthetic non-spaces' that testify to both the consumerist and political exploitation of current fears, the artist deploys interpolation as a means of exposing the ideological erosion and contamination of space.[38] In Schneider's pristine rooms of latent torture, the confrontation with the impending catastrophe of current ecologies of fear is ironically enacted. The work mobilizes not an apocalyptic dystopia, but rather the ethics of dwelling proposed by its unnerving, institutionalized, white emptiness.

Underpinning current policies of surveillance is also a widespread preoccupation across societies of economic uncertainties, the suspicion towards growing migration and the anxious perception of strangers. The results are xeno- and mixo-phobia expressed in attacks on specific groups as well as in more general instances of inclusion and exclusion.[39] The threat felt in Britain by domestic workers towards immigrants is just one example of an exclusionary anxiety that leads to discrimination and violence. This is paralleled by 'political agoraphobia' due to a permutation of the contours of national identity that increasingly determine the course of political and economic actions.[40] The growing popularity of national parties with contentious racial ideologies is an instance of growing preoccupations with modes of identification sanctioned by borders. Street violence, diffuse aggression and terrorism, whether national or international, are steeped in a climate of mistrust and anxiety. In the fluid circulation of contemporary life we are the more alert to the possibly intrusive other: we all are suspicious strangers, all spied-on citizens.

An intimation of a society built on suspicion and policing is at the heart of the video installation *Conspiracy Dwellings* (2007) by the British artist Pam Skelton. The work investigates the legacy of the state of surveillance in the former GDR between 1980 and 1989. Skelton traces the secret locations where members of the German Ministry of State Security (Stasi) would meet informants. These places included private apartments, rooms above shops, offices and other unassuming sites in the town of Erfurt, identified in the video by its code name and the Stasi's registration number (illus. 69). The result is unsettling as it mimics and disrupts the culture of dissimulation and conspiracy that it unravels. Skelton takes the viewer on a disorientating and anonymous tour of Erfurt, across housing estates and suburbs, shopping precincts, railway stations and bourgeois villas. As she comments: 'In the process of documenting *Conspiracy Dwellings* I became aware of the various positions that the act of recording induced. I was the observer, the voyeuristic lens of the camera, the eye of the informer and the all seeing Stasi.'[41]

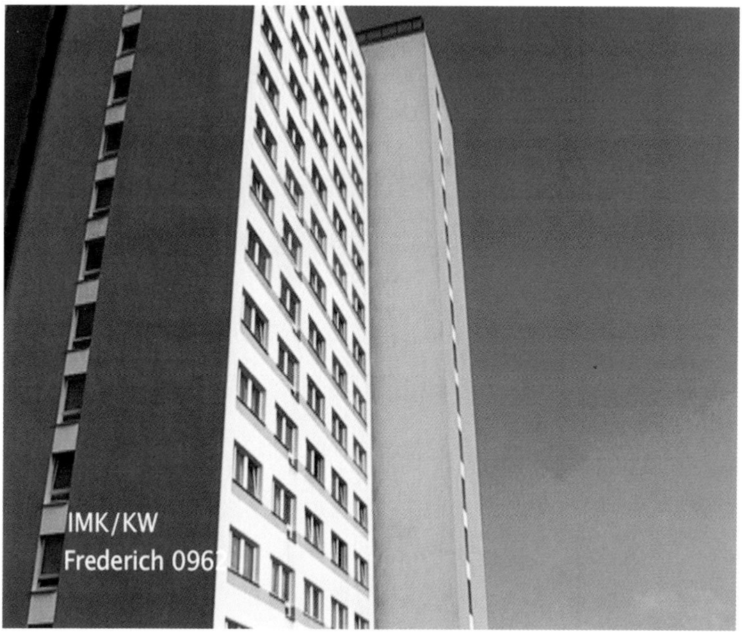

69 Pam Skelton, *Konspirative Wohnungen/ Conspiracy Dwellings*, 2007, video installation, 120 minutes.

The ambiguity of the observing gaze that Skelton describes evokes the uncertainty of a system in which everyone could be both victim and informant. Herta Müller's poignant evocation of Romanian dictator Nicolae Ceauşescu's equally oppressive regime of surveillance, where fear was like a habit and everyone was 'at home in their fear', resonates with Skelton's work.[42] As Müller writes: 'The factory and the bodega, the shops and the apartment blocks, the railway station and the train rides . . . all were listening. The streetcars, the hospitals, and the graveyards. The walls, the ceiling and the open sky.'[43] The viewer and the reader equally participate in this omnipresent conspiracy and share the ambivalence of the observing gaze, the uncertainty of who is looking and who is looked upon. The disparity between private and public expressions of belief and resistance that regulated East German society spanned the urban fabric. The sociologist Steven Pfaff notes that, 'With the legitimacy of the regime unknowable, the key to the regime's power resides in its ability to cajole and threaten members of society into conforming to this culture of dissimulation.'[44] Houses as well as public places are woven into an equally ambiguous tapestry of locations and of relations that betray an amorphous and ubiquitous web of surveillance, in which the private and public, the personal and the political, collapse in the act of conspiring, in ways that resonate with a globalized anxiety over such surveillance.

In this panorama, Jeremy Bentham's (1748–1832) idea of the Panopticon is a common metaphor to describe the culture of surveillance in which we live. A circular prison in which the cells could be continuously watched from a central observation tower without the prisoners being aware of it, the Panopticon aimed to instil inmates with self-discipline through the mere exercise of the authority of control. Not knowing whether they were watched or not, the prisoners would internalize the dynamics of surveillance.[45] Drawing on Michel Foucault's argument, this epitomizes the ideal structure of modern bio-politics that has only been superseded, technologically rather than ideologically, through ever more sophisticated devices of control, from CCTV cameras to biometric and digital forms of surveillance, and networks of transmission tracking. The internalization of the principle of control argued by Foucault is now realized both within and without the individual. The panoply of means of identifying, locating and measuring movement, transactions and interaction, through items such as mobile phones, and credit and registration cards, intensifies the spatial implosion suggested by Nancy through the continuous tracing of movements. The increased tagging of the digital trails that citizens daily produce creates new visibility through a map of retrievable information, including medical, financial and criminal records. This visibility is unsettling because it remains covert. Inadvertently, we leave behind traces of monetary and other transactions. In commenting on the currency of digital surveillance, Christian Parenti observes that 'the emerging architecture of the soft cage of total surveillance is perhaps most frightening because it is so mundane, decentralised, and even convenient.'[46] Fear thus seamlessly enfolds social living, giving new prominence to traditional fears such as agoraphobia and claustrophobia through the contemporary frames of surveillance and dislocation.

Agoraphobia

The urban uniformity that increasingly turns places into the homogenous 'non-places' of urban globalization, is the locus of contemporary agoraphobia.[47] The nineteenth-century Parisian arcade that fascinated Walter Benjamin at the beginning of the twentieth century has given way to massive shopping malls and supermarkets, to the large agglomerations of corporate buildings and the huge expanse of airports that characterize contemporary urbanization. Examples are numerous, including cities such as Los Angeles and Dubai, shopping towns such as the Mall of America in Minnesota or the Bluewater mall in Kent, underground shopping centres in Tokyo and Hong Kong, and hybrid places of transit filled with retail and other facilities such as Heathrow Terminal 5. In these places of passage, individuals move divested of individuality, all embodying the same shared codes of behaviour and interaction. The circumspect and nervously flirtatious wandering of the *flâneur* across the arcades and boulevards of the modern metropolises has been dissipated in the unnerving excitement and meaninglessness that pervades the dislocation of 'non-places'.[48] The protagonists of late modernity are travellers, shoppers, corporate employees, commuters and all the other incarnations of contemporary subjectivity. For this individual, vertigo is experienced as a distortion of one's surroundings in the interaction with machines that handle transactions, give announcements and barrier spaces, and in what appears as the ever-insidious and duplicating encounters with strangers whose scenarios and actions have the same deformed contours as our own.[49] Spatial alienation is thus symptomatic of the uneasy encounters of bodies in which social phobias are articulated through an apprehensive exchange of gazes.

The fluid, unsettling rhythm of the metropolis is the protagonist of the two-screen installation *Sleep Walk, Sleep Talk* (2009) by Suki Chan. With an unflinching eye, she offers us a portrait of London at night, pulsating with the contrasting feelings that the city evokes, whether tedious repetition or escape, paranoia or freedom. Urban crime translates in *Mount Fear* (2007), a series of works by the British artist Abigail Reynolds, in three-dimensional objects that are half model and half sculpture. Her 'emotion-scape' reproduces the density of reported crime events in specific urban areas such as East and South London for which the 'mount of crime' reaches a peak of five metres. The Chinese artist Xing Danwen, by contrast, captures the global uniformity of contemporary 'non-places' in *Urban Fiction* (*c.* 2004). In this work she layers and manipulates digital and film photographs of architectural models used by real-estate developments across China. A sign of the country's booming economic growth and expanding urbanization, the construction of skyscrapers and shopping malls are 'Western' to Chinese eyes. Characteristically, the models share an international, generic architectonic idiom informed worldwide by corporate culture, the initial inspiration of the work (illus. 70).

The miniaturization of this globalized vision is explicit in the architectural models that both endorse and sell the uniformity of 'non-places'. In staged scenarios featuring employees in suits, well-dressed women, youngsters on roller skates, the artificiality of a life-style – a

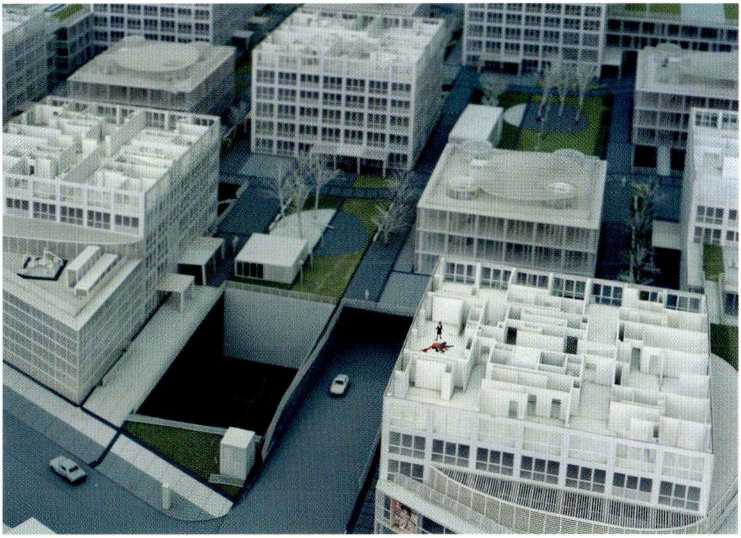

70 Xing Danwen, *Urban Fiction*, image 0, 2004.

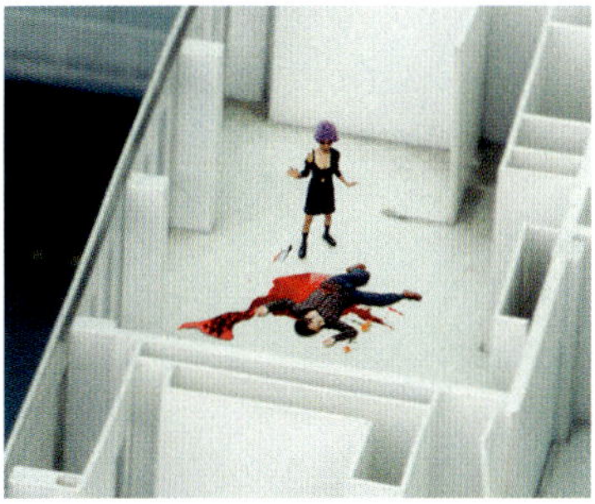

71 Xing Danwen, *Urban Fiction*, detail, image 0, 2004.

self-contained urban fiction – is rendered with playful ridicule and irony. Beyond glass walls and pristine concrete surfaces, dramas of violence and loneliness unfold: a murder on the top of a skyscraper, a car accident involving a woman in a vain call for help, a suicidal man in a suit balancing on the roof of a white building (illus. 71). Comfort and alienation seemingly interweave in these superficially idyllic, yet desperately marred, urban landscapes. Rather than mourning a loss of identity for China's buzzing cities in the new corporate conglomerates that denote the country's reinvention, Xing reflects upon the fictitious 'non-placeness' of these mushrooming urban developments, whose feeling of uniformity is perhaps their most eerie and disconcerting characteristic.

Similar themes of globalized urban homologation and individual alienation are explored in another of Xing's artworks that also uses manipulated photography of architectural models and animation. *Wall House* (2007) focuses on the interface between interiors and the external urban landscape of buildings, roads, and the continuous flow of people and vehicles. Its inspiration is the design of the American architect John Hejduk for Wall House 2 in Groningen, a building that challenges notions of closeness and isolation through the dislocation of architectural planes and the estrangement of domestic interiors. The installation creates a segmented structure of walls on which images of interiors of Hejduk's building show lonely figures, an isolated 'I' – the artist herself – while the exterior landscapes are a montage of Chinese cities. The lack of interpersonal connections is physically heightened by the angular structure of the installation, which translates the affective desolation of the pictures into disjointed perspectives from which one has the impression of spying into recognizable yet alienating scenarios. Xing exposes the tension between private and public places, the encounters of strangers whose gazes are intentionally averted, whose closeness is intentionally avoided.

Indeed, the alienating feelings of perpetually displaced urban encounters is present in the subtle psychological grammar of mirror images and conflicting gazes that characterizes many of the installations by the American artist Dan Graham. In Graham's work, the monitor reflects and doubles the individual's presence. In a dialogical continuum of internal and external reflections, we encounter technologically produced mirror images of ourselves and other people. Through monitor recordings we are shown unsettling projections of the affective dynamics circulating in the standardized locations of transparent and neutral environments that make up contemporary urban living. Graham's grammar of gazes sets up scenarios that resonate within the broader context of the contemporary syntax of space, interfacing architectural and urban design with social uses and emotional responses.

Rather than being faced with new questions, architecture and design respond to and endorse an ingrained demand of safety and protection that is increasingly paradigmatic in today's emphasis on risk and safety. This is apparent in the 'prosthetic' means of security that characterize buildings and urban environments, including alarm and CCTV systems, infrared barriers and iris scans.[50] The defences traditionally used to protect the perimeters of the city from external threats have been shifted within to protect the buildings themselves, rendering urban spaces 'a test tube of cultural control'.[51] According to architecture historian Nan Ellin, contemporary urban architecture functions within an innovative scientific milieu aimed at rationally forging and understanding the future. Nonetheless, as Ellin argues:

> Whereas modern fear and the scientific climate in which it occurred led to efforts to cope with it through rationally understanding and shaping the future, prevalent responses to postmodern fear, amidst the reigning anti-technocratic climate, are nostalgia and attempts on the part of designers to provide legible environments which are meaningful to their constituencies by referring to the context(s) or to mass imagery.[52]

Fear, as a veiled theme, thus conditions the design and hence the fruition of urban spaces.

Fear at the Discotheque (2009), a hypothetical project presented at an exhibition on urban design in Rotterdam by the designer group Nog Harder, conjures a menacing perception of the urban landscape in which agoraphobia metaphorically acquires new cultural connotations. The project imagines the case study of Mr Smith, a hyper-aware and paranoid character who shapes his psychotic anxieties through his perception of a street in Rotterdam, 1e Middellandstraat. Mr Smith is equally concerned about the proliferation of crime and with terrorist attacks, social and economic inequality, and surveillance policies, which he thinks endanger democracy. These fears manifest in the beliefs that the strategies to control criminality in Rotterdam, as well as in other cities, are in vain and that urban capsular places are but a manifestation of the doom lurking over democracy and freedom. Mr Smith's psychosis epitomizes the dysmorphophobic perception of urban space and society at large, since his fear is: 'simultaneously perceived as a local and global anxiety, and it is further subdivided into social and economic categories. He cannot distinguish between scales, and instead sees them as integrally connected. Mr Smith's fear of space is glocal.'[53] He configures the socio-economic motives shaping urban life in the technological systems of surveillance that interact at micro and macro levels, linking CCTV cameras in the local shop to satellite systems of protection. His 'agoraphobia' internalizes a contemporary hegemony of control as the contradictory endorsement of security and of a scripted scenario of fear. Like other means of control, CCTV cameras thus act as tools 'of deterrence enforcement and investigation', suggesting that surveillance 'is intimately bound up with the security of aesthetics of retail space, which itself is predicated on insider/outsider distinctions and codes of social hierarchy'.[54] Under the scrutinizing, disinterested gaze of the camera, any citizen is a potential victim or suspect. In commenting on *Fear at the Discotheque*, the sociologists Benjamin Barber and Joshua Karant observe, 'As Smith's anxiety demonstrates, far from cultivating a strong civil society or engaged citizenship, tactical surveillance only compounds individual fear and alienation.'[55] This condition is arguably describable as an architectonic and subjective internalization of the fears that endorse a Foucauldian vision of bio-politics.

In these impinging agoraphobic scenarios we could recognize the hypothetical Mr Smith in the anonymous man running across a bridge in Willie Doherty's *Re-Run* (2002). We cannot know who the man is, nor do we know what or whom he is running from or towards (illus. 72). The relentless run in the darkness is paved with uncertainty and an impending sense of threat. The menace evoked in the video matches Doherty's scrutinizing of the mechanisms of surveillance and tactics of inclusion and exclusion through the specific lens of the conflict in Northern Ireland. Since the early 1990s, Doherty has explored contemporary urban fear-scapes through a wide range of stylistic devices and visual references, which span from action film – as in *Re-Run* – to television

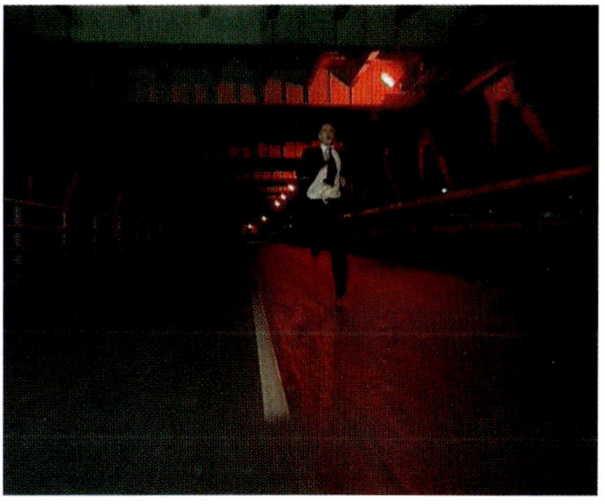

72 Willie Doherty, *Re-run*, 2002, video installation with projection on two screens.

reportage and documentary.[56] Murder scenes, controlled traffic areas, and cityscapes seen from the vantage point of military control points are some of the settings of his videos that investigate the stereotypes and uncertainties rooted in suspicion, violence, injustice and territoriality. Hence *Blackspot* (1997) focuses on an urban area with houses, shops, moving vehicles and people. Gradually the daylight dims into darkness, obscuring many of the details. The looped repetition of the same scene conjures the relentless pursuit of surveillance to a point of futility. The apparent tranquillity of the surroundings is contradicted by the title of the video, signalling a problem zone, which is endorsed by the position of the camera on the city walls in correspondence with British surveillance monitors. *Control Zone* (1999) and *Retraces* (2002) equally engage with the ambiguity of the boundaries of risk and safety, danger and protection enforced by continuous surveillance systems within the civic perimeter. In the latter, Doherty deploys footage taken from fixed cameras in a number of locations in Belfast and Derry, displayed in an installation of seven monitors. The speed and duration of the shots vary, and some are identified with a specific date and time according to documentary and reportage conventions, fixing their location and moment. Collectively the seven monitors produce a disturbing chart of nebulously disconnected places that are uncannily interwoven in the fixity of one point of view.

In this context, public fears become private, and private ones echo across the public sphere in ways that move beyond the local and historical specificity of the artworks. Doherty addresses what Rancière calls the presentation of a 'system of sensible evidence' that organizes images of space according to forms of ordering and distribution of places and roles. Rancière understands these systems through notions of policing that, according to the original meaning of the term, encompass forms of organization and distribution.[57] Fear thus becomes the affective means that, as in the case of bodies, circulate across social and symbolic boundaries to define the urban fabric, conditioning both literally and metaphorically the modalities of the perception, construction and representation of place.

Claustrophobia

In horror films and crime fiction the house is the haunted locus par excellence. This tenet is dense with other forms of 'phobic' unrest that challenge supposed topographies of security and containment. Many artworks come to mind that underscore contemporary ambivalences to places and which subvert the poetics of space predicated on Gaston Bachelard's nostalgic view of one's home as a metaphor of subjectivity. Instead the house is a spectral place filled with anxieties.[58] This is already suggested in Gordon Matta-Clark's iconic rupturing in artworks such as *Splitting* (1974), *Day's End* (1975) or *Conical Intersect* (1975), whereby the artist's intervention cuts through the architectural structure of existing buildings to reveal a threatening gap (illus. 73). With time the fracture within the domestic fabric seems to become ever more menacing and dislocating. Gregor Schneider's site-specific installation *Die Familie Schneider* (2004) uncannily unravels narratives of domestic violence through semi-concealed hints. These signals become apparent as the visitor is invited inside two identical flats and asked to witness the suspicious lives of their inhabitants, which in fact replicate each other. The Korean artist Do Ho Suh bears witness to the modern nomadic self through phantom-like house installations, including *North Wall* (2005) and *The Perfect Home* series (2002–5). Made with semi-transparent nylon tinted in pastel palettes of soft green, pink and blue, these ephemeral structures feel like skin; they are thin, faltering membranes that give way to solidity and permanence. Similarly, in the collision of two model houses (*Fallen Star* 1/5, 2008–11), dwelling is presented as disarticulated from traditional connotations, betraying opposite feelings of instability, insecurity and aggression (illus. 74). The

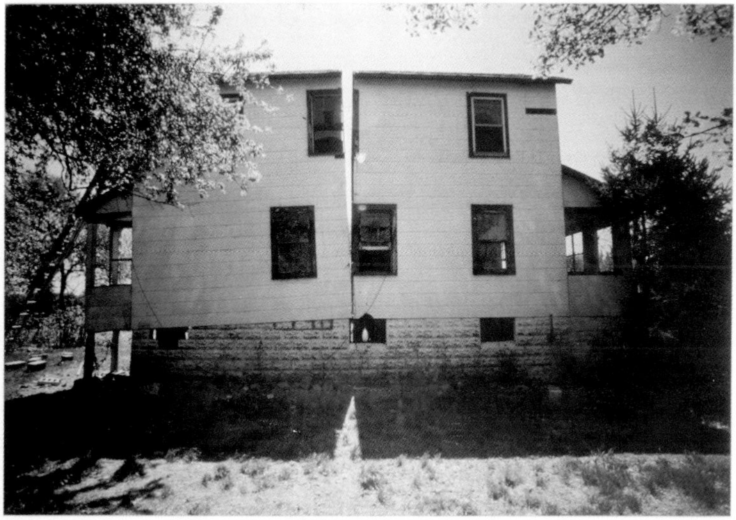

73 Gordon Matta-Clark, *Splitting*, 1974, silver dye bleach print (Cibachrome).

grounding somatic and psychic experience of the home that, for Bachelard, shapes the subject through traces of memory and belonging is antithetically presented in claustrophobic nervousness. This atmosphere challenges the prosaic intimacy of tastes and habits, reversing the familiar intimacy of the home in an unhomely opposite, saturated with bleak riddles and dark secrets. Instead we find a place within a place, furtively uncovered. Rather than the Gothic atmosphere of the haunted house, the accent is on the shadowy quality of the mundane and the ordinary.

In this context Bachelard's place of origin found a contemporary reformulation in Gregor Schneider's long-term project *Dead House – ur* (1985–97), in which the artist created a house within a house. Here the facade and interior duplicate, doors open into doors that deny access, windows open onto windows that are barred to the external world. The structure aberrantly closes itself from within. This disturbing withholding produces further distortions. As the artist comments, 'what is within the house must stay there', making enclosure a condition of being in place that is concretely realized through careful insulation, soundproofing, and the creation of a completely artificial environment of lighting and ventilation.

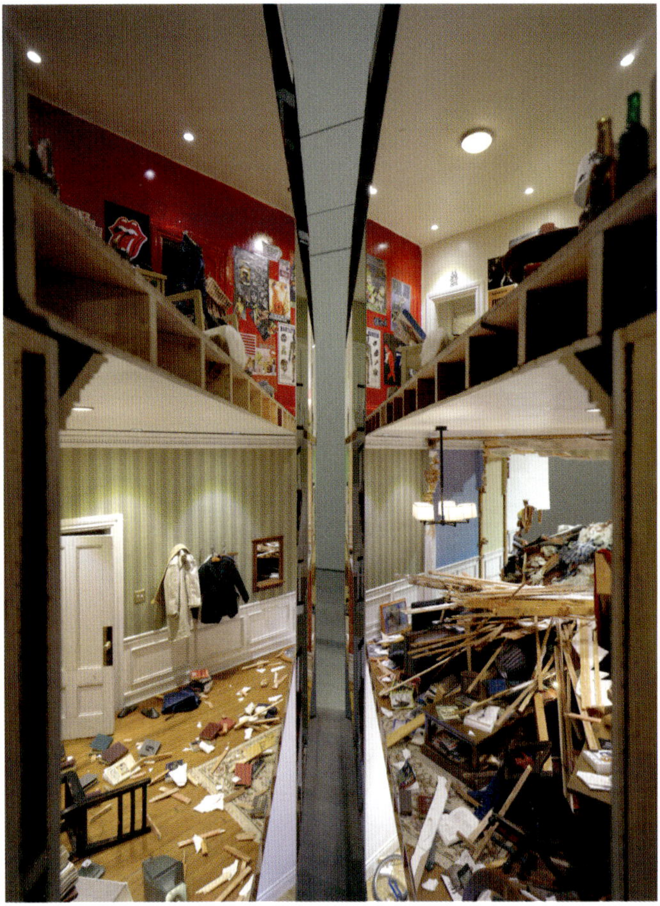

74 Do Ho Suh, *Fallen Star 1/5*, 2008–11, ABS, basswood, beech, ceramic, enamel paint, glass, honeycomb board, lacquer paint, latex paint, LED lights, pinewood, plywood, resin, spruce, styrene, polycarbonate sheets and PVC sheets.

Formerly belonging to Schneider's family and located at 12 Unterheydener Strasse in the German town of Rheydt, the house was declared uninhabitable because of its proximity to a lead factory also connected to the artist's family. 'Ur' refers both to the initial and final letters of the address and to the suffix of origin – the place of all beginnings. *Dead House – ur* resonates with personal references as well as with social changes in the small industrial town marred by a risk of contamination. What made the house unliveable is internalized in

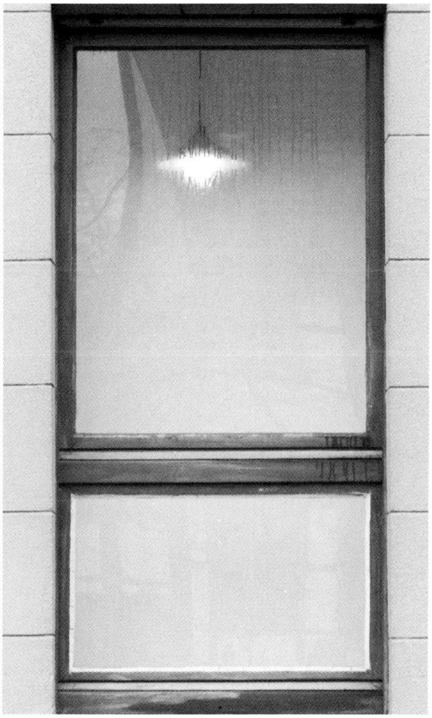

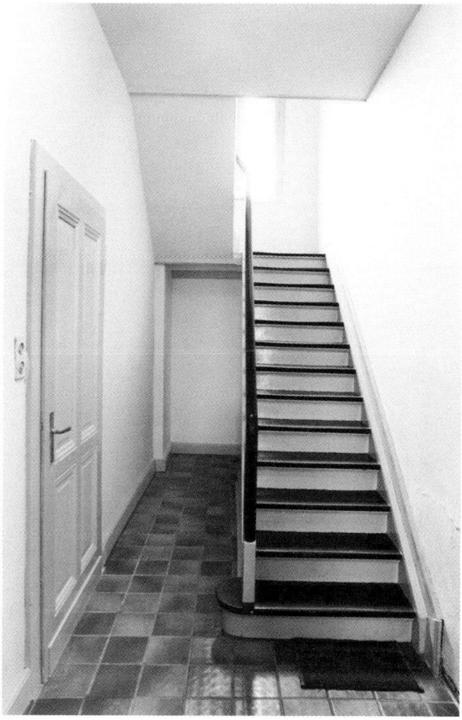

75 Gregor Schneider, *u r 4 Rheydt*, 1988, room within a room, plaster boards on a wooden construction, 1 lamp, grey carpet, white walls and ceiling.

76 Gregor Schneider, *u 25*, *Grosse Weisse Tür*, Rheydt 1989–93, wall in front of a wall, plaster boards, wooden construction, light yellow, 1 white door.

the sealing off of the building from the external world, contesting current assertions of safety in its complete enclosure (illus. 75). By using replica and repetition as formal motifs, Schneider literalizes the making of spatial interiority, rendering claustrophobia a tangible condition of inhabiting. Wall in front of wall, ceiling under ceiling, room within and around a room, all build a configuration of the uncanny that retains and objectifies the hidden (illus. 76). The pristine rooms on the upper floor are juxtaposed with the gloomy and almost psychotic atmosphere of the cellar, the room that for Bachelard locates the irrational depths of the mind. One of the rooms, like a modern *studiolo* or cabinet of curiosities, is crammed with objects. Stuffed animals, furniture, a shredded photograph of the artist's mother, a black and white star and other tokens insinuate secret stories, and a domestic world filled with the figments of imagination, and warped traces of life and memory.

Throughout, Schneider dissects and recomposes the original structure of the house, obliterating the original building in an unsettling simulacrum. Perhaps not accidentally, in the deepest room a mirror enacts a final duplication of the place in which beginning and end meet, and in which metaphorically we can envisage a return of archetypal fears. The place of origin also alludes to death, and the subject is trapped within the confinements of the mind and of the projections of one's psychic life. Schneider's *Dead House – ur* takes us back to Edgar Allan Poe's mysterious and ominous houses, which host within their walls hidden stories, and where bodies have been buried alive. As the artist describes:

> I suddenly found out that between the rooms things happened that I could not control anymore . . . When you opened [the wrong door] at the wrong time, you fell into a hole and you got deeper and deeper into the in-between rooms. You got the feeling that there was no way out.[59]

The hallucinatory and real merge uncomfortably, yielding to a space that evokes torture, isolation and entombment. The power of the claustrophobic distortion echoes an agony of being held captive. The artificial ambience of *Dead House – ur* is reminiscent of that of many contemporary buildings and 'non-places', including the white cube space of the art gallery. This 'familiarity' is both recognizable and disquieting. Schneider has lived and worked in the house, but he has also dismantled and transported the 'house' elsewhere, presenting reconstructed versions at the 49th Venice Biennale in 2001, among other venues. The stability of the house as a place that endures across time, firmly located in a place whether of origin or of transition or migration, is uprooted not by the possibility of making another house but rather by allowing the house to move. Schneider's *Dead House – ur* thus expresses a dislocation absorbed within the gaps and crannies that constitute it, a dwelling that refutes stability and continuity, making of dislocation 'a virtue of living'.[60]

Etymologically, to dwell means to lead astray, to delay. Hence, to inhabit a place signifies a diversion and detour that intimates another form of dislocation based on the relation of the self, on the one hand to interiors and interiorities, and on the other to the external world. The house built on the dichotomy between the exterior facade and the domestic interior is localized in a specific surrounding sanctioned by an address and normalized in the tropes of *habitus*: ownership, wealth, status and taste. However, dwelling only apparently stabilizes this dichotomy; indeed it only delays the engulfing disturbance produced by its enveloping structure. No less than the non-places of late modernity, the house is a site of ideological, if not physical, disorientation.

The British artist Rachel Whiteread has notoriously made casts of furniture, staircases, a room and a house. She has saturated and solidified these spaces, tangibly converting their emptiness into substance. In Whiteread's work, claustrophobia becomes a form of the visible. Dwelling is negated; sheltering and protection are refused. At the same time, signs of wear, the cracks and ruptures of walls, ceilings and floors, overtly mark the texture of the works. They become material memories of living, etched onto the surfaces of the sculptures. The fabric of these encased spaces is dense, opaque and ultimately claustrophobic. As Walter Benjamin observes:

> The nineteenth century was addicted to dwelling. It conceived the residence as a receptacle for the person, and it encased him with all his appurtenances so deeply in the dwelling's interior that one might be reminded of the inside of the compass's case, where the instrument with all its accessories lies embedded deep, usually in violet folds of velvet. What didn't the nineteenth century invent some sort of casing for! Pocket watches, slippers, eggcups, thermometers, playing cards – and in lieu of cases, there were jackets, carpets, wrappers, and covers.[61]

Whiteread turns the nineteenth-century receptacle inside out, to reveal the ideological remits of enclosure.

Ghost (1990), the cast of a Victorian parlour room in an abandoned house in Bethnal Green, East London, not dissimilar from the one in which the artist grew up, displays the hidden skin of the room (illus. 77). Nostalgia is both invoked and refuted in this solidification of inhabiting.[62] The parlour room as the place of intimate family life is a bare ruin. As its title suggests, the work searches for the ghostly possibility of dwelling, the archaic and archetypal place of the self, which is no longer to be found within the walls of a house but rather in the continuous displacement of being. The solidity of the Victorian home has given way to the fluid places of contemporary dislocation. The nostalgia and longing for the security of dwelling and its claustrophobic aversion both pervade and mar domestic architecture with the desire for the ideal home that resonates with Pierre Bourdieu's suspicion of class and

77 Rachel Whiteread, *Ghost*, 1990, plaster and steel frame.

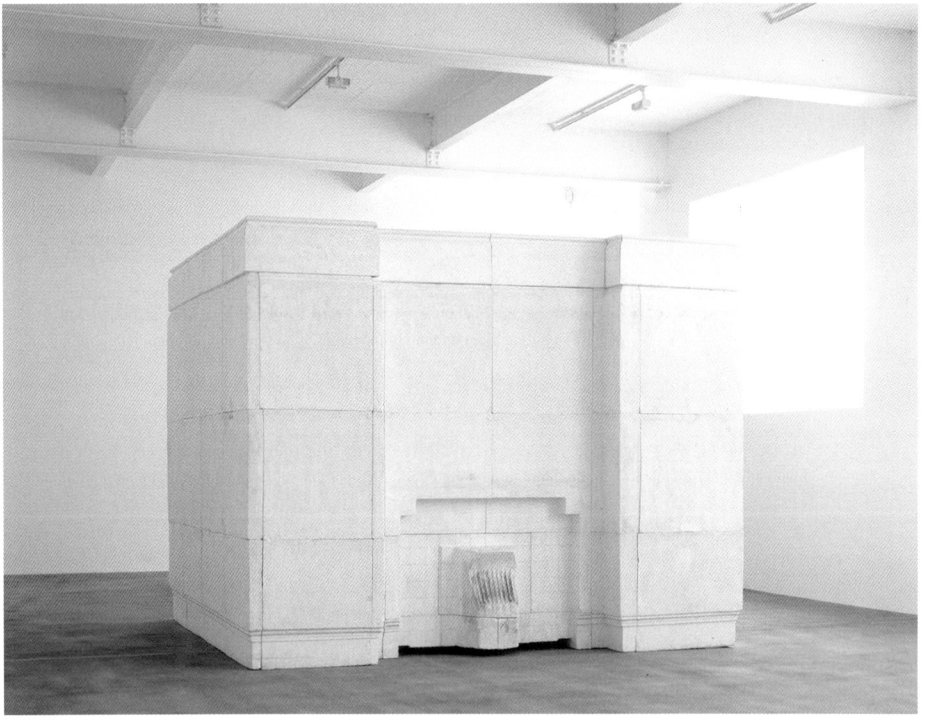

taste. Migration, homelessness and repossession render dislocation more than a figurative theme in today's life. At stake, beyond the harshness of the housing market, are policies, economics and practices of dwelling. Claustrophobia symbolically alludes to the vulnerability of the house in all its social and emotional connotations. It infers a fear of enclosure within a state predicated on contradictions and impossibility.

In this sense, Rachel Whiteread's project *House* (1993), the cast of the only extant, but condemned, Victorian terrace house on Grove Road in East London, significantly ruptured the apparent normality of dwelling represented by the building. Whiteread revealed its fragility within the specificity of local and national policies, but also its metaphorical significance (illus. 78). As the writer Iain Sinclair comments, 'Grove Road was on the border of everything: new money leaking out of Docklands, a local tradition of communal living in crumbling properties, eco parks running to the River Thames'.[63] *House* was a testimony to the past and to a process of demolition that betrayed the logic of new urban planning and new ideas of the 'home'. The project caused uproar in the press, and debate among residents and various constituencies. Opinions diverged. Its enigmatic presence, which confounded architectural model and sculpture, art and architecture, brought to the fore the debate over 'what is art?' Covered with graffiti, *House* stood at the boundaries of diverging local interest: as a work of art it was overtly public. Though it revealed the indentations and ruptures and cracks of domestic particulars, its formal dialogue with the surrounding buildings, whether apartment blocks, churches or shops, was explicit, an intimation of the social interaction that constitutes the tangible space and time of dwelling.[64] *House*, with its solid presence, occupying the place that it had always occupied, was, as geographer Doreen Massey suggests, 'clearly out of place', disrupting 'normality' as defined by use and social interactions.[65]

Whiteread further explores the aspirations and nostalgia embodied by the house in a more recent work, *Place (Village)* (2006–8). Consisting of hundreds of miniature dollhouses collected by the artist, the lighted interiors sparkle in the darkness and reveal themselves through windows, doors or the gaps left by them in the cut-out cardboard (illus. 79). These

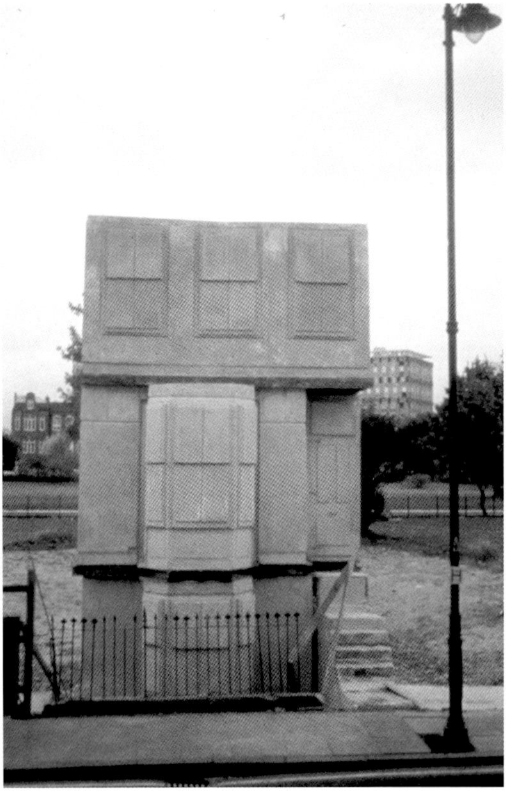

78 Rachel Whiteread, *House*, 1993, concrete.

miniature houses reveal the perpetuation and transition of taste, the class-saturated aspiration and myth of the 'house', the suburban dream of placeness, which is yet fictionalized, reduced to another image of dislocation. The miniature alludes to the child in the adult, to an inversion of proportions obsessively pursued, to a regression towards a model-like past. It is a regression enacted in the timelessness and placelessness of a nostalgia tinted by fantasy and immutability. Indeed, the dollhouse is the house within a house whereby the distinction between exterior and interior, exteriority and interiority, materializes as a secret. That which we spy when we peer within is the uncanny possibility of the familiar.[66] *Place* displays untold stories of dwelling, and is a locus for the imagination

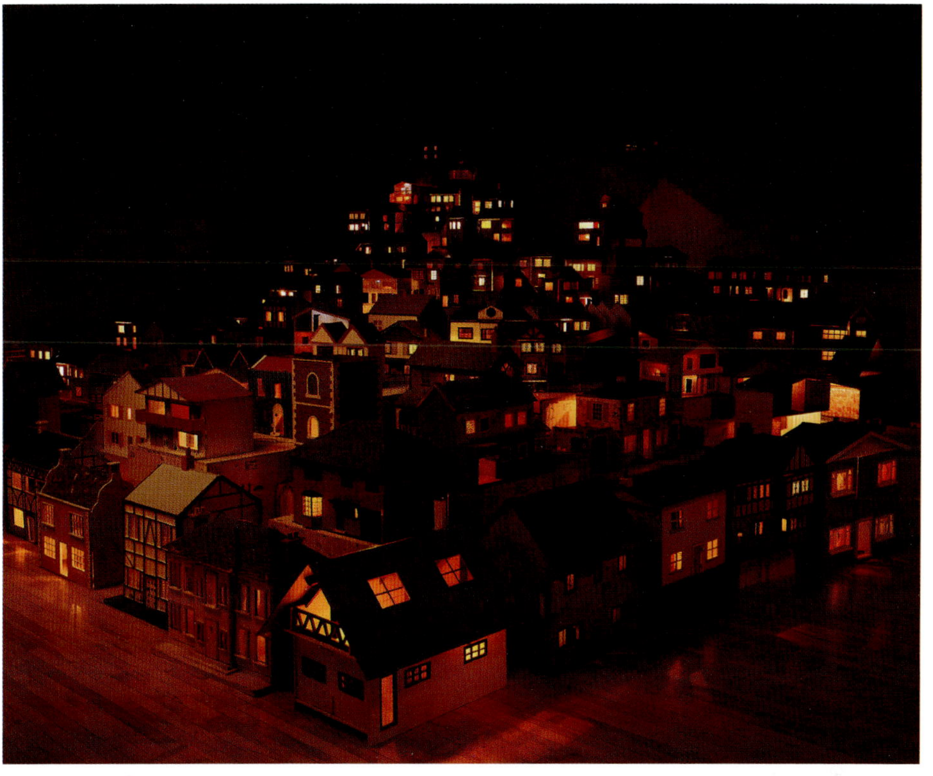

79 Rachel Whiteread, *Place (Village)*, 2006–8, mixed media: doll's house, crates, boxes, wood, eletrical fittings and fixtures, electricity.

to stage the constancy of domesticity. For Susan Stewart, 'the dollhouse has two dominant motifs: wealth and nostalgia' and, as such, 'the dollhouse is a version of property which is metonymic to the larger set of property relations outside its boundaries'.[67] As a manipulated fantasy, the dollhouse endorses 'the realization of the self as property, the body as container of objects, perpetual and incontaminable'.[68] Forever encased, enclosed and claustrophobic.

Bodies, objects, narratives and spaces converge in this figuration of dwelling that is both paralysed and paralysing. The defence system of the culture of fear realizes its ironic immobility. Yet its power to coerce opens up interstices, slippages and subversions in which the rich potential of reverting the 'fight or flight' mechanisms of this emotion can be exploited to move beyond the pervading sentiment of our time and realize the potentials of an aesthetics of fear as critique to the rhetoric and strategies that infuse us with pervading anxieties.

REFERENCES

INTRODUCTION

1 Cornelia Parker, 'Apocalypse Later', *Guardian*, 12 February 2008.
2 Voice-over in Cornelia Parker, *Chomskian Abstract* (2007), in *Cornelia Parker: Never Endings*, exh. cat., Ikon Gallery, Birmingham (2007), p. 55.
3 Frank Furedi, *Culture of Fear: Risk-Taking and the Morality of Low Expectations* (London, 2002), p. 23. See also Sara Ahmed, *The Cultural Politics of Emotions* (London, 2004), pp. 62–81; David L. Altheide, *Creating Fear: News and the Construction of Crisis* (New York, 2002); Frank Furedi, *Politics of Fear: Beyond Left and Right* (London and New York, 2005); Ulrich Beck, *Risk Society: Towards a New Modernity* (London, 1992); Sarah Dunant and Roy Porter, *The Age of Anxiety* (London, 1996); Brian Massumi, ed., *The Politics of Everyday Fear* (Minneapolis, MN, 1993); Lars Svendsen, *A Philosophy of Fear* (London, 2008); Paul Virilio, *City of Panic* (Oxford, 2005).
4 Frank Furedi, 'The only thing we have to fear is the "culture of fear" itself', *Spiked*, 4 April 2007, at www.spiked-online.com, last accessed 15 February 2012.
5 Peter N. Stearns, *American Fear: The Causes and Consequences of High Anxiety* (New York, 2006), pp. 5–14.
6 Zygmunt Bauman, *Liquid Fear* (Cambridge, 2006), pp. 1–21.
7 Joseph LeDoux, *Synaptic Self: How Our Brains Become Who We Are* (London, 2002), pp. 72–6; Joseph LeDoux, 'Emotional Colouration of Consciousness: How Feelings Come About', in *Frontiers of Consciousness: Chichele Lectures*, ed. Lawrence Weiskrantz and Martin Davies (Oxford, 2008), pp. 69–130. I refer to the amygdala in terms of 'alarm' rather than fear as a less determined reading that follows criticism of LeDoux's interpretation, see Jerome Kagan, *What Is Emotion? History, Measures, and Meanings* (New Haven, CT, and London, 2007), pp. 70–74.

8 Zygmunt Bauman, *Liquid Times: Living in an Age of Uncertainty* (Cambridge, 2007), p. 13. See also Joanna Bourke, *Fear: A Cultural History* (London, 2006); Elemér Hankiss, *Fears and Symbols: An Introduction to the Study of Western Civilization* (Budapest, 2001); Peter Sloterdijk, *Terror from the Air* (Los Angeles, 2009).
9 Ibid., p. 9. See also Richard Sennett, *The Culture of New Capitalism* (New Haven, CT, and London, 2006).
10 Furedi, *Politics of Fear*, p. 26.
11 Bauman, *Liquid Times*, p. 13.
12 Daniel Freeman and Jason Freeman, *Paranoia: The 21st-Century Fear* (Oxford, 2008), pp. 1–15. See also John Tulloch and Deborah Lupton, *Risk and Everyday Life* (London, 2003).
13 Zygmunt Bauman, *Intimation of Postmodernity* (London and New York, 1992), p. xviii; Nan Ellin, *Postmodern Urbanism* (Cambridge, MA, and Oxford, 1996), p. 26.
14 Furedi, 'The only thing we have to fear is the "culture of fear" itself'.
15 Bauman, *Liquid Times*, p. 9.
16 Paul Virilio, *Art and Fear* (London and New York, 2003), p. 27.
17 John Armitage, 'Art and Fear: an Introduction', ibid., p. 4.
18 Ibid., pp. 4–5.
19 Susan Buck-Morss, 'A Global Counter-Culture?', in *Thinking Past Terror: Islamism and Critical Theory on the Left* (London and New York, 2003), p. 64.
20 Ibid., p. 73.
21 Ibid.
22 Adam Lowenstein, 'Living Dead: Fearful Attractions of Film', *Representations*, 110 (Spring 2010), p. 108. See also Adam Lowenstein, *Shocking Representation* (New York, 2005), pp. 1–16. See also Walter Benjamin, 'The Work of Art in the Age of Mechanical Reproduction', *Illuminations* (London, 1970); Giuliana Bruno, *Atlas of Emotion: Journeys in Art, Architecture and Film* (London, 2002).
23 Lowenstein, *Shocking Representation*, p. 15.
24 Ibid.
25 Ibid.
26 Lowenstein, 'Living Dead', pp. 108–22.
27 Ibid., p. 122.
28 Ibid.
29 Ibid., p. 123.
30 *Oxford English Dictionary*, vol. I (Oxford, 1989).
31 Antonio Damasio, *Self Comes to Mind: Constructing the Conscious Brain* (New York, 2010), pp. 109–11.

32 Jean Piaget, *Six Psychological Studies* (London, 1967), p. 15.
33 The art critic and theorist W.J.T. Mitchell draws attention to the significance of visual culture in the War on Terror and underlines the critical function of contemporary art in the evaluation of images. W.J.T. Mitchell, *Cloning Terror: The War of Images. 9/11 to the Present* (Chicago, IL, and London, 2011).

ONE BODIES

1 Mary Richard, *Marina Abramović* (London and New York, 2010), pp. 87–92.
2 Joanna Bourke, *Fear: A Cultural History* (London, 2006), p. 8.
3 Joseph LeDoux, *Synaptic Self: How Our Brains Become Who We Are* (London, 2002), pp. 72–6.
4 Jerome Kagan, *What Is Emotion? History, Measures, and Meanings* (New Haven, CT, and London, 2007), p. 14.
5 For a discussion of the development of the historical concept of emotion, see Thomas Dixon, *From Passions to Emotions: The Creation of a Secular Psychological Category* (Cambridge, 2003); Rick Rylance, *Victorian Psychology and British Culture, 1850–1880* (Oxford, 2000); Michel Meyer, *Philosophy and the Passions: Towards a History of Human Nature* (University Park, PA, 2000), pp. 1–2; William M. Reddy, *The Navigation of Feeling: A Framework for the History of Emotions* (Cambridge, 2001).
6 Bourke, *Fear*, pp. 189–92.
7 Denis Diderot, 'Notes on Painting', in *Diderot on Art*, trans. and ed. John Goodman (New Haven, CT, 1995), p. 210.
8 Philippe Dubois, 'Glacé d'effroi. Les figures de la Peur, ou les Passions de l'expression à la représentation', in Philippe Dubois and Yves Winkin, *Rhétoriques du corps* (Brussels, 1988), p. 51.
9 Charles Bell, *Essays on the Anatomy and Philosophy of Expression* (London, 1824), pp. 105–6.
10 Phillip Prodger, 'Illustration as Strategy in Charles Darwin's *The Expression of the Emotions in Man and Animals*', in *Inscribing Science: Scientific Texts and the Materiality of Communication*, ed. Timothy Lenoir (Stanford, CA, 1998), p. 141. See also Barbara Larson and Fae Brauer, eds, *The Art of Evolution: Darwin, Darwinisms, and Visual Culture* (Lebanon, NH, 2009); Diana Donald and Jane Munro, eds, *Endless Forms: Charles Darwin, Natural Science and the Visual Arts*, exh. cat., Yale Center for British Art, New Haven, CT; Fitzwilliam Museum, Cambridge (2009); François Delaporte, *Anatomy of the Passions* (Stanford, CA, 2008).

11 Charles Darwin, *The Expression of the Emotions in Man and Animals* [1872] (London, 1999), p. 166.
12 G. B. Duchenne de Boulogne, *The Mechanism of Human Facial Expression* [1862], trans. and ed. R. Andrew Cuthbertson (Cambridge, 1990), pp. 89–91.
13 Ibid., p. 92.
14 Ibid., p. 92, figs. 61, 62 and 63.
15 Ibid., pp. 39–40.
16 Darwin, *The Expression of the Emotions*, p. 295; Herbert Spencer, *Principles of Psychology*, 4th edn (London, 1899), II, p. 628.
17 In another engraving included in the chapter, taken from a photograph of an insane woman, her frizzy hair has been augmented to increase the effect of it standing up under shock, like that of an animal.
18 Paolo Mantegazza, *Physiologie de la douleur* (Paris, 1888), p. 147.
19 J. Edward Chamberlin and Sander L. Gilman, eds, *Degeneration: The Dark Side of Progress* (New York, 1985); Sander Gilman, *The Jew's Body* (New York and London, 1991). For a discussion of the iconography of the modern woman, see Elizabeth K. Menon, *Evil by Design: The Creation and Marketing of the Femme Fatale* (Urbana, IL, 2006); Linda Nochlin, *Representing Women* (London, 1999); On homophobia see Paul Tardieu, *Étude médico-légale sur les attentats aux mœurs* (Paris, 1878); François Carlier, *La prostitution antiphysique* (Paris, 1887); Robert H. Allen, *The Classical Origins of Modern Homophobia* (Jefferson, NC, 2006); Louis-Georges Tin, *Dictionnaire de l'homophobie* (Paris, 2003); Richard Meyer, *Outlaw Representation: Censorship and Homosexuality in Twentieth-Century American Art* (Boston, MA, 2002).
20 Deborah Lupton, *Risk* (London, 1999), pp. 113–14; David L. Altheide, *Creating Fear: News and the Construction of Crisis* (New York, 2002), p. 21.
21 Lupton, *Risk*, p. 116.
22 John Tagg, 'A Means of Surveillance: The Photograph as Evidence in Law', *The Burden of Representation: Essays on Photographies and Histories* (Basingstoke and London, 1998), p. 76.
23 Barbara Stafford, quoted in Elizabeth Edwards, 'Ordering Others: Photography, Anthropologies, and Taxonomies', in *In Visible Light: Photography and Classification in Art, Science and the Everyday*, ed. Chrissie Iles and Russell Roberts, exh. cat, Museum of Modern Art, Oxford (1997), p. 58.
24 Alphonse Bertillon, *Identification anthropométrique: Instructions signalétiques* (Paris, 1893), p. xviii.
25 David G. Horn, *The Criminal Body: Lombroso and the Anatomy of Deviance* (New York and London, 2003), p. 6.

26 Ibid., pp. 146–7.
27 Alexander Bain, *The Emotions and the Will* (London, 1875), pp. 151–6; William James, *The Principles of Psychology* [1890] (Cambridge, MA, and London, 1981), vol. II, pp. 1065–9. See also Otniel E. Dror, 'The Scientific Image of Emotion: Experience and Technologies of Inscription', *Configurations*, 7 (1999), pp. 355–401; Otniel E. Dror, 'Fear and Loathing in Laboratory and Clinic', in *Medicine, Emotion and Disease, 1700–1950*, ed. Fay Bound Alberti (Basingstoke, 2006), pp. 125–43.
28 Angelo Mosso, *Fear*, trans. E. Lough and F. Kiesow (London, 1896), p. 19.
29 Ibid., pp. 82–3.
30 I am indebted to Prof. Marco Galloni for access to Mosso's archive.
31 Mosso, *Fear*, p. 68.
32 LeDoux, *Synaptic Self*, pp. 213–17, 221–6. See also Martin Davies, 'Consciousness and Explanation', in *Frontiers of Consciousness: Chichele Lectures*, ed. Lawrence Weiskrantz and Martin Davies (Oxford, 2008), pp. 1–53; Kagan, *What is Emotion*, pp. 70–83.
33 Edvard Munch, diary entry, Nice, 22 January 1892, quoted in Reinhold Heller, *Edvard Munch: The Scream* (London, 1973), p. 107.
34 Ibid., pp. 67–99; Vigilius Haufniensis [Søren Kirkegaard], *The Concept of Dread: A Simple Psychological Deliberation Oriented in the Direction of the Dogmatic Problem of Original Sin* [1844] (Eng. trans., Princeton, NJ, 1944), p. 55. See also Kynaston McShine, ed., *Edvard Munch: The Modern Life of the Soul*, exh. cat., Museum of Modern Art, New York (2006); Reinhold Heller, *Munch: His Life and Work* (London, 1984).
35 Sigmund Freud, *Beyond the Pleasure Principle* [1920], in *The Standard Edition of the Complete Psychological Works of Sigmund Freud*, ed. James Strachey, vol. XVIII (London, 1995), pp. 12–13.
36 Sigmund Freud, *Inhibition, Symptom and Fear*, Supplementary Remarks [1926], in *The Standard Edition of the Complete Psychological Works of Sigmund Freud*, ed. James Strachey, vol. XX (London, 2003), p. 233.
37 Sigmund Freud, *The Ego and the Id* [1923], in *The Standard Edition of the Complete Psychological Works of Sigmund Freud*, ed. James Strachey, vol. XIX (London, 2001), p. 147.
38 Freud, *Inhibition, Symptom and Fear*, p. 160.
39 Ibid., p. 162.
40 Ibid., p. 230. Freud identifies the repressed object with fear of castration and further links it to fear of death.
41 Adam Phillips, 'Fears', *Terrors and Experts* (London, 1997), p. 49.
42 Ibid., pp. 48–9.
43 See National Institute of Mental Health, 'Anxiety Disorders', at

www.nimh.nih.gov, last accessed 15 February 2012; BUPA UK, 'Anxiety Disorders', at www.bupa.co.uk, last accessed 15 February 2012; Daniel Freeman and Jason Freeman, *Paranoia: The 21st-Century Fear* (Oxford, 2008), pp. 16–65.

44 Sigmund Freud, 'New Introductory Lecture to Psychoanalysis' [1933], in *The Standard Edition of the Complete Psychological Works of Sigmund Freud*, ed. James Strachey, vol. XXII (London, 1995), pp. 58–9.

45 Susie Orbach, *Bodies* (London, 2009), p. 8.

46 Ibid., pp. 10–14, 77–111.

47 Renata Salecl, *On Anxiety* (London, 2004), p. 144. See also Sander L. Gilman, *Making the Body Beautiful: A Cultural History of Aesthetic Surgery* (Princeton, NJ, 1999).

48 Sander L. Gilman, *Fat: A Cultural History of Obesity* (Cambridge, 2008), pp. 3–9; World Health Organization, 'Obesity and Overweight' factsheet, March 2011, at www.who.int, last accessed 15 February 2012; Alice Julier, 'The Political Economy of Obesity: The Fat Pay All', in *Food and Culture: A Reader*, ed. Carole Counihan and Penny van Esterik, 2nd edn (New York and London, 2008), pp. 482–99. Julier underlines that issues of social deprivation, racism and discrimination denote the cultural image of the obese body and its failure to conform.

49 Isaacs in conversation with the author, Berlin, 22 April 2009.

50 Siri Hustvedt, *The Shaking Woman or A History of My Nerves* (New York, 2009), pp. 172–3.

51 Tamsin Blanchard, 'Arts: Sensation as ink and egg are thrown at Hindley portrait', *Independent*, 16 September 1997.

52 Marguerite Duras, 'Sublime, Necessarily, Sublime, Christine V', trans. Andrew Slade, *Janus Head*, 9/1 (2006), pp. 8–18.

53 Ibid., p. 18.

54 Paul Ekman, 'Introduction to the Third Edition', in Charles Darwin, *The Expression of the Emotions in Man and Animals* (London, 1999), pp. xxi–xxxvi; Paul Ekman and Richard J. Davidson, *The Nature of Emotion; Fundamental Questions* (New York, 1994). See also Giacomo Rizzolatti and Corrado Sinigaglia, *Mirrors in the Brain: How Our Minds Share Action and Emotion* (Oxford, 2008); Jonathan Cole, *About Face* (Cambridge, MA, and London, 1998). For a historical critique see Ruth Leys, 'How Did Fear Become a Scientific Object and What Kind of Object Is It?', in *Representations*, 110 (Spring 2010), pp. 66–104. My reading of the 'pose' differs from Leys, although it is indebted to her historical framework.

55 Roland Barthes, *Camera Lucida: Reflections on Photography*, trans. Richard Howard (London, 1993), p. 78.

56 LeDoux, *Synaptic Self*, p. 221. See also M. P. Ewbank, E. Fox and A. J. Calder, 'The Interaction between Gaze and Facial Expression in the Amygdala and Extended Amygdala is Modulated by Anxiety', *Frontiers in Human Neuroscience,* 4 (2010), p. 56; Ralph Adolphs, 'Fear, Faces, and the Human Amygdala', in *Current Opinion in Neurobiology*, XVIII/2 (2008), pp. 166–72; Matthias Gamer and Christian Büchel, 'Amygdala Activation Predicts Gaze Toward Fearful Eyes', *Journal of Neuroscience*, 29 (2009), pp. 9123–6.

57 Gen Doy, 'Visualizing the Invisible? Images of Migrants and Refugees in the New Europe', in *Art in the Age of Terrorism*, ed. Graham Coulter-Smith and Maurice Owen (Southampton, 2005), pp. 61–79.

58 Lupton, *Risk*, pp. 119–20.

59 Lisa Saltzman, *Making Memory Matter: Strategies of Remembrance in Contemporary Art* (Chicago, IL, and London, 2006), pp. 50–51.

60 Kriss Ravetto-Biagioli, 'The Visual Grammar of Suffering: Pia Lindman and the Performance of Grief', *PAJ: A Journal of Performance and Art*, 84 (2006), p. 77; Pia Lindman, 'The *New York Times*, Monuments, Art and Affect: Re-enactments in Grey-scale', in *Art in the Age of Terrorism*, ed. Coulter-Smith and Owen, pp. 81–95.

61 Ibid., p. 82.

62 Alan J. Fridlund, 'The New Ethology of Human Facial Expression', in *The Psychology of Facial Expression*, ed. James A. Russell and José Miguel Fernández-Dols (Cambridge, 1997), pp. 103–29; Kristen A. Lindquist and Lisa Feldman Barrett, 'Constructing Emotion: The Experience of Fear as a Conceptual Act', *Psychological Science*, XIX/9 (2008), pp. 898–903; Kagan, *What is Emotion?*, pp. 92–4.

63 Voice-over in Willie Doherty, *Non-Specific Threat* (2004), in *Willie Doherty: Anthology of Time-Based Works*, ed. Yilmaz Dziewior and Matthias Mühling, exh. cat., Kunstverein, Hamburg (2007), p. 138.

64 Ibid., p. 41.

65 John Pitts, *Reluctant Gangsters: The Changing Face of Youth Crime* (Cullompton, 2008), pp. 5–7.

66 *Black Male: Representations of Masculinity in Contemporary American Art*, ed. Thelma Golden, exh. cat., Whitney Museum of American Art, New York (1994), p. 19.

67 Voice-over in Shona Illingworth, *Bare Dust* (2000). I am grateful to Illingworth for pointing out the slang meaning of 'bare'.

68 Sara Ahmed, *The Cultural Politics of Emotions* (London, 2004), pp. 62–3.

69 Ibid., p. 67.

70 Robin Williams, Paul Johnson and Paul Martin, *Genetic Information*

and Crime Investigation: Social, Ethical and Public Policy Aspects of the Establishment, Expansion and Police Use of the National DNA *Database* (Durham, 2004), p. 11; report funded by the Wellcome Trust.

71 Ibid., pp. 68–9.

72 Ibid., p. 99.

73 Ibid., p. 14; Jonathan Michael Kaplan, *The Limits and Lies of Human Genetic Research: Dangers for Social Policy* (New York and London, 2000).

74 Jonathan Griffin, 'Tania Bruguera', *Frieze*, no. 118 (2008), at www.frieze.com, last accessed 15 Feburary 2012.

75 Philip G. Zimbardo, official website of the Stanford Prison Experiment (1999–2009), at www.prisonexp.org/psychology.

76 Ibid.

77 Ibid.

78 Paul Ekblom, *The 51st Framework: Knowledge transfer for innovative, adaptive crime prevention, security and community safety* (Basingstoke, forthcoming). I am grateful to the author for an early draft of the text and for drawing my attention to Coretta Phillips, Mary Considine and Rachel Lewis, 'A Review of Audits and Strategies Produced by Crime and Disorder Partnership in 1999', Home Office Briefing Note 8/00, November 2000.

79 Anthony Downey, 'The Lives of Others: Artur Zmijewski's *Repetition*, The Stanford Prison Experiment, and the Ethics of Surveillance', in *Conspiracy Dwellings: Surveillance in Contemporary Art*, ed. Outi Remes and Pam Skelton (Newcastle upon Tyne, 2010), p. 78.

80 Ibid., p. 78.

81 Elisabeth Bronfen, *Over her Dead Body: Death, Femininity and the Aesthetic* (Manchester, 1992), p. 62.

82 Oriana Baddeley, 'Teresa Margolles and the Pathology of Everyday Death', Professorial Platforms, Chelsea College of Art and Design, London, 4 November 2009.

83 Walter Benjamin, *The Origin of German Tragic Drama* (London, 1996), p. 166.

84 Mary Douglas, *Purity and Danger: An Analysis of Concept of Pollution and Taboo* (London, 1966), pp. 35–7.

85 Ibid., p. 37.

86 Ibid., p. 35. See also William A. Cohen and Ryan Johnson, eds, *Filth: Dirt, Disgust, and Modern Life* (Minneapolis, 2005); Virginia Smith et al., *Dirt: The Filthy Reality of Everyday Life*, exh. cat., Wellcome Collection, London (2011).

87 Anne McClintock, *Imperial Leather: Race, Gender and Sexuality in the*

Colonial Contest (London, 1995), p. 211; Erin O'Connor, *Raw Material: Producing Pathology in Victorian Culture* (Durham, NC, 2000).

88 Richard J. Evans, *Death in Hamburg: Society and Politics in the Cholera Years, 1830–1910* (Oxford, 1987), p. 271; Margaret Pelling, *Cholera, Fever and English Medicine, 1825–1865* (Oxford, 1978).

89 Andrew T. Price-Smith, *Contagion and Chaos: Disease, Ecology, and National Security in the Era of Globalization* (Cambridge, MA, 2009), p. 2.

90 Ibid., p. 20.

91 See the UK government's website 'Pandemic Flu' at www.direct.gov.uk/swineflu, last accessed 13 February 2012.

92 Oron Catts, Email exchange with the author, 12 December 2009.

TWO OBJECTS

1 Caterina Albano, 'Considerations of Representability: An Exhibition on Psychoanalysis' in *Psychoanalysis: The Unconscious in Everyday Life*, ed. Caterina Albano, Liz Allison and Nicola Abel-Hirsch, exh. cat., Science Museum, London (2010), pp. 18–19.

2 Nicholas Royle, *The Uncanny: An Introduction* (Manchester, 2003), p. 1.

3 Terry Castle, *The Female Thermometer: Eighteenth-Century Culture and the Invention of the Uncanny* (New York and Oxford, 1995), p. 8.

4 Tom Gunning, 'Invisible Worlds, Visible Media', in *Brought to Light: Photography and the Invisible, 1840–1900*, ed. Corey Keller, exh. cat., San Francisco Museum of Modern Art (2008), p. 52.

5 John Jervis, 'Uncanny Presences', in *Uncanny Modernity: Cultural Theories, Modern Anxieties*, ed. Jo Collins and John Jervis (Basingstoke, 2008), pp. 10–50; Jean-Luc Nancy, *The Ground of the Image* (New York, 2005); David Trotter, *Paranoid Modernism: Literary Experiment, Psychosis and the Professionalization of English Society* (Oxford, 2001).

6 Corey Keller, 'Sight Unseen: Picturing the Invisible', in *Brought to Light*, pp. 20–29, 34–6.

7 Jeffrey Sconce, *Haunted Media: Electronic Presence from Telegraphy to Television* (Durham, NC, 2000), p. 4.

8 Sigmund Freud, *The Uncanny* [1919], in *The Standard Edition of the Complete Psychological Works of Sigmund Freud*, ed. James Strachey, vol. XVII (London, 1985), pp. 219–56.

9 Ulrich Lehmann, 'The Uncommon Object: Surrealist Concepts and Categories for the Material World', in *Surreal Things: Surrealism and Design*, ed. Ghislaine Wood, exh. cat., Victoria & Albert Museum, London (2007), p. 19.

10 Ibid., p. 19.
11 Ralph Rugoff, Hal Foster and Michelle Kuo, *The New Décor*, exh. cat., Hayward Gallery, London (2010), p. 70.
12 For a discussion of the Uncanny and cybernetics, see Bruce Grenville, 'The Uncanny: Experiments in Cyborg Culture', in *The Uncanny: Experiments in Cyborg Culture*, ed. Bruce Grenville, exh. cat., Vancouver Art Gallery (2001), pp. 13–48.
13 Makiko Hara, 'Others in the Third Millennium', in *The Uncanny: Experiments in Cyborg Culture*, pp. 242–5.
14 Andrew Wilson, ed., *Lucia Nogueria*, exh. cat., Ikon Gallery, Birmingham (1993), n.p.
15 Michael Parsons, 'In Defence of the Uncanny', in *Psychoanalysis: The Unconscious in Everyday Life*, p. 102.
16 Freud, *The Uncanny*, p. 237.
17 Ibid., p. 234.
18 Parsons, 'In Defence of the Uncanny', p. 103.
19 Louise Bourgeois, 'On *Cells*' [1991], in *Destruction of the Father, Reconstruction of the Father: Writings and Interviews, 1923–1997*, ed. Marie-Laure Bernadac and Hans-Ulrich Obrist (London, 1998), p. 205; Mignon Nixon, *Fantastic Reality: Louise Bourgeois and a Story of Modern Art* (Cambridge, MA, 2008).
20 Bourgeois, 'On *Cell (You Better Grow Up)*' [1993], in *Destruction of the Father*, p. 231.
21 Sigmund Freud, 'Remembering, Repeating, and Working-through' [1914], in *The Standard Edition of the Complete Psychological Works of Sigmund Freud*, ed. James Strachey, vol. XII (London, 2001), p. 147.
22 Parsons, 'In Defence of the Uncanny', p. 105.
23 Mike Kelley, 'Playing with Dead Things: On The Uncanny', in *The Uncanny*, exh. cat., Tate Liverpool, Liverpool (2004), p. 73.
24 Ibid.
25 Royle, *The Uncanny*, p. 16.
26 Ibid., p. 18.
27 Ibid., pp. 17–18.
28 *Annette Messager: The Messengers*, ed. Sophie Duplaix et al., exh. cat., Hayward Gallery, London (2009).
29 Caterina Albano, 'Displaying Lives: The Narrative of Objects in Biographical Exhibitions', in *Museum and Society*, V/1 (March 2007), pp. 15–28.
30 Andrea Witcomb, 'Remembering the Dead by Affecting the Living: The Case of a Miniature Model of Treblinka', in *Museum Materialities: Objects, Engagements, Interpretations*, ed. Sandra H. Dudley (London

and New York, 2010), pp. 39–52; Ernst van Alphen, 'Toys and Affect: Identifying with the Perpetrator in Contemporary Holocaust Art', *Australian and New Zealand Journal of Art*, II/2 (2001), pp. 159–90.
31 Gannit Ankori, 'Mona Hatoum: Nomadic Bodies, Exilic Spaces', *Palestinian Art* (London, 2006), pp. 121–54.
32 Carol A. Breckenridge, Sheldon Pollock, Homi Bhabha, and Dipesh Chakrabarty, eds, *Cosmopolitanism* (Durham, NC, 2002); Julia Kristeva, *Strangers to Ourselves* (New York, 1991).
33 Quoted in Lutz Becker, 'Art, Death and Language', in *Parastou Forouhar: Art, Life and Death in Iran*, ed. Rose Issa, exh. cat., Leighton House, London (2010), p. 18.
34 Ibid., p. 19.
35 'Interview: Carlos Basualdo in conversation with Doris Salcedo', in *Doris Salcedo*, ed. Carlos Basualdo, Nancy Princenthal and Andreas Huyssen (London, 2000), p. 12.
36 Ibid.
37 Andreas Huyssen, 'Sculpture, Materiality, and Memory in an Age of Amnesia' , in *Displacements: Miroslaw Blaka, Doris Salcedo, Rachel Whiteread,* ed. Jessica Bradley and Andreas Huyssen, exh. cat., Art Gallery of Ontario, Toronto (1998), pp. 31–40; Achim Borchardt-Hume, 'Sculpting Critical Space', in *Doris Salcedo: Shibboleth*, exh. cat., Tate Modern, London, (2007), pp. 14–21.
38 Mieke Bal, 'Earth Aches: The Aesthetics of the Cut', in *Doris Salcedo: Shibboleth*, p. 43.
39 Julia Kristeva, *Powers of Horror: An Essay on Abjection* (New York, 1982), p. 154.
40 Catherine Grenier, ed., *Monumenta 2010: Christian Boltanski, Personnes*, exh. cat., Grand Palais, Paris (2010); Ernst van Alphen, *Caught by History: Holocaust Effects in Contemporary Art, Literature and Theory* (Stanford, CA, 1997).
41 Nancy Spector, ed., *Barney/Beuys: All in the present must be transformed*, exh. cat., Deutsche Guggenheim, Bonn (2007).
42 Dylan Trigg, *The Aesthetics of Decay: Nothingness, Nostalgia, and the Absence of Reason* (New York and Washington, DC, 2006), pp. XVI, 37–55.
43 *September 11: Bearing Witness to History,* online exh. cat., Smithsonian's National Museum of American History, Washington, DC (2002), at http://americanhistory.si.edu/september11
44 Ibid.
45 Iwona Blazwick and Ewa Lajer-Burcharth, eds, *Cornelia Parker*, exh. cat., Museo d'arte moderna e contemporanea, Turin (2001), pp. 59–65.
46 Kendell Geers, 'I TerrorRealist', in *Art in the Age of Terrorism*, ed.

Graham Coulter-Smith and Maurice Owen (Southampton, 2005), pp. 122–3.

47 *Cornelia Parker: Never Endings*, exh. cat., Ikon Gallery, Birmingham (2007), p. 6.

48 Ibid., pp. 6–7.

49 Dominique Laporte, *History of Shit* (Cambridge, MA, 2000), pp. 25–6; Joseph Stiglitz, *Freefall: Free Markets and the Sinking of the Global Economy* (New York, 2010).

50 Carlo Zanni in conversation with the author, 28 March 2010.

51 Jeremy Leggett, *Half Gone: Oil, Gas, Hot Air and the Global Energy Crisis* (London, 2005).

THREE NARRATIVES

1 Voice-over in Willie Doherty, *Ghost Story* (2007), in *Willie Doherty: Anthology of Time-Based Works*, ed. Yilmaz Dziewior and Matthias Mühling, exh. cat., Kunstverein, Hamburg (2007), pp. 162–3.

2 Marina Warner, *No Go the Bogeyman: Scaring, Lulling, and Making Mock* (London, 2000), pp. 257.

3 Stefan Germer, 'Peurs plaisantes: Géricault et l'inquiétante étrangeté à l'aube de XXe siècle', in *Géricault: La folie d'un monde*, ed. Bruno Chenique, exh. cat., Musée des Beaux-Arts, Lyon (2006), pp. 15–31.

4 Thomas De Quincey, *On Murder*, ed. Robert Morrison (Oxford, 2006).

5 Susan Sontag, *Regarding the Pain of Others* (London, 2003), p. 19. See also Caroline Brothers, *War and Photography: A Cultural History* (London, 1997); Ulrich Baer, *Spectral Evidence: The Photography of Trauma* (Cambridge, MA, 2002).

6 Roland Barthes, *The Pleasure of the Text* (London, 1975), p. 31.

7 Paul McCarthy in conversation with John C. Welchman, 'Risks Between: Trauma and Studio, Tape and World', in *The Aesthetics of Risk*, ed. John C. Welchman (Zürich, 2008), p. 324.

8 Ibid., p. 321.

9 Ibid., p. 322.

10 Slavoj Žižek, *The Fragile Absolute: or, Why is the Christian Legacy Worth Fighting For?* (London, 2000), p. 3.

11 Zygmunt Bauman, *Liquid Fear* (Cambridge, 2006), p. 55.

12 Ibid.

13 Terry Castle, *The Female Thermometer: Eighteenth-Century Culture and the Invention of the Uncanny* (New York and Oxford, 1995), pp. 141–2.

14 Walter Benjamin, 'The Work of Art in the Age of Mechanical Reproduction', *Illuminations* (London, 1970), p. 238.

15 Fred Botting, *Gothic* (London and New York, 1996), pp. 162–8; Anna Powell, *Deleuze and Horror Film* (Edinburgh, 2005), pp. 25–43, pp. 115–35.

16 Ibid., pp. 22–5.

17 Katrina M. Brown, *Douglas Gordon* (London, 2004); *Douglas Gordon What have I done*, ed. Douglas Gordon, Caroline Wetherilt and Jonathan Jones, exh. cat., Hayward Gallery, London (2002).

18 Fred Botting, *Limits of Horror: Technologies, Bodies, Gothic* (Manchester, 2008), p. 165.

19 Jean Baudrillard, *The Spirit of Terrorism; and Requiem for the Twin Towers* (London, 2003); Vincent Mosco, *The Digital Sublime: Myth, Power, and Cyberspace* (Cambridge, MA, 2004).

20 I am grateful to Carlo Zanni for many stimulating exchanges on his work and the realm of hyper-reality.

21 Gregory Flaxman, ed., *The Brain is the Screen: Deleuze and the Philosophy of Cinema* (Minneapolis, 2000), p. 29.

22 Botting, *Limits of Horror*, p. 86.

23 Andreas Jahn-Sudmann and Ralf Stockmann, eds, *Computer Games as a Sociocultural Phenomenon: Games without Frontiers, War without Tears* (Basingstoke, 2008); Rikke Schubart et al., eds, *War Isn't Hell, It's Entertainment: Essays on Visual Media and the Representation of Conflict* (Jefferson, NC, 2007); Heather Chaplin and Aaron Ruby, *Smartbomb: The Quest for Art, Entertainment, and Big Bucks in the Video Game Revolution* (Chapel Hill, NC, 2005); Alexander R. Galloway, *Gaming: Essays on Algorithmic Culture* (Minneapolis, 2006); Noah Wardrip-Fruin and Pat Harrigan, eds, *First Person: New Media as Story, Performance and Game* (Cambridge, MA, 2004).

24 Galloway, *Gaming*, p. 72.

25 Ibid., pp. 47–53.

26 Ibid., p. 69.

27 Ibid.

28 Gilles Deleuze, *Negotiations: 1972–1990* (New York, 1995), p. 123.

29 Steven Shaviro, *The Cinematic Body* (Minneapolis, MN, 1993), pp. 25–6.

30 *Oxford English Dictionary*, 2nd edn (Oxford, 1989).

31 Mark Micale, *Hysterical Men: The Hidden History of Male Nervous Illness* (Cambridge, MA, 2008), p. 120; Mark S. Micale, *The Mind of Modernism: Medicine, Psychology and the Cultural Arts in Europe and America, 1880–1940* (Stanford, CA, 2004).

32 Laurence J. Kirmayer, Robert Lemelson and Mark Barad, eds, *Understanding Trauma: Integrating Biological, Clinical, and Cultural Perspectives*, (Cambridge, 2007); Rebecca Cannon, 'Meltdown', *Journal of Media Practice*, VII/1 (2006), pp. 7–23.

33 Walter Benjamin, 'On Some Motifs on Baudelaire', in *Selected Writings, 1938–1940*, ed. Michael W. Jennings and Howard Eiland (Cambridge, MA, 2006), p. 328; see also Eugénie Shinkle, 'Video Games, Emotion and the Six Senses', *Media Culture and Society*, XXX/6 (2008), pp. 907–15.
34 James Der Derian, *Virtuous War: Mapping the Military-Industrial-Media-Entertainment Network* (Oxford, 2001); Daphnée Rentfrow, 'S(t)imulating War: From Early Film to Military Games', in *Computer Games*, ed. Jahn-Sudmann and Stockmann, p. 95; Edward F. Schneider, Annie Lang, Mija Shin and Samuel D. Bradley., 'Death with a Story: How Story Impacts Emotional, Motivational, and Physiological Responses to First-Person Shooter Video Games', *Human Communication Research*, 30 (2004), pp. 361–75.
35 Helga Tawil-Souri, 'The Political Battlefield of Pro-Arab Video Games on Palestinian Screens' in Schubart et al., eds, *War Isn't Hell*, pp. 215–37.
36 Antje Ehmann and Kodwo Eshun, *Harun Farocki: Against What? Against Whom?* (Cologne, 2009).
37 Julia Kristeva, *Powers of Horror: An Essay on Abjection* (New York, 1982), p. 141.
38 Siegmar Zacharias in phone conversation with the author, 16 April 2009.
39 Martin A. Conway et al., 'Brain Imaging Autobiographical Memory', *Psychology of Learning and Motivation*, vol. 41 (2002), p. 231.
40 Roger Luckhurst, *The Trauma Question* (London, 2008), p. 159.
41 Mathias Nilges, 'The Aesthetics of Destruction: Contemporary US Cinema and TV Culture', in *Reframing 9/11: Film, Popular Culture and the 'War on Terror'*, ed. Jeff Birkenstein, Anna Froula and Karen Randell (New York, 2010), p. 24.
42 See Marko Mäetamm World, at www.maetamm.net/index5, last accessed 15 February 2012.
43 Bauman, *Liquid Fear*, pp. 22–53.
44 Ruth Leys, *From Guilt to Shame: Auschwitz and After* (Princeton, NJ, 2007), p. 4. I am indebted to Leys' discussion.
45 Chris R. Brewin and Emily A. Holmes, 'Psychological Theories of Post-traumatic Stress Disorder', *Clinical Psychology Review*, 23 (2003), pp. 339–76.
46 Martin A. Conway, Kevin Meares and Sally Standart, 'Images and Goals', *Memory*, XII/4 (2004), pp. 521–31; Alan D. Baddeley and Jackie Andrade, 'Working Memory and the Vividness of Imagery', *Journal of Experimental Psychology: General*, 129/1 (2000), pp. 126–45; Anke Ehlers, Ann Hackmann and Tanja Michael, 'Intrusive Re-experiencing in Post-traumatic Stress Disorder: Phenomenology, Theory, and Therapy', *Memory*, XII/4 (2004), pp. 403–15.

47 Brewin and Holmes, 'Psychological Theories of Posttraumatic Stress Disorder', pp. 366–8.

48 Mark S. Micale and Paul Lerner, *Traumatic Pasts: History, Psychiatry and Trauma in the Modern Age, 1870–1930* (Cambridge, 2001), pp. 1–27; Chris R. Brewin, *Post-Traumatic Stress Disorder: Malady or Myth?* (New Haven, CT, 2003); Ruth Leys, *Trauma: A Genealogy* (Chicago, IL, 2000).

49 Cathy Caruth, *Unclaimed Experience: Trauma, Narrative, and History* (Baltimore, MD, 1996). For an exploration of contemporary art and trauma, see Jill Bennett, *Empathic Vision: Affect, Trauma, and Contemporary Art* (Stanford, CA, 2005).

50 Luckhurst, *The Trauma Question*, p. 177. Film was fundamental to the definition of PTSD and its treatment, especially in relation to post-traumatic memories. Psychologists Richard Lazarus and Mardi J. Horowitz notoriously conducted experiments on control groups to assess the emotional and psychological impact of stressful films. In particular Lazarus showed control groups a short black-and-white silent film, *Subincision* (also used by Horowitz), which showed a puberty initiation ritual that included extensive cutting scenes. Lazarus used different soundtracks to intimate varying degrees of threat related to the film content to demonstrate 'that the degree of stress from viewing the film was a function of the context, and that the viewer's response could be influenced by the "suggestive" character of the sound track . . . Lazarus had proposed that threat depended on the manner in which stimuli are appraised and interpreted'. Leys, *From Guilt to Shame*, pp. 113–14; Richard S. Lazarus and Elizabeth Alfert, 'The Short-circuiting of Threat by Experimentally Altering Cognitive Appraisal', *Journal of Abnormal and Social Psychology*, LXIX/2 (1964), pp. 196–205; Mardi J. Horowitz, 'Psychic Trauma: Return of Images after a Stress Film', *Archives of General Psychiatry*, XX/5 (1969), pp. 552–9; Emily A. Holmes, Chris R. Brewin and Richard G. Hennessy, 'Trauma Films, Information Processing, and Intrusive Memory Development', *Journal of Experimental Psychology: General*, 133/1 (2004), pp. 3–22.

51 Gilles Deleuze, 'On *The Movement-Image*', *Negotiations* (New York, 1995), pp. 46–56.

52 Martin A. Conway, 'Memory Drawing – Trauma Memory Details', in Shona Illingworth, *The Watch Man – Balnakiel* (London, 2011), pp. 52–3. Conway refers to the fluttering of leaves in Illingworth's *The Watch Man* as a non-traumatic imagery (visual and acoustic) that acts as a vector for the unconscious traumatic memories of the elderly man.

53 Flaxman, ed., *The Brain is the Screen*, pp. 365–72.
54 Shaviro, *The Cinematic Body*, p. 25; Powell, *Deleuze and Horror Film*, pp. 109–20.
55 A. F. Hurst and J.L.M. Symns, 'The Rapid Cure of Hysterical Symptoms in Soldiers', *The Lancet*, 3 August 1918, pp. 139–41. Michael Roper, *The Secret Battle: Emotional Survival in the Great War* (Manchester, 2009).
56 Voice-over in Shona Illingworth, *The Watch Man* (2007). I am grateful to the artist for the stimulating exchanges on the work, memory and trauma, and for access to related notes from her conversations with Martin Conway.
57 Walter Benjamin, 'Surrealism: The Last Snapshot of the European Intelligentsia', in *Reflections: Essays, Aphorisms, Autobiographical Writings*, ed. Peter Demetz (New York, 1978), p. 182.
58 Darcy Grimaldo Grigsby, *Extremities: Painting Empire in Post-Revolutionary France* (New Haven, NJ, 2002), pp. 172–205.
59 Shoshana Felman, *The Juridical Unconscious: Trials and Traumas in the Twentieth Century* (Cambridge, MA, 2002), p. 127. See also on memorial culture and narratives: James Young, *At Memory's Edge: After-Images of the Holocaust in Contemporary Art and Architecture* (New Haven, CT, 2000); Adrian Parr, *Deleuze and Memorial Culture: Desire, Singular Memory and the Politics of Trauma* (Edinburgh, 2008).
60 Lisa Saltzman, *Anselm Kiefer and Art after Auschwitz* (Cambridge, 1999), p. 136.
61 Ibid.
62 Ibid., p. 68.
63 Ibid., p. 69.
64 Roberto Andreotti and Federico De Melis, 'With History under his Skin', *Anselm Kiefer: Merkaba*, exh. cat., Hangar Bicocca, Milan (2006). p. 49.
65 Saltzman, *Anselm Kiefer*, p. 95.
66 Leys, *From Guilt to Shame*, pp. 11–12; Jacqueline Rose, 'Apathy and Accountability: The Challenge of South Africa's Truth and Reconciliation Commission to the Intellectual in the Modern World', in *On Not Being Able to Sleep: Psychoanalysis and the Modern World* (London, 2003), pp. 216–38.
67 Carolyn Christov-Bakargiev, 'On Defectibility as a Resource: William Kentridge's Art of Imperfection, Lack and Falling Short', in *William Kentridge*, exh. cat., Castello di Rivoli (2004), pp. 29–38; Bennett, *Empathic Vision*, pp. 70–77.
68 Jacques Rancière, *The Emancipated Spectator* (London and New York, 2010), p. 95.

69 Olivier Chow, 'Alfredo Jaar and the Post-Traumatic Gaze', at www.tate.org.uk, last accessed 15 February 2012.
70 Rancière, *The Emancipated Spectator*, p. 99.

FOUR SPACES

1 Anthony Vidler et al., *Antony Gormley: Blind Light*, exh. cat., Hayward Gallery, London (2007), pp. 53–6.
2 Ibid., p. 56.
3 Justin R. Davies, Adam D. Campbell et al., 'The Relationship between Fear of Falling and Human Postural Control', *Gait and Posture*, 29 (2009), p. 278. I am grateful to Prof. Brian Day for pointing out this article and for his insight into fear and postural control.
4 Jean-Luc Nancy, 'L'espèce d'espace pensée', preface to Benoît Goetz, *La dislocation: architecture et philosophie* (Paris, 2001), pp. 11–13.
5 Fredric Jameson, *Postmodernism, or the Cultural Logic of Late Capitalism* (London, 1990), p. 16; Andrew Thacker, *Moving through Modernity: Space and Geography in Modernism* (Manchester, 2003); David Harvey, *The Condition of Postmodernity: An Enquiry into the Origins of Cultural Change* (Oxford, 1990).
6 *Guillermo Kuitca: Burning Beds – A Survey, 1982–1994*, exh. cat., Contemporary Art Foundation, Amsterdam (1994).
7 Susan Stewart, *On Longing: Narratives of the Miniature, the Gigantic, the Souvenir, the Collection* (Baltimore, MD, 1984), p. 80.
8 Robert B. Mitchell et al., eds, *Global Environmental Assessments: Information and Influence* (Cambridge, MA, 2006), p. 79; Steve Connor and Michael McCarthy, 'World on course for catastrophic 6° rise, reveal scientists', *Independent*, 18 November 2009; Simon Morley, ed., *The Sublime* (London, 2010).
9 Marc Augé, *Non-places: An Introduction to an Anthropology of Supermodernity* (London, 1995), p. 77–8.
10 Carl Friedrich Otto Westphal, *Westphal's 'Die Agoraphobie' with Commentary: The Beginnings of Agoraphobia*, ed. Terry J. Knapp and Michael T. Schumacher (New York, 1988), pp. 70–73.
11 Anthony Vidler, *Warped Space: Art, Architecture, and Anxiety in Modern Culture* (Cambridge, MA, 2000), p. 34.
12 Benjamin Ball, 'On Claustrophobia', *British Medical Journal*, 6 September 1879, pp. 370–71.
13 Vidler, *Warped Spaces*, p. 42.
14 Joseph Leo Koerner, *Caspar David Friedrich and the Subject of Landscape* (London, 1990), p. 15.

15 Ibid., p. 92, pp. 119–21.
16 Jean-François Lyotard, *Lessons on the Analytic of the Sublime: Kant's Critique of Judgement* (Stanford, CA, 1994); Dylan Trigg, *The Aesthetics of Decay: Nothingness, Nostalgia, and the Absence of Reason* (New York and Washington, DC, 2006), pp. 107–18; Gene Ray, *Terror and the Sublime in Art and Critical Theory: From Auschwitz to Hiroshima to September 11* (New York, 2005).
17 François Debrix, *Tabloid Terror: War, Culture, and Geopolitics* (Abingdon and New York, 2008), pp. 126–7.
18 Ibid., p. 138.
19 Robert Storr, *Gerhard Richter: Forty Years of Painting*, exh. cat., Museum of Modern Art, New York (2002), p. 66.
20 Ibid., p. 68.
21 Quoted in ibid., p. 77.
22 Ibid., p. 77. Similarly, *September* (2005), which references the September attack on the Twin Towers in New York, is an unemphatic, though deeply affecting, meditation on horror. Menace lingers at the boundaries of the painted image, erasing any kind of facile voyeurism or fascination with terror. Indeed, the unwillingness to depict what 'cannot be painted' renders the harrowing presence of brutality ever more explicit. The painting shares the layering techniques of Richter's abstract works and, as art historian Robert Storr observes, acts like 'a focal point of thought that troubles the eye because of its small scale, intermediate depth of field and lack of vanishing point, while troubling the mind by condensing every uncertainty, contradiction, and ambivalence the viewer brings to it'. Robert Storr, *September: A History Painting by Gerhard Richter* (London, 2010), pp. 52 and 71.
23 Quoted in Debrix, *Tabloid Terror*, p. 138. See also Slavoj Žižek, *The Sublime Object of Ideology*, 2nd edn (London, 2008).
24 Mark Wigley, 'Inside the Inside', in Adam D. Weinberg, Mark Wigley and Anthony Vidler, *Architectural Unconscious: James Casebere + Glen Seator*, exh. cat., Addison Gallery of American Art, Andover, MA (2000), p. 17.
25 Adam D. Weinberg, 'James Casebere: Unconscious', in *Architectural Unconscious*, pp. 10–11.
26 Jeff L. Rosenheim, 'Do You Know What it Means', in Robert Polidori, *After the Flood* (Göttingen, 2006), pp. 10–11.
27 Hilarie M. Sheets, 'Seeing Life in Empty Rooms', *ArtNews*, 3 (2007), p. 126.
28 David L. Altheide, *Creating Fear: News and the Construction of Crisis* (New York, 2002), pp. 3 and 61.

29 Jacques Rancière, *Aesthetics and its Discontents* (Cambridge, 2009), p. 114.
30 Ibid., p. 114.
31 Ibid., p. 110.
32 Zygmunt Bauman, *Intimations of Postmodernity* (Abingdon and New York, 1992), p. xviii.
33 Lieven de Cauter, *The Capsular Civilization: On the City in the Age of Fear* (Rotterdam, 2004), p. 45.
34 Ibid., pp. 117–23; H. V. Savitch, *Cities in a Time of Terror: Space, Territory, and Local Resilience* (Armonk, NY, and London, 2008).
35 Rancière, *Aesthetics and its Discontents*, p. 129.
36 Dominic Eichler, 'Gregor Schneider', *Frieze*, 108 (June–August 2007); available at www.frieze.com, accessed 14 February 2012.
37 Ibid.
38 Ibid.
39 Zygmunt Bauman, *City of Fears, City of Hopes* (London, 2003), pp. 26–7; available at www.gold.ac.uk/media/city.pdf, accessed 14 February 2012.
40 Lieven de Cauter, *The Capsular Civilization*, pp. 117–23.
41 Pam Skelton, 'Konspirative Wohnungen/Conspiracy Dwellings: A Personal Report', in *Conspiracy Dwellings: Surveillance in Contemporary Art*, ed. Outi Remes and Pam Skelton (Newcastle upon Tyne, 2010), p. 11. I am grateful to the artist for an early draft of the essay and for discussions of her work.
42 Herta Müller, *The Land of Green Plums* (London, 1993), p. 31.
43 Ibid., pp. 31–2.
44 Steven Pfaff, *Exit-Voice Dynamics and the Collapse of East Germany: The Crisis of Leninism and the Revolution of 1989* (Durham, NC, 2006), p. 73.
45 Michel Foucault, *Discipline and Punish: The Birth of the Prison* (London, 1991), pp. 195–228.
46 Christian Parenti, *The Soft Cage: Surveillance in America from Slavery to the War on Terror* (New York, 2003), p. 78.
47 Augé, *Non-places*, p. 94.
48 Elizabeth Wilson, *The Sphinx in the City: Urban Life, the Control of Disorder, and Women* (London, 1991), p. 136; Anthony Vidler, *The Architectural Uncanny: Essays in the Modern Unhomely* (Cambridge, MA, 1992).
49 Augé, *Non-places*, pp. 93–115.
50 Bert de Muynck, 'The Prosthetic Paradox', in *Fear and Space: The View of Young Designers in the Netherlands*, exh. cat., Urban Affairs, Rotterdam (2004), p. 10; available at http://movingcities.org, last accessed 14 February 2012.

51 Ibid., p. 12.
52 Nan Ellin, *Postmodern Urbanism* (Cambridge, MA, and Oxford, 1996), p. 153.
53 Nog Harder, 'Fear at the Discotheque', in *Fear and Space*, p. 27.
54 Parenti, *Soft Cage*, p. 111.
55 Benjamin R. Barber and Joshua Karant, 'Prognosis', in 'Fear at the Discotheque', p. 48.
56 *Willie Doherty: Anthology of Time-Based Works*, ed. Yilmaz Dziewior and Matthias Mühling, exh. cat., Kunstverein, Hamburg (2007), p. 126.
57 Jacques Rancière, 'Politics and Aesthetics: An Interview', *Angelaki*, VIII/2 (August 2003), pp. 191–211. See also Jacques Rancière, *The Politics of Aesthetics: The Distribution of the Sensible* (London, 2004).
58 Gaston Bachelard, *The Poetics of Space* (New York, 1964); Pierre Bourdieu, *Distinction: A Social Critique of the Judgement of Taste* (London, 1984).
59 Paul Schimmel, *Gregor Schneider* (Milan, 2004), p. 106; Zoë Brant, 'Gregor Schneider's *süßer duft* at La Maison Rouge', *Whitehot Magazine of Contemporary Art* (March 2008).
60 Goetz, *La dislocation*, pp. 97–8.
61 Walter Benjamin, *The Arcades Project*, ed. Rolf Tiedemann (Cambridge, MA, 1999), pp. 220–21.
62 Charlotte Mullins, *Rachel Whiteread* (London, 2004), pp. 23–4.
63 Iain Sinclair, 'PS Buildings', in *Psycho Buildings: Artists Take on Architecture*, exh. cat., Hayward Gallery, London (2008), p. 159.
64 James Lingwood, 'Introduction', in *Rachel Whiteread: House*, ed. James Lingwood (London, 1995), p. 8.
65 Doreen Massey, 'Space-Time and the Politics of Location', in *Rachel Whiteread: House*, p. 36.
66 Stewart, *On Longing*, pp. 44–61.
67 Ibid., pp. 61–2.
68 Ibid., p. 62.

ACKNOWLEDGEMENTS

My curiosity in the contemporary culture of fear began as a puzzled observer of the events of the last two decades. I increasingly became aware of the ordinary reactions and behaviour around me, in London where I live, of the language and ways in which we tell each other stories, the ways in which we relate to environments and objects. Fear seems to be everywhere and pervade everything. My curatorial work also drew my attention to the contemporary art scene and to the ways in which fear has become a potent theme across different art forms. During the writing of the book, I curated and collaborated on a number of other projects that have enriched and layered the exploration of some of the topics discussed, providing interesting links. Throughout, help has come in many, unexpected and inspiring ways.

I would like to acknowledge Central Saint Martins College of Arts and Design for the endorsement and support for the research of the book. In particular I am grateful to Prof. Jane Rapley, Head of College, Prof. Janet McDonnell, Head of Research, and to Dani Salvadori, Head of Innovation.

Throughout my research librarians and staff at the British Library, Cambridge University Library, Wellcome Collection and Wellcome Library (London), National Art Library and University of London Library have been very obliging and cooperative. The Centre for the History of Emotions at Queen Mary University of London has provided a stimulating forum of ideas. Many institutions and art galleries have variously helped with the project and illustrations. I would like to acknowledge Alexander and Bonin (New York), Alte Nationalgalerie (Berlin), Archivio Scientifico e Tecnologico (Università di Torino), Louise Bourgeois Trust, Cambridge University Library, Paul Ekman Group, The Estate of Sir Jacob Epstein, Frith Street Gallery, Flowers Galleries, Gagosian Gallery, Green Cardamom, Marian Goodman Gallery (Paris/New York), Rose Issa Gallery, Kerlin Gallery, Galerie Peter Kilchmann, Lisson Gallery, The Estate of Gordon Matta-Clark, Lehmann Maupin Gallery, Musée du Louvre (Paris),

Museum of Modern Art (New York), National Museum for Art, Architecture and Design (Oslo), Nationalmuseum (Sweden), Roslyn Oxley9 Gallery (Sydney), San Francisco Museum of Modern Art, Smithsonian's National Museum of American History (Washington, DC), Sperone Westwater (New York), State Museum Auschwitz-Birkenau in Oświęcim, Tate Gallery (London), White Cube Gallery, Yamamoto Gendai, Wellcome Library, Gallery Zandari, David Zwirner Gallery (New York).

Artists have very generously assisted me by showing and discussing their work, commenting on the writing and helping with illustrations. In particular I would like to thank Christian Boltanski, Lee Byund-ho, James Casebere, Jota Castro, Oron Catts and Jonat Zurr, Xing Danwen, Willie Doherty, Sophie Ernst, Harun Farocki, Parastou Forouhar, Kendell Geers, Douglas Gordon, Antony Gormley, Marcus Harvey, Mona Hatoum, Shona Illingworth, John Isaacs, Alfredo Jaar, Luke Jerram, William Kentridge, Guillermo Kuitca, Gerhard Lang, Pia Lindman, Marko Mäetamm, Teresa Margolles, Annette Messager, Tracy Moffatt, Tony Oursler, Cornelia Parker, Robert Polidori, Abigail Reynolds, Gerhard Richter, Doris Salcedo, Gregor Schneider, Lorna Simpson, Pam Skelton, Eddo Stern, Do Ho Suh, Rachel Whiteread, Kenji Yanobe, Siegmar Zacharias and Carlo Zanni.

My colleagues at Artakt, Marina Wallace, Thereza Wells, Julie Hill and Amelie von Harrach, offered a supporting and humorous environment during the writing of the book. I am especially grateful to Julie Hill for helping with the illustrations. Laurence Scott was an excellent editor and his comments were invaluable. I would like also to thank the editorial team at Reaktion for their help with this book.

Friends and colleagues have assisted me by sharing ideas, reading parts of the manuscript, patiently letting me obsess about fear and in other unrelated ways. A special thank you to Simon Agate, Ken Arnold, Nigel Atkinson, Federico Audisio di Somma, Sebastiano Barassi, Peter Baxter, Lutz Becker, Gilla Bertotti, David and Patricia Brewerton, Joanna Bourke, Robert Bud, Elena Cologni, Valeria Danesino, Marco Galloni, Michaela Giebelhausen, Manel Güell, Greg Hilty, Kuei Lin Hsu, Martin Kemp, Alessandra Marsoni, Brendan Murdock, Christopher Osborn, Helen Roberson, Chris Ross, Marc Turner and Nigel Warner. As ever my family has been fantastically supportive and encouraging; a special thanks goes to my father and my sister. This book is dedicated to my father.

PHOTO ACKNOWLEDGEMENTS

© ADAGP, Paris and DACS, London 2012: 33; Courtesy of Alexander and Bonin New York, and White Cube, London (Photographer: Paolo Pellion), Turin: 31; Alte Nationalgalerie, Berlin: 61; Courtesy of the Archivio Scientifico e Tecnologico dell'Università di Torino, Turin: 4; Image courtesy of Cambridge University Library: 3; © James Casebere. Courtesy of the artist and Lisson Gallery, London: 64, 65; Courtesy Studio Jota Castro: 38; Courtesy of the artist (Xing Danwen): 70, 71; © Paul Ekman Ph.D/Paul Ekman Group, LLC: 11; Image courtesy the artist (Sophie Ernst) and Green Cardamom: 15 (© Sophie Ernst/Photo Vipul Sangoi); © Harun Farocki. Courtesy of the artist (Harun Farocki): 44; Courtesy of the artist (Kendell Geers): 36; Courtesy of Yamamoto Gendai: 22 (Photo by Hideki Hiromoto); Collection of the Fondation Cartier pour l'art contemporain. Paris (acq.1996): 41 (Photo © Jean Louis Losi: ADAGP, Paris and DACS, London 2012. © Douglas Gordon); Collection Ydessa Hendeles Art Foundation, Toronto: 23 (Photo: Marcus Leith/ © Louise Bourgeois Trust/DACS, London/VAGA, New York 2012); © Shona Illingworth, Courtesy of the artist (Shona Illingworth): 16, 52, 53; Courtesy of the artist (Alfredo Jaar), N.Y: 57, 58; Courtesy of the artist (Luke Jerram): 20 (Photograph by Luke Jerram); Courtesy of the artist (William Kentridge) and Marian Goodman Gallery, New York/Paris: 55, 56; Courtesy of Kerlin Gallery, Dublin, and the artist (Willie Doherty): 14, 72; © Gerhard Lang. Courtesy of the artist (Gerhard Lang): 17; Courtesy of Collection Angela and Massimo Lauro, Il Giardino Dei Lauri, Città della Pieve (PG) Italy: 39 (Photo by Mirko Rizzi); © Pia Lindman. Courtesy of the artist (Pia Lindman): 13; © Marko Mäetamm. Courtesy of the artist (Marko Mäetamm): 47, 48; Courtesy of the artist (Teresa Margolles) and Gallerie Peter Kilchmann, Zurich: 18; Image courtesy of the artist (Tracey Moffatt) and Roslyn Oxley9 Gallery, Sydney: 45, 46; Collection of Musée d'art moderne de la Ville de Paris. Courtesy Annette Messager et Galerie Marian Goodman Paris/New York: 25; Musée du Louvre, Paris. © RMN/Daniel

Arnaudet. Courtesy of the Musée du Louvre, Paris: 54; © Gerhard Richter Digital image: © 2012 The Museum of Modern Art, New York/Scala, Florence: 63 (Catalogue Raisonné: 668); © Nasjonalmuseet for kunst, arkitektur og design/The National Museum for Art, Architecture and Design, Norway: 5; Division of Armed Forces History, National Museum of American History, Smithsonian Institution: 34; Nationalmuseum, Stockholm: 40; Courtesy of the artist (Tony Oursler) and Lisson Gallery: 8, 9; Courtesy of the artist (Cornelia Parker) and the Frith Street Gallery, London: 35, 37; © Robert Polidori, courtesy of Flowers Gallery, London: 66, 67; The Rachofsky Collection: 24 (© Louise Bourgeois Trust/DACS, London/VAGA 2012. Photo: Peter Bellamy); Courtesy of Rose Issa Gallery, London: 28, 29; Doris and Donald Fisher Collection at the San Francisco Museum of Modern Art: 62 (© Gerhard Richter); Courtesy of San Francisco Museum of Modern Art, Accessions Committee Fund: gift of Carla Emil and Rich Silverstein, Patricia and Raoul Kennedy, Elaine McKeon, Lisa and John Miller, Chara Schreyer and Gordon Freund, and Robin Wright; © Doris Salcedo: 30; © Gregor Schneider/VG Bild-Kunst, Bonn/DACS, 2012: 68, 75, 76; Courtesy of the artist (Lorna Simpson): 12; © Pam Skelton. Courtesy of the artist: 69; The archives of the State Museum Auschwitz-Birkenau, Oświęcim: 32; © Eddo Stern, Mark Allen. Courtesy of the artist: 43; Courtesy Studio lost but found: 49, 50, 51; Courtesy of the artist (Do Ho Suh) and Lehmann Maupin Gallery, New York © Do Ho Suh 2008–2011: 74; © Tate, London 2012 & The Estate of Sir Jacob Epstein: 21; Image courtesy of the Tissue Culture & Art Project (Oron Catts & Ionat Zurr). The Tissue Culture & Art Project is hosted at SymbioticA – The Centre of Excellence in Biological Arts, School of Anatomy and Human Biology, The University of Western Australia: 19; Courtesy of the Wellcome Library, London: 1, 2; Courtesy Wellcome Trust Collection, London: 7 (Photo: John Isaacs); Courtesy Sperone Westwater, New York: 60; Courtesy of the White Cube: 10 (© the artist (Marcus Harvey)/White Cube. All rights reserved, DACS 2012. Photo Stephen White); Courtesy of the White Cube: 26 (Photo: Hugo Glendinning), 27 (Photo: Hugo Glendinning); Installation White Cube, Mason's Yard, London. Photograph by Stephen White, London, Courtesy of the artist (Antony Gormley): 59; © 2011 Rachel Whiteread. Courtesy Gagosian Gallery: 77 (Photo by Mike Bruce), 78 (Commissioned and produced by Artangel/Photo by Sue Omerod), 79 (Photo by Mike Bruce); Courtesy of Gallery Zandari: 6; Courtesy of the artist (Carlo Zanni – www.zanni.org/average): 42; Image courtesy of David Zwirner: 73 (© 2012 Estate of Gordon Matta-Clark/Artists Rights Society (ARS), New York, DACS London).

INDEX